MATTHEW SARDON

Memento Mori

How the Memory of Death Awakens the Christian Life

Copyright © 2025 by Matthew Sardon

All rights reserved. No part of this publication may be reproduced, stored or transmitted in any form or by any means, electronic, mechanical, photocopying, recording, scanning, or otherwise without written permission from the publisher. It is illegal to copy this book, post it to a website, or distribute it by any other means without permission.

Matthew Sardon asserts the moral right to be identified as the author of this work.

First edition

This book was professionally typeset on Reedsy. Find out more at reedsy.com

*To the One who conquered death,
and to every soul learning to live awake.*

"Teach us to number our days,
that we may gain a heart of wisdom."

— Psalm 90:12

Contents

Prologue   1

I   THE FORGOTTEN WISDOM

1 The First Wisdom: "Teach Us to Number Our Days"   7
2 Dust and Glory: The Christian View of Mortality   28
3 The Desert Fathers and the Holy Art of Remembering Death   47
4 When the Heart Awakens: Mortality as the Doorway to Christ's...   71

II   THE WARNINGS OF THE LORD

5 "Stay Awake": Jesus' Full Teaching on Vigilance   77
6 Parables of Sloth, Delay, and Neglect   99
7 Lukewarmness: "I Will Spit You Out"   123
8 When Death Becomes Desire: From Holy Fear to the Longing for...   143

III   THE MONASTIC BATTLE WITH SLOTH

9 Acedia: The Noonday Demon   149
10 Nepsis: Watchfulness of Heart and Mind   170
11 "My Master Is Delayed": The Lie That Damns Souls   191

12 When Death Becomes Desire: From Holy Fear to the Longing for...   208

IV JUDGMENT, LOVE, AND THE BRIDEGROOM

13 What We Will See: The Face of Christ at Death   215
14 Death as the Arrival of the Bridegroom   232
15 Purgatory: The Last Mercy Before the Wedding Feast   249
16 The Nearness of the Bridegroom: Letting the End Shape the...   273

V A LIFE THAT IS READY

17 Daily Practices of Memento Mori   279
18 Detachment: Freedom from the Tyranny of Comfort   308
19 Urgency Without Panic, Love Without Delay   331

Epilogue   351
About the Author   363

Prologue

There comes a moment—quiet, unplanned, and often unwanted—when the truth of our mortality steps out from the shadows and refuses to be ignored. It is not summoned. It is not chosen. It arrives like a visitor who has been waiting patiently for years, and suddenly decides the time has come to speak.

For me, it happened on a completely ordinary afternoon. Nothing dramatic was unfolding. The sky was unremarkable. The tasks of the day were unexceptional. I was healthy. I was safe. Nothing external hinted at anything momentous. Yet in the middle of all that ordinariness something pressed in—not an emotion, not a panic, but a clarity. It was as though the veil over the most obvious truth of human existence had been quietly lifted.

In a single heartbeat, the words spoken to Adam became personal: "You are dust, and to dust you shall return."

I had read those words countless times. That day, I felt them. Suddenly the horizon of my life—so often treated as wide, predictable, and comfortably distant—contracted into something far more honest. My life was not an endless plain. It was a gift with boundaries. A story with an ending already written. A breath held in the hands of God.

The moment was not dark. It was clarifying.

It was not fear. It was truth.

The modern world coaches us to avoid such clarity. We medicalise death until it seems like a technical failure rather than a spiritual reality. We hide it behind hospital curtains, distract ourselves with entertainment, and dress it in euphemisms to soften its edge. We have created an age in which a person can live decades without ever seeing death face-to-face—and can therefore live decades without ever confronting life's deepest questions.

Yet Scripture refuses to play along with this cultural amnesia.

The Psalmist prays, "Teach us to number our days, that we may gain a heart of wisdom." Wisdom does not grow in the soil of denial. It grows in the soul that remembers it will one day meet the God who made it. Ecclesiastes tells us that it is better to enter a house of mourning than a house of feasting, not because sorrow is superior to joy, but because reality is superior to illusion. And reality is this: we are mortal.

That afternoon, this biblical wisdom—so ancient, so steady—became immediate. The illusion of "later" collapsed. I saw how easily the human heart drifts into presumption, how naturally we assume there will be more time: more days to convert, more years to repent, more opportunities to love. Without knowing it, we build our lives around an unspoken guarantee we were never given.

Jesus never allowed His disciples such comfort.

His warnings ring through the Gospels with remarkable consistency:

"Stay awake."

"Be ready."

"You know not the hour."

He speaks of thieves in the night, servants waiting for their master, virgins trimming their lamps, stewards tempted to delay obedience, trees expected to bear fruit, branches that wither when detached from the vine. His images change. His message does not. A life lived unprepared is a life lived in spiritual illusion.

When I began searching the Scriptures in the days that followed,

I found this theme everywhere. Jesus warns more about spiritual drowsiness, delay, and lukewarmness than most modern Christians ever notice. His sharpest words are not reserved for public sinners, but for those who become sleepy: those who neglect the lamp, bury the talent, postpone conversion, or assume holiness can be deferred. He speaks not only of judgment but of the tragedy of wasted time.

It startled me to realize that some of the most serious warnings in the entire New Testament are directed toward the passive heart—the heart that drifts. Sloth, acedia, postponement, indifference: Jesus calls these postures foolish, perilous, even damning. These are not minor footnotes in the spiritual life. They are among its greatest dangers.

Around this same time, something else surfaced with striking clarity.

The purpose of remembering death is not to cultivate gloom. It is to awaken desire. If death is the moment we meet Christ, then every day lived in its shadow becomes a day lived in anticipation of the Bridegroom. Early Christians prayed "Maranatha"—Come, Lord—not because they were morbid, but because they were in love.

Death is not the end of our story. It is the moment our story is revealed.

It is the unveiling of truth.

It is when illusion dies and reality stands forth in the light of God.

Seen in this way, memento mori is not a meditation on decay. It is a meditation on destiny. It does not shrink life—it enlarges it. It orders our desires. It purifies our priorities. It cuts away the spiritual lethargy that so easily settles over the soul. It exposes the false security of "later" and replaces it with the joyful discipline of "today."

That quiet afternoon awakened a clarity I did not know I had lost. It exposed how deeply I had mistaken comfort for peace, delay for prudence, and routine for readiness. It revealed how much of discipleship I had subconsciously moved to the tomorrow that may never come.

I did not become afraid of dying.

I became afraid of living unprepared.

This is what the saints understood. This is why monks placed skulls on their desks, why the Fathers preached vigilance, why Christians for centuries prayed for "a good and holy death." They were not fixated on the grave. They were fixated on Christ. They remembered their death so they could remember their destiny.

Memento mori does not darken the Christian life. It illumines it.

It teaches the believer to live every hour with the clarity that only eternity can give.

This book was born from that moment of revelation. My hope is that it grants you the same grace: a wisdom that sobers without crushing, a vigilance that awakens without frightening, a desire for Christ that makes every day an act of preparation and every act a step toward love.

Because the day you remember you will die is the day you finally begin to live ready.

I

THE FORGOTTEN WISDOM

1

The First Wisdom: "Teach Us to Number Our Days"

The beginning of wisdom, according to Scripture, does not emerge from achievement, intelligence, or even religious devotion. It begins with something far more humbling: the recognition that our days are numbered. Human beings resist limits. We are uncomfortable with finitude. We plan decades ahead and speak of our future as though it were guaranteed. Yet the biblical worldview begins not with self-confidence, but with creatureliness. It begins with a truth we spend our whole lives instinctively trying to avoid: we will die. This is not melodrama. It is revelation. And Scripture presents it not as the end of wisdom, but as its doorway.

Israel learned this early. When the Lord led His people through the wilderness, He took them into a place where their mortality could no longer be hidden by the illusions of Egypt. The desert exposed everything—strength, weakness, fear, faith. It became the classroom where God taught His people the truth of their dependence. In the wilderness, life was fragile by design. Food appeared one morning at a time. Water came only by God's intervention. The horizon was empty, the nights long, the days unforgiving. Every breath was a reminder that they lived only because God sustained them. The desert removed the noise that once kept their minds occupied and their souls distracted. It made room for reality. It made room for wisdom.

From this wilderness schooling comes Psalm 90, one of the oldest prayers in the Scriptures, attributed to Moses himself. It is a prayer that does not flatter the worshipper. It lays the truth of human existence before the Lord with startling clarity: "You turn man back to dust, and say, 'Return, O children of men.' For a thousand years in Your sight are but as yesterday when it is past, or as a watch in the night." Moses does not soften the contrast between God's eternity and our temporality. He places it front and centre. He wants Israel to see that the God who has no beginning or end has chosen to enter into covenant with creatures whose lives pass like shadows. This is the context for one of the most important petitions in all of Scripture: "Teach us to number our days that we may gain a heart of wisdom." The numbering of days is not a mathematical exercise. It is the recognition that we live our entire existence before the eyes of the Eternal One. Wisdom begins when a person recognizes that every day is a gift measured out by God, and that none of them are guaranteed beyond His generosity.

The wisdom tradition develops this theme with remarkable consistency. In Psalm 39, David cries out with raw honesty, "Let me know my end and the measure of my days; let me know how fleeting I am." David is not surrendering to despair. He is asking for truth. He wants to see his life as God sees it. In the same psalm he confesses, "Surely every man stands as a mere breath." He uses the Hebrew word *hebel*, the same word that appears throughout Ecclesiastes: vapor, mist, breath. It is the word used to describe the insubstantial nature of human striving apart from God. David is confronting the fact that his strength, his kingship, his ambitions—all of it rests on a foundation no more solid than vapor unless anchored in the Lord. He wants the reality of his finitude to become the foundation of humility and prayer.

The book of Job deepens this recognition. Job is often remembered for his suffering, but his greatest awakening comes not simply from pain, but from the realization of his smallness before the Creator. "My days are swifter than a weaver's shuttle," he laments. "They come to an end without hope." He describes his life as "a breath," "a cloud that vanishes," "a shadow that declines." Yet these are not the words of nihilism. They are the words of a man being educated in the mystery of human existence. Job's encounter with God at the end of the book—that overwhelming revelation of divine majesty—rests entirely on this foundation: Job is a creature. His days are known to God. His life, with all its trials, is held within the wisdom of the One who laid the foundations of the world. Job's mortality becomes the lens through which God reveals His glory.

Ecclesiastes brings this truth into even sharper focus. If ever there were a book that confronts the illusions of modern man, it is this one. The Teacher surveys every human attempt at meaning—pleasure, wealth, toil, success, knowledge, legacy—and shows how each collapses under the weight of death. "What does man gain by all the toil at which he toils under the sun?" he asks. Generations come and go; projects are completed and forgotten; fortunes are built and dissolve; knowledge accumulates but cannot protect from mortality. Every earthly achievement ends at the grave, and no human effort can stop time from erasing what we try to preserve. Qoheleth is not cynical. He is honest. He is doing the spiritual work of dismantling illusions. His aim is not to depress but to liberate—to strip away the false security that blinds the heart to God. Ecclesiastes prepares the ground for faith by tearing down the idols we use to avoid thinking about death.

The Bible's relentless honesty about mortality is not cruelty. It is mercy. God reveals our frailty not to humiliate us but to heal us. Wisdom requires truth, and the truth is that human beings are not sovereign over their own existence. We are contingent. We are dependent. We are fragile. And when this truth is forgotten, everything else in the spiritual life begins to slide. Idolatry, pride, presumption, spiritual laziness—these are all downstream from the refusal to acknowledge that we are creatures and that our days are limited.

The world around us takes the opposite approach. Modern society does everything possible to keep death out of sight and out of mind. We hide the elderly in facilities, avoid cemeteries unless necessary, speak of death in softened euphemisms, and design a culture of endless entertainment so that no one has to sit in silence long enough to confront their own frailty. Medical advancements, which are good and necessary in themselves, have unintentionally contributed to a worldview in which death appears to be a failure rather than a fact. Our culture reduces the human person to a body, then treats the body as a malfunctioning machine, hoping that with enough technology, enough medication, enough intervention, mortality itself can be ignored indefinitely. This is not wisdom. It is denial.

In such a world, the biblical call to number our days stands as a radical counter-proposal. Scripture invites us to remember what the world tries to forget. It calls us to acknowledge our limits, not as humiliation but as illumination. Mortality becomes the lens through which everything else becomes clear: our need for God, the urgency of repentance, the value of each moment, the real purpose of life. When we forget death, we forget God. When we remember death, we remember who God is and who we are in relation to Him.

This is why the wisdom literature ties mortality so closely to conversion. When Moses prays, "Return, O Lord," he pairs it with

God's command, "Return, O children of men." Human beings return to dust; God returns in mercy. The acknowledgement of finitude becomes the place where covenant faithfulness is renewed. To know that you will die is to know that you need salvation. To know that you are dust is to understand the wonder of being loved by the One who formed you from that dust. Mortality reveals the gulf between God's eternity and our frailty, but it also reveals His desire to bridge that gulf.

This is why the early chapters of Genesis present death not merely as punishment but as revelation. When the Lord declares, "You are dust," He is not merely announcing a consequence. He is telling Adam and Eve the truth about their nature—a truth they were tempted to forget the moment they reached for the fruit that promised to make them "like gods." Death reveals the lie of self-divinization. It exposes the impossibility of human autonomy. It calls us back to humility, to dependence, to covenant trust. Mortality becomes a boundary within which grace operates.

The Christian tradition takes this even further. In Christ, death is not only revealed—it is redeemed. By taking on human flesh, the eternal Son embraced the full reality of our condition. He did not merely speak about death; He entered into it. And by doing so, He transformed it from the inside. Death, once the great enemy, becomes in Him the passageway to life. The resurrection proves that mortality does not have the final word. But it does have a necessary word. We cannot understand the resurrection unless we understand death. We cannot grasp eternal life unless we grasp the brevity of earthly life. Mortality becomes the teacher that prepares the heart for hope.

And yet, for reasons as old as Eden and as modern as digital distraction, the human soul continues to avoid the one truth that would heal it. We surround ourselves with noise so that silence cannot speak. We drown ourselves in activity so that reflection cannot pierce through. We cling to illusions of control so that we never have to face the fact that our breath is not our own. All of this leads to spiritual drowsiness, the sleep of the soul that Jesus warns against so often. But the Scriptures refuse to let us sleep. They call us back to a truth that awakens.

This awakening is not gloomy. It is luminous. To remember death is to remember the God who overcame it. It is to remember that your life has a purpose beyond the immediate horizon. It is to remember that everything passes except the One who holds all things in His hands. When the heart finally accepts that its days are numbered, the priorities of life shift. Forgiveness becomes urgent. Love becomes precious. Repentance becomes daily. Worship becomes natural. The trivial loses its power. The eternal becomes visible. This is the beginning of wisdom.

When mortality takes its rightful place in the Christian imagination, something remarkable happens. The fear that once surrounded the idea of death begins to dissipate, not because death becomes pleasant, but because it becomes honest. Scripture never sentimentalizes death. It never pretends that death is a friend. Saint Paul calls it "the last enemy." Jesus Himself weeps at Lazarus' tomb, even though He knows He will raise him. The Christian does not conquer the fear of death by pretending it is natural; we conquer that fear by learning what death truly means in the light of God's covenant. Death is an enemy, yet an enemy that Christ has subdued. It remains painful, but no longer omnipotent. It still wounds, but no longer defines. When viewed apart from God, death is darkness. When viewed in the light of Christ, death becomes a lamp that exposes every false attachment and summons the soul to readiness.

But the Bible does something else here, and it is crucial for understanding why memento mori—"remember your death"—is not a marginal spiritual practice, but a central one. Scripture places death at the hinge point of wisdom because death reveals our identity. We are creatures, not gods. We are stewards, not owners. We inhabit time, not eternity. Everything in our lives unfolds within boundaries we did not choose and cannot escape. The numbering of days is not meant to instil dread; it is meant to restore relationship. When you remember that your life has a limit, you remember that your life also has a Lord. Finitude becomes the frame in which faith grows.

This is why Psalm 90 connects wisdom to repentance. Moses does not simply say, "Teach us to number our days." He says, "Return, O Lord… satisfy us in the morning with Your steadfast love." The recognition of mortality drives the soul not into despair, but into God's mercy. We learn to number our days so that we may return to the One who governs them. The Psalm moves from acknowledging God's eternity, to confessing our frailty, to seeking God's compassion, to asking for His favour on the work of our hands. This is covenant spirituality in its purest form: mortality → humility → repentance → dependence → divine blessing. When Christians today rediscover this pattern, they rediscover the heart of biblical spirituality.

Yet nothing in modern life trains us to think this way. Instead of numbering our days, we count our achievements. Instead of contemplating our end, we obsess over our next step. Instead of receiving life as a gift, we treat it as a project to be optimized. Instead of seeing ourselves as creatures, we try to function as gods. The cultural promise that we can design the perfect life, extend our health indefinitely, and keep mortality out of view is not progress—it is a form of forgetfulness. And forgetfulness is spiritually dangerous. The Bible's repeated warnings are not about the horrors of the afterlife; they are about the dangers of living without remembering our end.

There is a reason why the Old Testament continually returns to the image of dust. "Dust you are, and to dust you shall return" is not merely a sentence pronounced over Adam. It becomes the grammar of human existence. Abraham describes himself as "dust and ashes" when he intercedes for Sodom. Job cries out, "Remember that You have made me of clay; will You turn me to dust again?" The Psalms speak of the Lord's compassion in terms of His knowledge of our frame: "He remembers that we are dust." Dust is not a poetic flourish. It is a theological statement. It is the truth that humbles pride, breaks illusions, and opens the heart to grace. When God remembers our frailty, it is mercy. When we remember it, it is wisdom.

To lose sight of this is to drift into what Scripture calls folly. The fool in the Bible is not merely unintelligent; he is someone who lives without reference to God. He has forgotten his origins and neglected his end. His life becomes a restless attempt to secure what cannot be secured and ignore what cannot be escaped. The Psalms treat this as a form of spiritual blindness. The prophets describe it as a hardening of the heart. Jesus describes it as sleep. This is why the biblical call to vigilance is always preceded by the reminder of mortality. "All flesh is grass," cries Isaiah, "and its beauty like the flower of the field." Yet the prophet does not leave us in fragility. He lifts our gaze to the only truth strong enough to sustain us: "The word of our God stands forever." Mortality is the frame; God's promise is the substance within it.

As the biblical narrative unfolds, the themes of mortality and wisdom become inseparable. Solomon, despite all his wisdom, falls when he forgets his dependence on God. Ecclesiastes, written in the twilight of wisdom, corrects the very illusions Solomon fell into. The prophets remind Israel that exile is the result of forgetting who they are and who God is. Again and again, the Scriptures return to this foundational truth: wisdom begins when the creature remembers he is a creature.

But something extraordinary happens when this truth is carried into the New Covenant. Jesus does not abolish the old wisdom; He intensifies it. He does not soften the reality of mortality; He steps directly into it. The Eternal Word becomes flesh, not as a symbolic gesture, but as a real entrance into the human condition, with all its limits and vulnerabilities. He grows, hungers, sleeps, weeps, bleeds, and dies. By taking on our mortality, He reveals its meaning. In His death, He shows that mortality is not ultimate. In His resurrection, He proves that mortality is not final. And in His teachings—especially His parables—He shows that remembering death is essential for readiness.

It is striking how often Jesus returns to this theme. He tells His disciples to stay awake, not because He intends to return in fearsome unpredictability, but because He knows the human tendency to delay, to drift, to assume there will always be more time. He warns about the rich fool who built bigger barns but forgot that his soul could be required that very night. He describes the five foolish virgins who failed to bring oil, the servant who said, "My master is delayed," the tree that bore no fruit, the wedding guest who arrived without a garment. These warnings are not scattered teachings; they form a pattern. Jesus is teaching His disciples that the remembrance of death is not meant to be a rare moment of solemnity—it is meant to be the rhythm of a faithful life.

But we must be careful to understand this correctly. Jesus does not call His followers to live in fear. He calls them to live in truth. The remembrance of death is not anxiety about the future; it is clarity about the present. When a Christian remembers his mortality, he is not consumed by dread—he is liberated from illusion. He becomes attentive to grace, alert to temptation, grateful for time, eager for holiness. He begins to see his life not as an endless stretch of self-directed plans, but as a pilgrimage under the Father's care. This clarity is the seed of joy. It is the antidote to lukewarmness. It is the safeguard against spiritual sleep.

The early Church understood this deeply. The martyrs went to their deaths not with bravado, but with the conviction that life is found on the other side of fidelity. The desert fathers kept human bones on their desks—not out of morbidity, but out of desire for purity of heart. The monastic tradition held memento mori as the first step toward freedom from the passions. The saints of every age have echoed the same truth: when you remember that you will die, you begin to understand how to live.

And all of this prepares us for the most important insight of all: mortality is not only a limitation to accept; it is a teacher sent by God. When we remember that our days are numbered, we learn to value each day differently. We learn to love differently, to forgive differently, to pray differently. We learn to see sin as something that robs us of time and holiness. We learn to see grace as something that prepares us for eternity. Mortality becomes a tutor in conversion. It teaches us that our lives are not random or accidental; they are a series of God-given opportunities to become saints.

This is why the numbering of days is the first wisdom. Without it, nothing else in the spiritual life can be understood correctly. Virtue loses urgency. Sin loses danger. Grace loses preciousness. Mission loses focus. Prayer loses depth. When a person forgets his end, he begins to drift without knowing it. But when the truth of mortality settles into the heart, life becomes sharp, intentional, awake. Love becomes sacrificial. Repentance becomes frequent. Hope becomes strong. Faith becomes joyful. The heart becomes wise.

When the heart finally receives this wisdom, even subtly, a quiet reordering begins. The things that once seemed urgent—reputation, productivity, approval, comfort—lose their grip. Their shine fades because they cannot endure the weight of eternity. Mortality puts them in their proper place. But at the same time, the things that once seemed small—prayer, repentance, reconciliation, charity—rise into view with a new clarity. These are no longer background duties. They become treasures, because they shape the soul for its meeting with God. This is the paradox Scripture reveals: remembering death does not diminish life. It sanctifies it.

This helps explain why the biblical call to remember our days always comes with a corresponding invitation to joy. In Psalm 90, immediately after Moses acknowledges that our lives are like a passing sigh, he prays, "Satisfy us in the morning with Your steadfast love, that we may rejoice and be glad all our days." The numbering of days is not meant to induce gloom but to open space for divine joy. When you know your life is passing, you stop grasping at what cannot last and begin receiving what God wishes to give. Mortality creates a kind of spiritual hunger that only God can satisfy. It breaks open the heart so that divine love can fill it.

The modern world does not understand this because it does not understand the soul. It interprets wisdom in terms of knowledge, success, or self-actualization. It treats happiness as the achievement of personal desire. It sees discomfort as an obstacle and death as an insult. But Scripture, with its divine realism, points us to something deeper: true wisdom is not self-generated but God-given. It comes through humility, surrender, and truthfulness. And nothing reveals truth as forcefully as mortality. The person who remembers his end becomes teachable. He stops defending illusions. He begins to see himself as God sees him. This is why the Bible treats the numbering of days as a prayer. Only God can teach the heart what mortality truly means.

The early fathers of the Church saw this clearly. They understood that the remembrance of death is not a morbid fascination but a spiritual discipline. Saint Basil described the forgetfulness of death as "the root of every sin," because once a person forgets that his time is limited, he delays repentance, downplays temptation, and assumes that conversion can wait for a more convenient hour. Saint

Gregory of Nyssa warned that the failure to remember death leads to a life of distraction and self-deception, whereas the remembrance of death awakens the soul to the seriousness of grace. Even Augustine, who spent much of his youth chasing pleasures that never satisfied, confessed that nothing sobered him more than the realization that his life was passing swiftly. For the fathers, memento mori was not a slogan—it was the first step on the road to sanctity.

This is why the Church has always commemorated the dead, prayed for them, honoured their memory, and kept the reality of mortality before the eyes of the faithful. We meditate on the four last things not because we love severity but because we love truth. We pray "now and at the hour of our death" not to generate anxiety but to invite God into the most vulnerable moment of our future. We celebrate funerals not to dwell on sadness but to proclaim hope. Everything in Catholic tradition, from the ashes of Lent to the prayers at Compline to the requiem liturgies, teaches us to live in the light of our end. Not because death is the centre of our faith, but because Christ is—and remembering death reveals our need for Him.

Modern Christians often struggle with this because we have imbibed more of the world's assumptions than we realize. We are conditioned to think of death as something accidental, undesirable, or peripheral. Yet the biblical worldview does not allow us to treat mortality as an afterthought. It draws it into the centre of reflection so that life can be interpreted correctly. The prophets do this. The psalmists do this. The wisdom authors do this. Jesus Himself does this. Every major thread of Scripture pulls mortality into the foreground, not to frighten us but to awaken us. Memento mori is not a medieval oddity. It is a biblical command.

But if the numbering of days is the beginning of wisdom, then forgetting our days is the beginning of foolishness. The person who never reflects on his mortality begins to live as though he will never die. He treats time as limitless. He assumes that repentance can wait, that prayer can wait, that forgiveness can wait, that holiness can wait. This is the spiritual psychology behind lukewarmness. Jesus warns repeatedly that delay is dangerous not because He wishes to condemn but because He wishes to save. When the heart assumes that there is always more time, it stops watching, stops praying, stops examining itself. It grows numb. It becomes spiritually sleepy. And spiritual sleep is the prelude to spiritual disaster.

This is why memento mori is not a negative practice. It is a protective one. It guards the heart against the illusions that lead to sloth. It keeps the soul awake. It trains the mind to assess life through the lens of eternity rather than convenience. It helps us discern which desires are holy and which are hollow. It clarifies our vocation. It purifies our intentions. It makes the will eager for God. There is nothing morbid about this. It is the clarity that leads to peace.

When a Christian truly begins to number his days, his relationship to time changes. Time is no longer a commodity to control but a sacrament to receive. Each day becomes an opportunity to love, to repent, to forgive, to grow. When a person understands that he may not have another year or another month—or even another day—then each moment becomes precious. He does not spiral into anxiety but rises into fidelity. He becomes less attached to the passing world and more attached to the eternal one. This detachment does not diminish his love for earthly things; it purifies it. He begins to love people more, not less, because he understands that love is the only thing that carries into eternity.

This shift is the fruit of wisdom. It is not learned in a classroom. It is not acquired by studying theological textbooks. It is the grace that comes from facing truth in the presence of God. When a believer meditates on mortality, he is not simply contemplating the natural end of life. He is contemplating the moment when he will stand before the God who made him. This is why the fear of the Lord is called "the beginning of wisdom." The fear Scripture speaks of is not terror but reverence—the recognition that life is a gift entrusted to us, and that we will one day answer for what we made of it. Mortality brings this truth into sharp focus.

The numbering of days also exposes idols. Much of what we cling to loses its power when seen in the light of eternity. Wealth, status, beauty, influence—these fade quickly. Sin becomes weighty rather than appealing. Virtue becomes luminous rather than burdensome. Prayer becomes natural rather than difficult. The remembrance of death reveals the poverty of everything that is not God and the richness of everything that is. When we forget death, we become enslaved to idols without even noticing it. When we remember death, idols lose their allure.

This awareness builds gradually, like dawn breaking over the horizon. At first, it is unsettling. Then it becomes clarifying. Eventually it becomes freeing. A Christian who remembers his mortality does not live with dread; he lives with purpose. He sees time not as something to be filled, but as something to be sanctified. He sees his family not as possessions but as souls entrusted to his care. He sees his work not as self-definition but as stewardship. He sees suffering not as accident but as purification. He sees death not as destruction but as completion. Wisdom makes all of this possible.

This wisdom, once it enters the heart, begins to reshape the entire spiritual landscape of a person's life. It does this quietly at first, like a seed planted deep in the soil, unnoticed by others and barely perceived by the one in whom it has taken root. But over time, the transformation becomes unmistakable. The person who remembers his mortality becomes someone who sees life as a sacred trust rather than a personal possession. He becomes someone who measures his decisions not by convenience but by eternity. He becomes someone who learns, slowly but seriously, to live as a disciple who is passing through this world on the way to the next.

This is why Scripture insists that wisdom is not merely knowledge—it is posture. Job gains knowledge when God speaks, but he gains wisdom when he recognizes his smallness before God. David gains knowledge when he receives the law, but he gains wisdom when he prays for God to reveal the measure of his days. The Teacher of Ecclesiastes gains knowledge through experience, but he gains wisdom through disillusionment. Wisdom is born when the heart humbly acknowledges reality: we are creatures made for God, and life is short.

And this humility, grounded in the remembrance of death, opens the soul to grace in ways nothing else can. Grace does not enter a proud heart. It enters through cracks—moments of weakness, moments of vulnerability, moments when we recognize that we are not in control. Mortality creates such cracks. It exposes our limits. It invites God into the places where our illusions once stood. The person who remembers his death becomes, perhaps surprisingly, a person of deeper faith, because he has learned to rely on God rather than himself.

This is why the saints, almost without exception, speak about death with a kind of quiet confidence. They do not romanticize it, and they do not seek it prematurely. But they understand that death is the moment when faith becomes sight, when hope becomes fulfillment, when love becomes complete. Saint Francis called death a sister not because it was pleasant but because it led him to Christ. Saint Thérèse of Lisieux described her approaching death not with terror but with longing. Saint Paul could proclaim, "To die is gain," because he knew that death was the doorway to communion with the One he loved. This confidence is not natural; it is the fruit of grace. But that grace begins with wisdom, and wisdom begins with numbering our days.

Still, for many believers, the remembrance of death is uncomfortable. It feels heavy. It feels intrusive. It feels like an unwelcome interruption to the rhythms of daily life. This is natural. The human heart resists what it cannot control. But the discomfort itself is part of the gift. When we resist thinking about death, we discover how deeply we cling to this world. When we recoil from our mortality, we learn how much we fear surrender. These reactions become moments of self-revelation. They show us where our trust is thin, where our attachments are excessive, where our love is divided. The remembrance of death becomes, in this way, a mirror that reveals the truth we usually keep hidden.

The fathers often described this mirror with surprising tenderness. Saint Isaac the Syrian said that the remembrance of death "is the mother of prayer." Saint John Climacus wrote that it "awakens the heart" and "plants the seeds of purity." The fathers were not interested in frightening the faithful; they were interested in freeing them. They understood that a person who forgets death becomes enslaved to distractions, consumed by anxieties, and spiritually numb. But a person who remembers death becomes focused, peaceful, and attentive to God. The remembrance of death is not darkness; it is dawn.

This dawn gradually reshapes everything. It leads to a new relationship with the present moment. Instead of rushing through the day, the believer becomes attentive to grace: the quiet prompting to pray, the subtle nudge toward generosity, the inner conviction to repent. These movements become sharper because mortality clarifies what matters. When a person knows he will die, he becomes less interested in wasting time and more interested in redeeming it. He becomes less concerned with appearing holy and more concerned with becoming holy. He becomes less preoccupied with comfort and more committed to love. In this way, the remembrance of death becomes a daily invitation to live intentionally in the presence of God.

This intentionality does not make life smaller; it enlarges it. The person who numbers his days begins to see the world with fresh eyes. He notices the beauty he once ignored. He appreciates the blessings he once took for granted. He cherishes relationships more deeply. He forgives more quickly. He becomes both more serious about holiness and more joyful about life. And this combination—seriousness and joy—is the hallmark of the Christian heart awakened to wisdom. It reflects the mind of Christ, who faced His own death with unwavering fidelity and extraordinary love.

All of this prepares the soul for what Scripture calls "the fear of the Lord," which is not dread but reverence, not anxiety but awe. This holy fear is the foundation of wisdom because it teaches the heart to stand rightly before God: grateful, humble, attentive. It teaches us to receive life as a gift and to treat every moment as sacred. It teaches us that each day is an opportunity to grow in the likeness of Christ. It teaches us that time is not merely passing—it is shaping us for eternity.

When we number our days in this way, we begin to see the spiritual life not as a set of duties but as a journey. God becomes not a distant ruler but a faithful companion. Mortality becomes not a threat but a guide. Each moment becomes a step toward the One who loves us more than we can comprehend. And this journey leads us to the very centre of Christian wisdom: the knowledge that our end is our beginning, that our death is our passage, that our meeting with Christ is the purpose for which we were created. The remembrance of death is the first wisdom because it leads us to the One who is Wisdom Himself.

Yet as the heart learns this wisdom, something even deeper unfolds. The remembrance of death, which once felt sombre or unsettling, becomes a source of profound consolation. It reminds us that this world, with all its burdens and sorrows, is not our home. It reminds us that suffering does not have the last word. It reminds us that our lives are not random but written into the vast story of God's redeeming love. The person who remembers his death becomes, paradoxically, a person of hope, because he begins to see the trajectory of his life not as a slow movement toward darkness but as a pilgrimage toward light. The horizon of his existence shifts. What once loomed as an ending begins to appear as a beginning.

This shift takes time. It cannot be forced, and it cannot be faked. But it can be cultivated. And Scripture gives us the means to cultivate it. When Moses prayed, "Teach us to number our days," he was asking for instruction from the only One who sees time perfectly. He was asking to see life as God sees it. This is the heart of biblical wisdom. To number our days is to acknowledge that our lives are lived within a story larger than ourselves—a story in which God is the Author, we are the creatures, and eternity is the horizon. It is to understand that every choice we make is shaping our soul for the moment when we stand before God. It is to understand that life is not a possession but a preparation.

This is why remembering death does not produce despair in the believer but order. It reorganizes the interior life according to truth. It teaches the heart to seek first the Kingdom of God. It exposes the hollowness of sin and the urgency of grace. It draws the soul away from procrastination and toward perseverance. It shifts the focus from comfort to holiness. When a Christian knows that his time is limited, he becomes more responsive to the movements of the Holy Spirit. He becomes sensitive to the invitations of grace and resistant to the whispers of temptation. He begins to take the spiritual life seriously, not out of fear but out of love.

And love is the true heart of this wisdom. The remembrance of death is not primarily about avoiding judgment; it is about preparing to meet the One who has loved us into existence. When we meditate on our mortality, we are not contemplating nothingness—we are contemplating the moment when we will see God face-to-face. The believer who lives with this awareness does not shrink from that moment; he longs for it. He organizes his life around it. He shapes his desires in anticipation of it. His faith becomes not an obligation but a yearning. He longs to be found faithful. He longs to be found ready. He longs to hear the words, "Well done, good and faithful servant."

This longing is a grace, and it grows as mortality becomes a companion rather than a stranger. It is the longing of Saint Paul, who declared, "Our citizenship is in heaven, and from it we await a Savior." It is the longing of the psalmists, who cried out for God as a deer longs for running water. It is the longing of Israel, who waited for the Day of the Lord with tearful expectation. It is the longing of the Church, who prays, "Come, Lord Jesus." When mortality is remembered rightly, it does not stifle this desire—it intensifies it. It makes heaven more real, Christ more present, eternity more nearby.

And it does something else: it brings peace. A strange and steady peace settles over the soul that lives with its end in view. Not the peace of denial, but the peace of acceptance. Not the peace of distraction, but the peace of trust. A person who remembers that life is short learns to hold lightly to what passes and to cling tightly to what lasts. He learns to forgive quickly, because resentment wastes precious time. He learns to love generously, because love is the only currency that endures. He learns to pray earnestly, because prayer aligns the heart with the God who will soon be its all. He learns to work joyfully, because work becomes participation in God's creative plan rather than a frantic attempt at self-definition. This peace is the fruit of wisdom, and wisdom is the gift of remembering our days.

But what happens if we do not remember? Scripture is clear about this as well. The person who forgets his mortality becomes spiritually drowsy. He loses the sense of urgency that once animated faith. He drifts through life assuming that tomorrow will always come. He postpones repentance, minimizes sin, and treats grace casually. His heart becomes divided, his conscience dull, his zeal faint. This is the condition Jesus warns against so repeatedly—the sleep of the soul. The sleep of complacency. The sleep of a heart no longer alert to the things of God. And that sleep is dangerous precisely because it feels comfortable. That is why Scripture shakes us awake with the remembrance of death. It cries out, "Today, if you hear His voice, do not harden your heart." Not tomorrow. Not later. Today.

The remembrance of death rescues us from this sleep. It does not frighten; it focuses. It does not paralyse; it purifies. It does not burden; it liberates. It clarifies the purpose of life, reveals the weight of eternity, and protects the soul from the deadly illusion that time is ours to waste. A Christian who remembers his death does not wander aimlessly. He lives intentionally, gratefully, joyfully. He sees everything—his family, his work, his sufferings, his opportunities—as gifts entrusted to him by God, to be used for God's glory. His days become not a series of interruptions or obligations, but a sequence of chances to love.

In this way, the remembrance of death becomes the doorway to wisdom's greatest fruit: desire for God. The more a person lives with his end before him, the more he realizes that nothing in this world can satisfy the soul. The more he contemplates his meeting with Christ, the more he hungers for holiness. The more he recognizes the brevity of life, the more he longs for the life that never ends. Mortality reveals not only the shortness of time but the length of eternity, not only the limits of the world but the boundlessness of God. It reveals that we were made for more than this life can give.

When this desire awakens, the heart becomes ready. Ready to obey. Ready to repent. Ready to love. Ready to persevere. Ready to suffer. Ready to die. Not out of stoicism, but out of faith. Not out of resignation, but out of hope. The remembrance of death teaches us to lift our eyes toward the horizon of eternity and to live each moment with the knowledge that our end is not annihilation but encounter. It is the moment when the veil lifts and the truth of our lives come fully into view. It is the moment when all our choices converge into a single revelation: what we have become in the sight of God.

This is the first wisdom. It is the wisdom that clears the mind, strengthens the will, purifies the heart, and deepens faith. It is the wisdom Israel learned in the desert, the wisdom the psalmists prayed for, the wisdom the prophets proclaimed, the wisdom the fathers cherished, and the wisdom Christ Himself embodied. It is the wisdom that prepares the soul for every chapter that follows.

2

Dust and Glory: The Christian View of Mortality

To understand what death truly means for the Christian, we must return to the place where the story begins—not to a cemetery or battlefield, but to a garden. Genesis does not introduce humanity with fear or frailty. It introduces us with intimacy. God forms the first man from the dust of the ground, yet He does not speak the man into existence as He did the light, the stars, the seas. Instead, He stoops. He shapes. He breathes. The very posture of God in the act of creation tells us something about who we are: creatures fashioned with intention, loved before we are even alive, bearing a dignity that does not come from ourselves. "Then the Lord God formed the man of dust from the ground and breathed into his nostrils the breath of life" (Gen 2:7). Dust and divine breath—humility and glory—woven together into one mystery.

The fathers of the Church never tired of contemplating this moment. Augustine marvelled that the God who fills heaven and earth chose to form a creature out of such lowly material, not to diminish man's dignity but to magnify His own generosity. Basil the Great, preaching on the days of creation, described the human person as "the meeting place of the visible and the invisible," a being who stands with one foot in the soil and the other lifted toward God. Athanasius, with his characteristic clarity, spoke of humanity as a creature made from nothing yet destined for participation in the divine life. None of these fathers saw dust as humiliation. They saw it as theology, as revelation, as a sign that human life is a gift sustained entirely by the breath of God.

There is no shame in dust because there is no shame in being a creature. Quite the opposite. Dust is the reminder that our existence is not self-generated, not self-directed, and not self-sustained. We are dependent from the first moment of our lives, and dependence is not a defect—it is a design. To be made of dust is to stand in humility before God; to receive breath is to be lifted into glory by God. This is why, even before death enters the story, the Bible speaks of the human person with wonder. We are dust touched by the Spirit, matter ignited by divine breath, images of the God who made heaven and earth.

Yet this exalted beginning also reveals a truth that many modern people resist: we are not gods. We are not immortal by nature. We are not self-existent. Our life comes from God's breath, and our identity comes from His image. The serpent's great deception in Genesis 3—"you will be like God"—was not the promise of freedom but the seed of death. Augustine wrote that pride is the beginning of all sin because it attempts to reverse the order of creation. Pride forgets dust. It forgets dependence. It forgets the hands that formed us and the breath that sustains us. Pride attempts to seize glory apart from God, and the result is not freedom but collapse. The fall is not simply disobedience; it is the refusal to remain creaturely.

This is why the divine sentence pronounced after the fall—"you are dust, and to dust you shall return" (Gen 3:19)—is not arbitrary punishment but the revelation of a truth humanity had attempted to forget. Athanasius explains this with striking simplicity in *On the Incarnation*: to turn away from the Source of life is to return to non-being, to corruption, to the dissolution inherent in matter apart from grace. Death enters not because God delights in suffering, but because separation from God cannot sustain life. When Adam and Eve stepped outside the covenant of love, they stepped outside the breath that made them alive. Dust without breath always collapses.

And yet, even in this moment of judgment, mercy is hidden like a seed beneath the soil. The fathers insist that mortality after the fall is both consequence and compassion. Gregory Nazianzen described death as "the limit placed upon sin," a boundary that prevents evil from becoming immortal. Maximus the Confessor, with theological brilliance, spoke of death as a "bitter medicine," permitted by God to keep humanity from plunging endlessly into pride. Benedict XVI echoed this when he wrote that mortality, though painful, prevents the human heart from enthroning itself as god. In this sense, "to dust you shall return" is not only a sentence; it is a safeguard. It is the reminder that we are not what the serpent promised. We are dust beloved by God, not divinity in disguise.

This means that mortality is not simply a fact of biology but a sign of theology. It is a truth about who we are and who we are not. It is the revelation that life is not self-contained. It is the confession that existence is received, not earned. The very structure of human life—including its end—whispers a covenant language: you belong to the One who made you; your life is not your own. When Job cries, "Remember that You have made me like clay; and will You return me to dust?" (Job 10:9), he is not lamenting insignificance; he is appealing to relationship. Clay remembers its potter. Dust remembers the hands that shaped it.

This is why Scripture never speaks of death as simple cessation. Death is relational. It is the rupture of communion, the undoing of the unity between dust and breath, body and soul. Ecclesiastes captures this with sombre poetry: "the dust returns to the earth as it was, and the spirit returns to God who gave it" (Eccl 12:7). There is nothing random or mechanical here. Death is the moment when the gift of life returns to its Giver. It is tragic because it was not meant to be this way. It is holy because even in tragedy, God remains faithful to His creature. "He remembers that we are dust," David sings in Psalm 103, and this remembrance is not condescension—it is compassion. God never forgets our fragility even when we forget it ourselves.

This interplay between dust and glory—between creatureliness and divine breath—forms the heart of the Christian understanding of mortality. We are not angels trapped in bodies nor animals ruled by instinct. We are embodied souls, animated dust, images of the invisible God. To be made of dust is to be humble; to bear God's breath is to be exalted. To be mortal is to be needy; to belong to God is to be loved. The Bible does not resolve this tension; it reveals it as the very place where grace works. The Christian view of death cannot be understood without this paradox. It is the stage upon which both the tragedy of sin and the triumph of redemption are displayed.

And yet, if Genesis shows us the origin of mortality, it does not show us its end. The story of dust is unfinished in the garden. Something—or rather Someone—must enter the dust in order to transform it. Someone must step into the place of dissolution, corruption, and loss in order to bring forth life. The entire Old Testament strains toward this hope with groanings and promises, sacrifices and prophecies, shadows and signs. Humanity returns to dust because of the fall, but the Scriptures whisper of a deliverer who will enter the dust not as victim but as victor.

The mystery deepens when we consider what Scripture dares to proclaim: the God who formed humanity from dust will Himself enter that dust. The One who breathed life into Adam will one day breathe His last. The Word through whom all things were made will take on the very flesh that withers. Nothing in Genesis prepares us for this except the boundless love of the Creator. Humanity's return to dust becomes, in Christ, the place where God Himself chooses to meet us. Athanasius writes with astonishment that the Word "took to Himself a body capable of death," not because He was subject to it by nature but because He desired to destroy death from within. The Incarnation is not merely God drawing near; it is God stepping into the condition of mortality we brought upon ourselves.

Before Christ takes on flesh, death is a curse. After Christ takes on flesh, death becomes the battlefield where the decisive victory of salvation is won. Hebrews gives us the clearest window into this wonder: "Since the children share in flesh and blood, He Himself likewise partook of the same nature, that through death He might destroy him who has the power of death" (Heb 2:14–15). The author of Hebrews does not say Christ avoided death; he says Christ used death as a weapon. The very thing that had enslaved humanity becomes, in the hands of God, the instrument of liberation. Death is undone by death. The grave becomes the place where Satan loses his claim. The fear that once held the human race captive is shattered because the Son of God entered the dust willingly.

This is why the cross, from a distance, appears as defeat but is in truth the great inversion of history. Augustine wrote that Christ's death contained "the medicine of immortality," because the poison of sin must be healed through the very nature that had been wounded. Basil taught that the body of Christ was like a hook hidden within the bait of human flesh—Satan, thinking he had conquered another mortal, seized Him and was dragged into his own destruction. The fathers saw the cross not as accident but as strategy. God uses mortality to conquer corruption. He uses the fragility of dust to reveal the invincibility of divine love.

If Genesis reveals what humanity is without God, the Gospels reveal what humanity becomes when God joins Himself to our condition. Christ does not merely sympathize with our mortality; He sanctifies it. He touches the leper, not to show compassion alone but to show that corruption cannot infect the incorruptible. He raises the dead not simply to restore life but to signal the coming defeat of death itself. He weeps at the tomb of Lazarus because He knows the grief that has burdened humanity since Eden. Yet He cries out with divine authority, "Lazarus, come forth!" not as a temporary gesture but as a sign of the resurrection that will spring from His own tomb.

Every miracle Christ performs is an unveiling of His mission to conquer death. His healing of the sick is a foretaste of the renewal of creation. His authority over demons is the prelude to the destruction of the one who wielded death as his weapon. His Transfiguration is the revelation of the glory that awaits humanity when the power of death is broken. Even His silence before Pilate is an act of sovereignty; He is not a victim swept into execution but the Lamb who offers Himself freely. Athanasius reminds us that Christ could not die unless He willed it. Immortality cannot be forced into death. The moment He bows His head on the cross is the moment He chooses to enter the dust on behalf of the dust He created.

This is why the early Christians did not fear martyrdom. They saw in death not annihilation but union with Christ. The catacombs bear witness to a people who understood the paradox: death is the last enemy, but it is a defeated enemy. The grave is still dark, but it has been filled with the presence of the One who is Light. Chrysostom could preach on Pascha, "O death, where is your sting? O hell, where is your victory?" because the sting has been blunted and the victory reversed. Paul's proclamation in 1 Corinthians 15 is not poetic flourish; it is theological fact. Christ's resurrection is not merely the end of His story; it is the beginning of ours. The dust that once doomed humanity now becomes the very soil from which resurrection life springs.

But this does not mean death becomes natural or pleasant or neutral. Christianity never romanticizes death. Scripture calls death "the last enemy," and the Church never forgets it. The pain of separation is real. The wound of mortality is real. Yet for the believer, death is no longer a wall but a door. No longer a curse but a passage. No longer the triumph of sin but the moment when grace reaches its fullest expression. The Christian stands at the grave with tears, but not as those who have no hope. The grief is human; the hope is divine. Death has not been erased; it has been transformed.

This transformation begins in the tomb of Christ. The dust of Adam returns to the ground because of sin, but the dust of Christ lies in the earth for three days and emerges glorified. The resurrection is not simply resuscitation; it is recreation. The body that rises is the same and yet entirely new—mortal flesh now transfigured by divine life. Paul calls Christ the "first fruits," a term loaded with covenant meaning. Where the first Adam brings death, the second Adam brings life. Where the first Adam returns to dust, the second Adam rises from it so that all who belong to Him may share His destiny. The resurrection reveals that death is not the final truth about humanity. Union with Christ is.

And this truth casts a new light on every page of Scripture. Adam's formation from dust is no longer merely a sign of fragility; it becomes a prophecy of redemption. If God formed humanity from dust once, He can form us again in the resurrection. If He breathed life into Adam at the beginning, He can breathe eternal life into us at the end. The body, far from being disposable, becomes the vessel through which God will reveal His glory. Irenaeus loved to repeat that "the glory of God is man fully alive," and this fullness is possible only because Christ has entered our mortality and filled it with His immortality.

The Christian view of death, then, is not denial, despair, or detachment—it is hope grounded in history. The resurrection is not metaphor; it is event. The transformation of dust is not symbolic; it is promised. Augustine insisted that God loses nothing of what He has made, that every particle of the human body, no matter how scattered, will be gathered again by the One who fashioned it. This confidence is not wishful thinking; it is covenant theology. The God who remembers that we are dust is the God who refuses to abandon the dust He formed. Mortality reveals fragility, but it also reveals fidelity. God's faithfulness is displayed precisely in the place where human weakness is undeniable.

The fathers pressed this truth with a boldness that continues to astonish. They saw in Christ's descent into the grave not simply an act of solidarity with humanity but a cosmic reversal. Ephrem the Syrian imagined death as a monstrous mouth that had swallowed every generation since Adam, widening with each corpse, confident in its dominion. Yet when Christ entered, Ephrem says, death "swallowed Him" only to choke, as if it had attempted to contain fire. The grave collapsed inward; corruption recoiled from in corruption. For the first time since Eden, death tasted something it could not digest. Ephrem's imagery is poetic, but the theology is precise: Christ did not merely avoid decay—His very presence reversed it, conquering the corruption embedded in human mortality.

Athanasius explains this same mystery from a different angle. Humanity, he says, was sliding toward non-being, dissolving back into the nothingness from which it had been made. Sin was not simply moral failure; it was metaphysical decay. But the Word took on a body precisely to halt and reverse that descent. "He surrendered His body to death in place of all," Athanasius writes, "and offered it to the Father." In that offering, death lost its legal claim. The penalty was paid, the curse exhausted, the dominion shattered. This is not abstract theology—it is the very architecture of Christian hope. If death is undone in the body of Christ, then it cannot hold those who belong to Christ.

Augustine approaches the mystery with characteristic realism. He marvels that the Word became flesh not merely to teach or to heal but to die. In his *City of God*, he writes that Christ "submitted to death of His own will" so that humanity, enslaved to death against its will, might be freed. Augustine lingers on the humility of God entering our frailty—dust embracing dust—not because He lacked power, but because love compelled Him. For Augustine, the Incarnation is the ultimate revelation of God's fidelity to His creation. The God who formed humanity from dust will not abandon humanity to dust. He enters the story we ruined so that He might restore the destiny we lost.

This restoration is not merely personal; it is cosmic. Basil the Great, preaching on creation, envisioned humanity as the crown of the visible world, the creature through whom all matter was meant to praise God. When humanity fell, the harmony of creation was wounded, not because dust rebelled but because the one who bore God's image misused his freedom. In Christ, Basil sees the healing not only of humanity but of the world. The flesh assumed by the Word becomes the beginning of a renewed creation. Dust is not discarded; it is redeemed. Matter is not despised; it is sanctified. The resurrection of the body is not an afterthought—it is the fulfillment of God's original plan.

If Christ's entry into mortality is the turning point of history, His resurrection is its unveiling. The empty tomb is not simply the sign of victory; it is the sign of identity. What God did in the body of Christ becomes the promise of what He will do in the bodies of all who belong to Him. Paul draws this parallel with stunning clarity: "As we have borne the image of the man of dust, we shall also bear the image of the man of heaven" (1 Cor 15:49). Resurrection is not escape from dust; it is the glorification of dust. The human body, which once returned to the earth in sorrow, will rise from the earth in splendour. Death, which once marked the dissolution of the person, will become the doorway to the full revelation of the person in Christ.

This is why the Christian tradition insists on the dignity of the body even in death. We bury the dead, not discard them. We treat the body with reverence, not because it retains biological function, but because it retains theological identity. The flesh that dissolves in the earth is the flesh God formed, the flesh Christ assumed, the flesh destined for resurrection. Early Christians adorned tombs with images of Jonah, Daniel, the three young men in the furnace—all signs of deliverance through death, all foreshadowing's of resurrection. They understood that the grave is not the final word; it is the place where God speaks His definitive promise.

If death has been transformed in Christ, then the entire experience of human mortality takes on a new meaning. Mortality no longer signals abandonment; it signals need. It reveals the truth that we depend on God not only for breath but for destiny. Mortality teaches us humility, yes, but also trust. The God who formed us from the dust remembers that dust. He remembers its fragility, its limitations, its fears. And He remembers it not with frustration but with fidelity. Psalm 103 says, "He remembers that we are dust," and those words are not indictment—they are comfort. God does not forget the material from which He made us. He does not despise our frailty; He takes it up into Himself.

This divine remembrance is the heart of redemption. God's fidelity is not abstract. It appears in the very place where human existence is most fragile—in sickness, in aging, in the moment when breath fails and the body yields. Christ entered that moment to fill it with His presence so that we would never face it alone. The resurrection reveals that the God who made humanity in the beginning remains faithful to humanity in the end. Dust and glory belong together because God holds them together. This is the Christian view of mortality: death as enemy, conquered; death as doorway, opened; death as consequence, transformed; death as the meeting place of divine fidelity and human frailty.

This movement now prepares the final half of the chapter, where the meaning of mortality for the Christian life will unfold more deeply: what it reveals about God's love, what it reveals about our destiny, and how Christ's victory reframes the entire drama of death.

If the resurrection recasts death as the place where God's fidelity shines, it also recasts life as preparation for glory rather than a slow march toward decay. The Christian does not deny mortality; he interprets it. He sees in his frailty not a sign of insignificance but a summons to communion. Mortality becomes the reminder that life is relational at its core: we came from God, we depend on God, and we return to God. Without this relationship, death is terror; within this relationship, death is truth. It reveals what has always been the case—that our existence is not self-contained. We live by a breath that is not our own. We stand on grace every moment of our lives. Mortality does not diminish this truth; it reveals it.

This revelation reshapes the entire biblical narrative. The fall introduces death, but the covenant answers it. Abraham's story only makes sense because God binds Himself to a mortal man whose days are numbered. Moses is not immortal; he dies within sight of the Promised Land, yet Scripture tells us his eyes were undimmed because his life was anchored not in longevity but in promise. David sings of mortality with honesty—"Man is like a breath; his days are like a passing shadow"—yet he sings with confidence because God's love endures forever. The pattern is always the same: humanity is fleeting, but God is faithful. Dust returns to dust, but the covenant does not crumble. It is sealed by the God who remains.

This contrast between human weakness and divine fidelity becomes even more striking in the prophets. Isaiah declares that "all flesh is grass," yet immediately affirms that "the word of our God will stand forever." Ezekiel is commanded to preach to dry bones, not to display their hopelessness but to reveal the power of God to create life where only death is visible. Hosea speaks of God ransoming His people "from the power of Sheol," a promise that seems impossible until Christ fulfills it. Mortality becomes the canvas upon which God paints His mercy. The more fragile the canvas, the more radiant the mercy appears.

This is why the New Testament reads differently once we understand death through the lens of Christ. Jesus does not treat death as something natural or inconsequential. He weeps at Lazarus's tomb because death is an intruder, a vandal in the house of creation. Yet He confronts that intruder directly. He allows death to touch His own flesh so that He might rob it of its victory. When He rises, He does not merely return to life—He inaugurates a new kind of life, one no longer subject to corruption. Paul calls this the "imperishable" body, the body sown in weakness and raised in power, sown in dishonour and raised in glory. What Christ reveals is not immortality of the soul alone but the destiny of the whole human person, body and soul reunited in splendour.

This hope changes the meaning of every human experience of suffering, aging, or loss. The body that weakens is not losing its purpose; it is advancing toward revelation. The body that bends, breaks, or falters is not betraying us; it is teaching us. It teaches us dependence. It teaches us humility. It teaches us longing for the world to come. In this sense, mortality is not the enemy of faith but its tutor. Athanasius insisted that humanity's corruption after the fall was precisely what made the Incarnation necessary, and in that necessity lies a strange hope. Our frailty called forth God's closeness. Our need drew down His mercy. If we were immortal by nature, we would not have known the God who conquers death. If we were unbreakable, we would not have known the God who heals. Mortality reveals the God who will not let dust have the final word.

Paul expresses this with gripping intensity when he writes that "creation itself will be set free from its bondage to decay." This is not mere metaphor. It is ontology. Decay does not define creation; redemption does. The dust from which we were made is not the dust of oblivion but the soil awaiting resurrection. Irenaeus insisted that God never relinquishes what He has made. If He formed humanity from the earth once, He will form us again. If He breathed life into Adam once, He will breathe eternal life into us at the resurrection. Redemption is not spiritual escape—it is the completion of creation.

This, in turn, sheds light on a profound truth: death is both the last enemy and the final teacher. As enemy, it wounds. It separates. It makes exile palpable. As teacher, it humbles. It awakens. It directs the heart toward the One who alone can grant life beyond the grave. The fathers spoke of death as a "boundary" given by God—not to harm us but to prevent sin from becoming endless. Maximus the Confessor saw in death the limit that keeps humanity from worshiping itself. The limitation of mortality is the space where grace enters. It is the place where pride loses its footing. Dust teaches what Eden forgot: creatureliness is not a burden but a blessing.

Seen through this lens, the Christian does not merely accept mortality—he interprets it as revelation. Mortality reveals that God keeps His promises. It reveals that God enters our story not when we are strong but when we are weak. It reveals that divine love is not abstract; it is incarnate, tangible, embodied. Christ's resurrection transforms mortality from a verdict into a vocation. Death becomes the hour when faith becomes sight, hope becomes fulfillment, and love becomes communion. It is the moment when the God who formed us from dust calls us by name and raises us from the earth in glory.

This transformation is not only future; it is present. Every encounter with our own limitation becomes an encounter with grace. Every reminder of our frailty becomes a reminder of God's fidelity. Mortality turns the heart toward the things that endure—mercy, holiness, forgiveness, covenant. The believer who lives with death before him does not grow morbid; he grows wise. He begins to understand that life is not measured by length but by love. He begins to desire not simply more years but deeper union with Christ. Mortality, in this sense, becomes the teacher that leads the soul into maturity.

The believer who meditates on mortality in this way begins to see that death is not simply something that happens at the end of life but something that shapes the meaning of life as it unfolds. Christ has transformed death from a termination into a revelation. When a Christian contemplates the grave, he does not contemplate nothingness; he contemplates the faithfulness of God. He sees that the God who breathed life into Adam will breathe new life into all who die in Christ. He sees that the God who raised Jesus from the dead will "give life to our mortal bodies also through His Spirit who dwells in us" (Rom 8:11). This promise is not peripheral to the Gospel; it is the Gospel's final unveiling. Salvation is not complete until the body rises, until dust is clothed in light, until mortality is swallowed up by immortality.

This is why death, even now, carries a sacramental character. It reveals what every moment of life is pointing toward: union with God. The Christian tradition has always understood death in this dual sense—enemy and threshold, rupture and consummation. Death is the enemy because it tears apart what God joined; it separates soul from body, loved ones from one another. Jesus Himself grieved this separation when He stood before Lazarus's tomb. Yet death becomes the threshold of glory because Christ has passed through it. The Christian does not enter the grave alone; Christ waits on the other side. Death becomes the place where the covenant reaches its climax, where God keeps the final promise: "I will be your God, and you shall be My people."

This covenant fidelity unfolds in ways that touch every corner of the Christian life. Mortality teaches us to pray with sincerity, because prayer is not a hobby of the religious but the conversation of the dying with the Giver of life. Mortality teaches us to forgive, because resentment wastes the limited time we have. Mortality teaches us to love, because every act of love participates in the eternity we seek. Mortality teaches us gratitude, because each day is unearned. In this sense, the remembrance of death is not an escape from life but an entrance into its deepest meaning. It is the lens through which the Christian learns to see every gift as gift and every moment as grace.

The fathers knew this well. They taught that death, rightly understood, becomes a spiritual discipline. It awakens watchfulness. It shakes away illusions. It cuts through the false securities that so easily distract the soul. Ephrem the Syrian wrote that "death is the scholar of truth," because it reveals what we truly are and what we truly love. The desert monks often kept skulls in their cells, not as morbid decoration but as tutors in wisdom. They believed that if a man remembered his death, he would never squander his life. This was not pessimism; it was clarity. They saw in mortality the invitation to live with intention, to seek holiness with urgency, to love God with purity of heart.

But the greatest clarity mortality offers is not self-awareness; it is God-awareness. When the believer contemplates death, he comes face-to-face with the faithfulness of the One who refuses to abandon His creation. Augustine captured this with piercing simplicity: "God is closer to us than we are to ourselves." Mortality exposes this truth because in our weakness, God's nearness becomes visible. As our strength fades, His providence becomes palpable. As our breath shortens, His breath sustains. As our days diminish, His promise grows. Mortality becomes the stage on which divine fidelity is displayed in unmistakable light.

This fidelity is not seen only in the resurrection to come but in the way God accompanies His people in the valley of the shadow of death. Psalm 23 does not promise exemption from the valley; it promises presence within it. "You are with me" is the heart of the psalmist's confidence. God's rod and staff do not remove death; they transform the way we walk toward it. The Christian who knows he will die walks differently from the one who denies it. He walks with trust, not fear; with hope, not despair; with purpose, not panic. He recognizes that death is not the negation of life but the unveiling of what life was always pointing toward: communion with God.

This communion is not ethereal or abstract. It is embodied. The resurrected Christ bears wounds, not scars. His risen body is not a rejection of the flesh but the fulfillment of it. He eats with His disciples, speaks with them, breathes peace upon them. The resurrection does not erase the physical; it transfigures it. This is why Christian hope is always hope in the resurrection of the body. Dust matters because God chose dust. Flesh matters because God took flesh. Death matters because God entered death. And the body's destiny matters because Christ's own body stands as the pledge and pattern of our future.

In this light, mortality becomes not only a reminder of our origin but a sign of our destiny. The body that returns to dust will be raised in glory. The breath that leaves the body at death will be restored in a new creation. The weakness that characterizes our present condition becomes the very place where God promises to reveal His power. "What is sown in weakness is raised in power," Paul writes. This is the grammar of redemption: God transforms what He touches.

Dust touched by God becomes humanity. Humanity touched by God becomes the Body of Christ. The Body of Christ, risen and glorified, becomes the promise extended to all who are united to Him.

This promise reshapes not only our theology but our imagination. When the Christian looks at the world, he sees signs of resurrection everywhere. Seeds falling into the earth to die before they bear fruit. Winter yielding to spring. Night giving way to dawn. Even the cycle of human breath—inhale, exhale, return—mirrors the deeper rhythm of life and death and life again. Creation whispers what Scripture proclaims: death is not the final sound in the orchestra of existence. It is the silence before the final movement, the moment where the Conductor raises His hand and creation waits to erupt with new life.

The more deeply this truth settles into the heart, the more mortality becomes not a threat but a teacher of hope. It instructs the Christian in the art of waiting—not with dread, but with expectation. The God who formed humanity from dust at the beginning is the same God who will raise humanity from dust at the end. His hands have not weakened. His breath has not dimmed. His desire has not wavered. What He began in Eden, He will complete in the New Creation. Mortality is the paradoxical reminder that our lives are carried by a promise larger than we can see. Every wrinkle, every ache, every limitation becomes a quiet homily: "You are being prepared for glory."

This preparation unfolds not in some distant spiritual realm but in the very texture of daily life. The Christian who remembers that he is dust finds that he becomes more attentive, more grateful, more humble. He learns to live deliberately because he knows his time is limited. He learns to love generously because he knows love alone survives the grave. He learns to cling to God rather than to passing things because he knows that God alone can raise what death tries to claim. Mortality purifies desire. It clarifies purpose. It strips away illusions. It leads the soul toward the one truth that cannot die: God is faithful.

This is the truth that death reveals with uncompromising clarity. When a believer stands at a graveside, he encounters not only the reality of human frailty but the stubborn fidelity of God. The body returns to the earth, yet the promise of resurrection remains unshaken. The soul departs, yet the covenant endures. The grave appears final, yet it is already marked by the presence of the One who rested there for three days and rose never to die again. Death threatens to take everything, yet Christ has taken its power. It can still wound, but it cannot win. It can still grieve, but it cannot govern. The risen Christ stands at the centre of the Christian view of mortality, transforming every fear into invitation.

He invites us to trust. He invites us to surrender. He invites us to see death not as the collapse of meaning but as the unveiling of it. For the one who dies in Christ, death becomes the moment when all of life's scattered pieces finally converge. The threads of longing, the struggles against sin, the acts of mercy, the tears of repentance—all are gathered by the hands that once formed us from dust. The Christian dies into the embrace of God. And from that embrace, God will call forth the body itself, restored, renewed, and radiant.

This hope does not minimize the sorrow of death. Jesus wept at Lazarus's tomb precisely because death is not trivial. It wounds the heart because it was never meant to be part of the human story. Yet Jesus wept only before He commanded Lazarus to rise. He grieved what death had done, then revealed what God would do. This is why Christian mourning is honest yet hopeful. It acknowledges the rupture while proclaiming the promise. It allows tears without surrendering to despair. It stands between the grave and the resurrection with the same faith that Martha uttered: "I know that he will rise again in the resurrection on the last day."

Christ answers her—and us—not with doctrine alone but with self-revelation: "I am the resurrection and the life." He does not simply teach the meaning of death; He embodies the victory over it. In Him, death becomes not just conquered but redefined. What once signified the end becomes the beginning. What once signified defeat becomes triumph. What once signified separation becomes communion. For the believer in Christ, death no longer declares the final word; it yields to the Word made flesh.

The fathers spoke of this transformation with poetic intensity. Ephrem envisioned Christ entering the grave like a king entering a tyrant's palace, seizing its treasures—human souls—and leading them out in triumph. Augustine imagined Christ as the Bridegroom entering the bridal chamber of the tomb, sanctifying it for His beloved. Maximus saw in Christ's passage through death the healing of the rupture between body and soul. Each father, in his own way, grasped the truth that death, though still present, has been stripped of its absoluteness. It remains a passage, but not a prison.

This brings the chapter to its deepest conclusion: mortality is not simply a human problem but a divine promise. It is the place where God reveals His unwavering commitment to His creation. If we were not mortal, we would never know the God who conquers death. If we did not return to dust, we would never know the God who raises dust to glory. Mortality is the stage upon which divine fidelity is displayed in its most radiant form. It is the arena where Christ manifests His victory. It is the reminder that God does not abandon what He makes. Dust is not disposable; it is destined.

3

The Desert Fathers and the Holy Art of Remembering Death

The Christian tradition has always known that remembering death awakens the soul, yet nowhere does this truth burn more fiercely than in the deserts of Egypt and Palestine, where the first monks—those strange, holy men who fled the world to find God—made memento mori the heartbeat of their lives. Their world seems far from ours: barren landscapes, caves carved into cliffs, cells woven from reeds, and long nights stretched out in prayer beneath an unbroken sky. Yet the wisdom they discovered in those silent places remains startlingly relevant, because the desert only made visible what has always been true. It exposed the illusion that human beings live by habit and chance and comfort. It revealed the truth that life is fragile, that time is short, that death is not an enemy to fear but a teacher to heed.

When Athanasius wrote the *Life of Antony*, he gave the Church not only a biography of its first great monk but a window into a spiritual vision shaped by mortality. Antony was young when he entered the desert—barely more than a boy—and yet from the moment he stepped beyond the boundaries of ordinary life, he lived with the clarity of someone who understood that every day could be his last. Athanasius records that Antony often visited the tombs just outside the village of his youth. The ancient world placed the dead outside city gates, and for Antony these tombs were not places of dread but places of prayer. Here he confronted the truth of human frailty and asked God for the grace to live in the light of judgment. According to Athanasius, he prayed in the tombs "as if seeing his own death before him," and it was in these early vigils that his spiritual sight sharpened. Death no longer frightened him—it humbled him, sobered him, and awakened him.

This was the beginning of a pattern that would mark the entire monastic tradition. The desert was never a romantic escape; it was a return to reality. Life in the cities, even in antiquity, had its comforts and distractions. The desert stripped these away. There, a person faced the truth without mediation: the frailty of the body, the limits of the mind, the ease with which temptation arises, the vulnerability of a heart that lives on dependence rather than autonomy. In the desert, you could not pretend you were immortal. The heat reminded you. The silence reminded you. The bones scattered across the sands reminded you. The sight of a monk praying in a burial cave reminded you. Everything taught the lesson the Scriptures had already given: "Teach us to number our days," not to depress us, but to awaken wisdom.

Antony's story makes this remarkably clear. Athanasius recounts that when he first began his solitary life, the devil tried to terrify him with visions of beasts and ghosts—illusions meant to overwhelm him. Antony did not flee. He confronted them by remaining fixed in the remembrance of death. He knew he belonged to Christ; he knew judgment would come; he knew the One who defeated death had made the grave powerless. His calm baffled the enemy. Athanasius says that Antony answered these assaults with an almost disarming simplicity: *"Where were you when I was dying to myself? You have no power over those who remember God."* Whether Athanasius gives us Antony's exact words or a theological portrait, the message remains the same: the remembrance of death anchors the mind in God and frees the heart from fear.

If Antony gave the Church the first portrait of Christian memento mori, it was Macarius who gave it its depth. Macarius is one of the great desert luminaries—quiet, gentle, unassuming, yet fierce in spiritual warfare. The *Sayings of the Desert Fathers* preserve a teaching attributed to him: "If you remember death and keep it before your eyes, you will never sin." These words are not moralistic; they are metaphysical. Macarius understood the human heart. He knew how easily thoughts wander, how quickly desires flare, how quietly pride rises. He knew that sin thrives on forgetfulness—forgetfulness of God, forgetfulness of judgment, forgetfulness of the brevity of life. Remembering death does not frighten the heart into righteousness; it awakens the heart to the truth. It makes sin look as small as it truly is. It reminds the soul that every moment has eternal weight.

One story from Macarius captures this perfectly. The elders told of a young monk who struggled with lustful thoughts. He approached Macarius ashamed, hoping for a difficult rule to purge the temptation. Macarius did not give him one. Instead, he led the young man to a small burial place where the desert winds had left one of the old skulls exposed. "Brother," he said, "place this before you, and remember that you will one day be as he is." The young monk obeyed. Days passed, and the temptation lost its power. The remembrance of death did not suppress the young man's humanity—it restored it. He saw his life clearly, without illusion, without the noise of false desire. He regained freedom.

The desert monks were not fascinated with death; they were fascinated with truth. Death was simply the most honest teacher they knew. Antony's vigils in the tombs, Macarius' counsel, the cell rituals that many monks adopted—all these practices aimed to keep the heart awake. Pride dies when a man remembers that he is dust. Anger fades. Vanity dissolves. Envy looks absurd. Gluttony looks childish. Lust loses its fire. Acedia—the demon of spiritual sloth—no longer whispers convincingly that there will be time "later," because the monk knows that "later" is not promised. The remembrance of death pierces through illusion and brings a man back to the reality that his life belongs to God and is meant to be offered to God now.

The monks lived this with an astonishing literalness. A famous saying tells of Abba Arsenius, once a tutor of the Roman emperor's children, who became a solitary in the desert. He slept with his own burial shroud folded beside him. Each night he spread it out before lying down, praying the words of the psalm: "Into Your hands I commend my spirit." At dawn he folded it again. For Arsenius, this was not dramatics; it was devotion. It was a way of reminding his heart that every day is borrowed, every breath is grace, every moment is preparation for the hour he would meet the Lord. This, for the monks, was the essence of memento mori—not dread, not despair, but readiness.

The desert became a school of vigilance. The monks understood that human beings do not drift into holiness. They knew that the heart, left unguarded, falls asleep. They took Jesus' command seriously: "Stay awake." This command echoed through everything they did. If the apostles struggled to keep watch for one hour in Gethsemane, the monks trained themselves to keep watch for a lifetime. They sought wakefulness, clarity, sobriety, the opposite of spiritual drowsiness. And remembrance of death was the key that opened the door.

This is the world into which we now step—a world in which Christian men and women learned to live fully awake by learning to remember that they would die. The wisdom that grew in those lonely places still speaks with force and beauty, because the human soul has not changed. We still fall asleep to what matters. We still drift into distraction. We still believe we have endless time. The Desert Fathers knew better. They woke themselves with the truth, and in so doing, they discovered a life filled with God.

The deeper one goes into the stories of the Desert Fathers, the clearer it becomes that their entire spirituality rests on a single conviction: clarity is the beginning of holiness. The desert offered no disguises. Everything was exposed—the sky, the sand, the harshness of the climate, the fragility of the body, the instability of the mind. In that exposure, the monks learned the most fundamental truth about themselves: they were mortal. Nothing in the desert allowed them to pretend otherwise. Food was uncertain, water was scarce, sickness was common, and wild animals prowled the edges of their solitude. Yet the monks did not run from this vulnerability. They embraced it, because they saw in it a path to wisdom. Their mortality reminded them who they were, who God is, and what their lives were for.

One of the most striking witnesses to this truth comes from the sayings of Abba Poemen, a spiritual father revered for his discernment. Poemen rarely spoke forcefully; he was known for gentleness and measured counsel. Yet when he spoke about the remembrance of death, his tone sharpened, as though he were touching something absolutely essential. The *Apophthegmata* records him saying, "A man who remembers death is immune from care." At first hearing, that sounds almost unbelievable. How could thinking about death remove anxiety? But Poemen was not speaking of a morbid fixation. He was naming the freedom that comes when a person sees life through eternal eyes. When you remember you are going to die, you stop clinging to what cannot last. You stop fearing what cannot harm your soul. You let go of the illusions that make you restless. The anxieties that once consumed you begin to fall away. You become free to seek God without distraction.

A story preserved in the same collection illustrates this. A brother came to Poemen, overwhelmed by anger toward another monk. He had repeated the offense in his mind a hundred times, turning it over, fuelling his resentment. Poemen listened carefully, then asked, "Brother, when you stand before Christ on the day of judgment, will this matter hold weight?" The brother fell silent. Poemen continued, "If it will not matter then, it should not master you now." This was Poemen's way of teaching memento mori—not through skulls or graves, but through perspective. He lifted the brother's eyes to the horizon of eternity, where petty disputes dissolve and only love remains. By remembering the judgment, the brother regained peace.

Macarius and Poemen often complement each other this way—Macarius with his practical austerity, Poemen with his pastoral depth. Both understood that spiritual clarity arises when a person lives in the light of death. It was not unusual for monks to keep a skull in their cell, not as a macabre trophy but as a sacrament of honesty. A skull is the most truthful object in the world. It tells you who you are without pretence. It tells you what every person you envy, resent, or imitate will someday become. It tells you that the only thing worth pursuing is holiness, because holiness alone survives death. In the presence of a skull, pride becomes ridiculous. Vanity becomes pitiable. Acedia becomes dangerous. The remembrance of death gives birth to humility, and humility gives birth to wisdom.

Evagrius, the great theologian of the desert, offers a more intellectual articulation of this same truth. In his *Praktikos*, he describes acedia—the noonday demon—as a force that convinces the monk that "the day is long, and the time is abundant." Acedia is not laziness in the modern sense; it is the deep spiritual resistance to the present moment. It whispers, "You can pray later. Repent later. Change later. Forgive later." Evagrius understood that acedia thrives on the illusion of endless time. Remembering death destroys that illusion. When a monk holds his mortality before his eyes, acedia loses its power. The thought "I will repent tomorrow" becomes absurd. Evagrius therefore teaches that remembrance of death is not optional; it is an antidote. He insists that only the monk who remembers death will persevere in prayer and remain faithful to his calling.

Cassian, who carried the wisdom of the Egyptian fathers to the West, confirms this same insight. In his *Conferences*, he teaches that the monk should meditate daily on the hour of his death, not to fall into fear but to "acquire the compunction that purifies the heart." Cassian is gentle in tone, yet firm in conviction. He knows that remembering death disciplines the will, sharpens desire, and humbles pride. He knew, as the desert fathers knew, that the remembrance of death is the foundation of purity. When a person sees life from the vantage point of its end, the trivialities fall away. He prays with sincerity. He forgives with urgency. He repents with honesty. Cassian saw this over and over in the monasteries of Egypt: the monks who remembered death were the monks who loved best.

All of this helps us understand why the desert was not a place of despair, but a place of joy. The fathers did not brood over death. They were not melancholy or fearful. They lived with a kind of radiant sobriety, a peace born from knowing that death had been conquered by Christ. Their remembrance of death was always Christ-centred, rooted in the Resurrection. They remembered death not to dwell on the grave but to stay awake to grace. They remembered death because they believed the promise of eternal life. The more they meditated on their mortality, the more they longed for God. The more they confronted the brevity of earthly life, the more they invested themselves in the life that would never end.

The monks also saw death as a weapon against self-deception. Human beings are remarkably skilled at lying to themselves. We rationalize sin. We justify delay. We exaggerate our virtues and minimize our faults. We want to believe we have more time. The monks understood this instinct deeply, because they faced it in their own hearts. They found that the remembrance of death cut through every falsehood. It forced honesty. When a monk asked himself, "What will matter at the hour of my death?", the truth became clear. Pride never survives that question. Neither does lust, greed, envy, or anger. Death is the great clarifier. Remembering it daily keeps the soul anchored in reality.

If Antony, Macarius, Poemen, Evagrius, and Cassian form the theological backbone of this chapter, then the lived examples of the lesser-known monks flesh out the picture. The desert tradition preserves countless stories of brothers who overcame spiritual struggles simply by remembering their death. One tale tells of a monk who was plagued by constant irritation with others. His elders advised him to imagine standing at the threshold of his deathbed every morning. He obeyed, and over time, the irritation melted into compassion. Another tells of a brother repeatedly tempted to return to the world. He began visiting a graveyard each day, praying, "Lord, grant me to remember my last day." Slowly his desire for the world faded, replaced by a hunger for holiness. These stories are not meant to be dramatic. They show how remembrance of death, applied faithfully, reshapes the heart.

The desert did not teach the monks something exotic. It taught them something profoundly human. Every person, whether in Egypt or Melbourne or anywhere else in the world, is bound for death. Every person lives in the fragile space between birth and judgment. The monks simply refused to forget that truth. They embraced it. They prayed with it. They allowed it to purify their motives and strengthen their desire for God. This is why their wisdom endures. The remembrance of death is not a monastic eccentricity; it is a Christian necessity.

THE DESERT FATHERS AND THE HOLY ART OF REMEMBERING DEATH

Among the Desert Fathers, no one explored the spiritual psychology of remembrance as deeply as Abba Moses the Black. Once a violent bandit, later a monk aflame with humility, Moses understood mortality in a way most of us never do. He knew what it meant to waste a life. He knew what it meant to be preserved from destruction by mercy alone. The *Apophthegmata* recounts that when he first entered the monastery, still carrying the rough memories of his former life, he asked an elder how he might purify his thoughts. The elder placed his hand on Moses' chest and said, "The door of the heart opens when you remember that you will die." This became Moses' guiding wisdom. He told the younger monks, "Sit in your cell, and your cell will teach you everything." What did the cell teach? Silence, vulnerability, and above all, mortality—the truth that strips away illusions and turns the heart toward God.

Moses' story is dramatic, yet the heart of his teaching is not. It is profoundly simple: a man becomes wise when he remembers that his life is short. Moses had lived foolishly, assuming he would always have more time, more chances, more opportunities to change. When grace arrested him and drew him into the desert, he discovered that the remembrance of death was the beginning of freedom. He no longer postponed repentance. He no longer excused anger or pride. He learned to forgive quickly, to pray earnestly, to serve humbly. When asked how he overcame the temptations that once dominated him, he replied, "I have expected my death every day." This expectation did not darken his soul—it purified it. It made him tender, gentle, unguarded, incapable of holding grudges. The remembrance of death softened him into a saint.

In the wider monastic tradition, symbols of death served as tools for transparency. Modern readers may recoil at the image of a monk praying beside a skull, but the monks knew exactly what they were doing. A skull is the great leveller. It removes illusions of superiority.

It unmasks pretension. It speaks a word the ego does not want to hear: *"You are dust."* Yet the skull also whispers a second word: *"You are destined for resurrection."* For the Christian monk, the skull was not a symbol of despair but of truth. It reminded him that death is neither the whole story nor an incidental part of it—it is a doorway Christ Himself walked through, a doorway He has transformed by His victory.

John Climacus, writing in the sixth century, gathered the wisdom of generations into his *Ladder of Divine Ascent*, a work that shaped monastic spirituality for centuries. In Step 6, devoted entirely to the remembrance of death, he writes, "He who has died to himself remembers death constantly." Climacus understood that remembrance of death is not a psychological exercise. It is a spiritual posture. It is the placing of one's life under the light of eternity. It is the recognition that our choices are not trivial but weighty, not fleeting but eternal. Climacus observes that the man who remembers death "will never fear the world" because he sees himself as already belonging to another kingdom. He also teaches that remembrance of death gives rise to repentance, and repentance gives rise to tears—those tears the fathers called "the second baptism." In other words, remembering death cleanses the soul.

One of Climacus' most striking insights is that remembrance of death is inseparable from joy. This seems paradoxical, yet the monks lived it. They wept for their sins, yet they rejoiced in God. They grieved their mortality, yet they exulted in the resurrection. Climacus writes, "Happy is the man who continually expects his death; happy because he will be prepared for every event." Preparation produces peace. Vigilance produces freedom. The man who remembers that he will die is no longer enslaved by the opinions of others. He no longer fears loss. He no longer clings to possessions or reputation. He lives lightly, gladly, ready to meet Christ.

This joy appears repeatedly in the monastic tradition. Abba Sisoes, nearing his death, was surrounded by brothers who saw his face radiant with light. They asked him what he saw, and he replied, "I behold the Lord, and I am not afraid." The man who has spent his life remembering death does not fear its arrival. He welcomes it as the coming of the Bridegroom. Athanasius hints at this when describing Antony's final moments. As Antony lay dying, he spoke gently to his disciples, urging them not to grieve but to persevere in their calling. He had lived with death before his eyes for decades; therefore, the hour of his departure was not a surprise but a fulfillment. It was the hour he had prepared for every day of his life.

Evagrius gives the intellectual key to this paradox: only the person who remembers death sees life clearly. Acedia—his great preoccupation—is the refusal to see clearly. It is the spiritual fog that convinces us that today does not matter, that holiness can wait, that prayer can be postponed. Evagrius says that acedia is "the most oppressive of demons" because it blinds the soul to the urgency of love. It whispers that time is abundant. It persuades us to live as though God is far away and judgment is distant. Remembrance of death shatters this deception. It restores sight. It reminds the soul that every moment is precious because every moment is offered to God. The monks were not fighting laziness; they were fighting the delusion that they had endless tomorrows.

Cassian expands this insight by noting that remembrance of death produces compunction—a word often misunderstood today. In the monastic vocabulary, compunction is the wound of love, the sorrow that awakens desire for God. It is not despair. It is not shame. It is the ache that longs for healing, the longing that leads to repentance. Cassian says that compunction cleanses the heart, not by crushing it but by opening it. And remembrance of death is its source. When a person remembers that he will die, he begins to mourn his sins with honesty. He prays with purity. He forgives without delay. Compunction is not a mood; it is a grace. It springs from the recognition that life is short and God is merciful.

The monks treasured this grace. They believed that a man cannot grow in holiness unless he has first been humbled by the truth of his mortality. Pride dies when a person remembers death. Self-assertion collapses. The ego loses its grip. The monk becomes teachable, gentle, eager for God. This humility becomes the soil of virtue. Antony, Macarius, Moses, Poemen—all of them exhibit a striking lack of self-importance. They do not care about being admired. They care only about being faithful. They measure their actions not by human praise but by the hour of judgment. They do not compare themselves to others; they compare themselves to Christ. The remembrance of death liberated them from the tyranny of ego.

This liberation produced extraordinary charity. The monks who remembered death were among the most forgiving people in the world. They knew their lives were brief, their sins were many, and God's mercy was great. They forgave easily because they saw everything through the lens of eternity. Poemen once said, "If a man remembers his sins, God will forget them; if he forgets his sins, God will remember them." Remembrance of death helped them remember their sins without despair, because they remembered them before the mercy of God. The desert fathers knew nothing of self-hatred. They knew repentance, humility, and freedom—three gifts born from remembering their mortality.

The remembrance of death also shaped how the monks understood spiritual warfare. They believed the devil's greatest weapon was not temptation but distraction. If the enemy could draw the mind away from the present moment, away from prayer, away from the truth of mortality, the soul would weaken. But if the mind remained fixed on the hour of death, temptations lost their force. Anger softened. Lust cooled. Greed loosened. Pride shrank. The remembrance of death pulled the mind back to reality and made it difficult for the passions to dominate. Climacus writes that when a monk remembers death, "the heart becomes unassailable." This is language of battle, but it is also language of love. The monk is not defending himself against the world; he is protecting his capacity to love God.

This is why remembrance of death sits at the heart of monastic vigilance. The monk keeps watch not because he fears punishment but because he desires union with God. Jesus' words—"Stay awake"—echo in the cells of the desert. The monks understood that staying awake meant remembering death. The man who knows he will die does not waste time. He does not squander grace. He lives with purpose, attentiveness, and longing. He prepares not only for judgment but for the Bridegroom's arrival. This was the spiritual logic that animated the desert: memento mori was not about avoiding sin but about awakening desire for God.

The monastery of Scetis, one of the great centres of desert spirituality, preserved stories that illuminate this longing with extraordinary clarity. One such story recounts a young monk who approached Abba Joseph, troubled by spiritual dryness and the sense that God felt distant. Joseph listened and then did something unexpected: he stood, stretched out his arms, and his fingers became like ten flames of fire. "If you will," he said, "you can become all flame." The story is famous, often cited as an illustration of divine transformation. Yet its monastic context makes something else clear: becoming "all flame" requires wakefulness, and wakefulness requires the remembrance of death. Joseph was not speaking of a mystical spectacle. He was speaking of the purified heart—the heart that sheds illusions, renounces procrastination, and burns with longing because it knows time is short.

The monks understood that remembrance of death ignited desire for God. It was not meant to extinguish joy, but to intensify it. They saw their mortality not as a prison but as an impetus toward love. The very fact that life is brief made every moment precious. A brother once asked an elder how he might pray more faithfully. The elder replied, "Pray as if you were about to die." The instruction sounds severe, but it is actually liberating. It frees a person from divided attention. It unifies the heart. It makes prayer sincere. When a man prays with death before his eyes, he does not waste words. He becomes honest. His heart becomes simple, undistracted, ready.

This readiness shaped the monks' daily rhythm. They worked, prayed, fasted, and kept vigil with the knowledge that each day could be their last. They did not live in fear of death; they lived in the expectation of meeting Christ. This expectation gave their asceticism a luminous quality. The monks were not trying to escape the world; they were trying to enter eternity. They pursued holiness with urgency because they believed life was a pilgrimage toward a final encounter. Remembering death illuminated that path. It reminded them that their labour, their sacrifices, their renunciations were all ordered toward the joy of seeing God.

The Desert Fathers saw death as the great purifier of intention. Nothing clarifies motive like the question, "Will this matter at the hour of my death?" A monk tempted to anger found the question disarmed his resentment. A monk tempted to lust found it cooled his desire. A monk tempted to pride found it humbled his heart. The remembrance of death forced them to evaluate their lives in light of eternity. What seemed urgent lost its urgency. What seemed trivial became essential. The monks did not judge their days by productivity but by fidelity. They measured their hearts not by accomplishment but by readiness.

It is striking, in this regard, how often the sayings of the fathers emphasize the fragility of life. "Today," they would say, "is the day of salvation." This echoes the words of St. Paul, but it also captures the monastic instinct. The monks refused to live in the illusion of tomorrow. They understood that the devil's favourite lie is postponement. Evagrius says that acedia persuades the monk to believe that "later" is always available. The remembrance of death dismantles this lie. It teaches the heart that the only moment given is the present one. This is not meant to create panic; it is meant to awaken love. When a person realizes that his days are numbered, he begins to use them wisely.

The monks also believed that remembrance of death sharpened compassion. A man who knows he will die does not have the luxury of judging others harshly. He sees them as fellow pilgrims, fragile and flawed, walking the same path toward God. Poemen once said that the remembrance of death makes a man "slow to anger and quick to mercy." He understood that forgiveness becomes easier when viewed in the light of mortality. Why hold a grudge when both you and the person you resent will stand before God in a short time? Why cling to bitterness when the grave looms? The remembrance of death softened the monks, made them patient, gentle, merciful. It cured the harshness that so often accompanies religious zeal.

This mercy extended even to self-judgment. The monks were not hard on themselves in the modern sense. They did not wallow in guilt or spiral into despair. They acknowledged their sins with clarity and entrusted themselves to God with confidence. Remembrance of death gave them humility, but it also gave them boldness. They knew they would die, but they also knew Christ had conquered death. They confessed their sins because they trusted God's mercy. They repented quickly because they desired to be free. Climacus notes that the remembrance of death produces a "bright sorrow"—a sorrow that does not crush but cleanses. This sorrow leads to repentance, and repentance leads to joy.

The more one reads of the desert, the more apparent it becomes that the monks were guided by a singular vision: life on earth is a preparation for the hour of death. That hour is not a moment of annihilation but a moment of unveiling. It is the moment when the truth of a person's life is revealed. The monks did not fear that moment. They longed to be ready for it. Remembering death trained their hearts to love God above all things. It gave them freedom from the tyranny of the present moment. It freed them from fear. It made them courageous. Abba Theodore once said that a person who remembers death "has already begun to rise." The remembrance of death was not a meditation on endings; it was a meditation on beginnings.

This is why the monks cherished silence. Silence made room for remembrance. In the quiet of the cell, a monk faced himself and God without distraction. He confronted his mortality. He saw his passions clearly. He allowed the remembrance of death to break his pride. He let repentance take root. Silence cleansed the mind. It strengthened the will. It created space for prayer. Cassian describes how the monks would spend long nights awake in silent meditation, sometimes repeating the simple prayer, "Lord, have mercy," while imagining themselves standing before God. This practice was not theatrical. It was training in vigilance. It prepared them to meet the Lord with humility and longing.

The remembrance of death also shaped the monks' understanding of community. Monastic life was not solitary in the absolute sense. Even the hermits had relationships with elders, disciples, and neighbouring monks. These relationships were shaped by the shared awareness of mortality. They were marked by patience, forgiveness, mutual support, and a refusal to cling to petty disputes. When a monk remembered that both he and his brother would die, he learned to see the other not as a rival or a burden but as a companion on the journey. Memento mori fostered charity.

Perhaps the clearest glimpse of the monastic approach to death appears in their funerals. When a monk died, the brothers gathered around the body, not with despair but with solemn joy. They sang psalms that spoke of hope. They prayed for his soul. They touched his body with reverence. They saw death not as defeat but as the completion of a pilgrimage. Many early texts describe monks dying with faces radiant or peaceful, their hands clasped in prayer. Their remembrance of death throughout life had prepared them for a holy death. They had prayed for this moment daily. Now they met it with serenity.

The Desert Fathers believed that every Christian, regardless of vocation, is called to this same remembrance. The monk's cell and the modern home may look different, but the soul's journey is the same. We live in a world that distracts, numbs, entertains, and postpones. The desert shows us another way: to live awake. To remember death. To let that remembrance anchor our hearts in eternity. To allow it to purify our desires, soften our judgments, strengthen our repentance, and deepen our love for God.

One of the most revealing features of the desert tradition is how seamlessly the remembrance of death wove itself into the monks' ordinary activities. It was not reserved for moments of crisis or contemplation but permeated their daily work. A monk weaving baskets repeated verses from the Psalms about the brevity of life. A monk drawing water reflected on the Samaritan woman who encountered the Messiah unexpectedly. A monk tilling the soil meditated on the words spoken over Adam: "For dust you are, and to dust you shall return." Their labour became liturgy. Their tasks became reminders. They lived their days under the shadow of eternity, not to darken them, but to keep them bright with purpose.

This orientation toward death transformed how they understood time. Time, for the desert fathers, was a sacred trust. It was not to be squandered or dismissed. It was to be received as a gift. Cassian notes that one of the greatest temptations in monastic life was not lust or gluttony or anger—it was wasting time. To waste time was to squander the opportunity to love God. It was to lose sight of the hour of judgment. The monk who remembered death guarded his time carefully. He prayed when it was time to pray. He worked when it was time to work. He rested when it was time to rest. He did not entertain idle thoughts. He did not indulge in pointless conversation. He lived his day as though it were his last, not out of anxiety but out of reverence.

This reverence extended even to the way the monks understood their bodies. In the modern world, the body is often seen either as an idol to perfect or an obstacle to escape. The desert fathers saw the body as neither. They saw it as the vessel through which a man prepared for eternity. They fasted not to punish the body but to discipline the soul. They laboured not to exhaust themselves but to keep their minds attentive. They rested not to indulge comfort but to restore strength for prayer. The remembrance of death taught them to treat the body with humility and gratitude. It reminded them that the body, too, would return to dust—and that, in the resurrection, it would be raised in glory.

The monks' approach to suffering reveals this even more clearly. They did not seek suffering, but they accepted it when it came. They saw suffering as a teacher, a purifier, a participation in the sufferings of Christ. Climacus writes that remembering death gives rise to courage in the face of trials. When a monk meditates on his mortality, he becomes less attached to comfort and more attached to God. He endures hardship with patience. He offers his pain as prayer. He sees suffering not as a random misfortune but as a moment of grace. The remembrance of death prevented suffering from becoming meaningless. It framed it within the story of salvation.

Yet the monks were not stoics. Their remembrance of death did not numb their emotions or isolate them from human relationships. Quite the opposite. It made them tender-hearted. They mourned the death of a brother with real sorrow, yet their sorrow was suffused with hope. They knew that death was not the final word. They knew that Christ had trampled down death by death. They knew that the grave was a temporary resting place, not a permanent defeat. Their mourning bore a resemblance to the early Christian funeral liturgy, which speaks of death in tones of solemn joy: "For to your faithful people, Lord, life is changed, not ended." The monks lived those words long before they were written.

Their tenderness extended to strangers. The monks of Egypt were renowned for their hospitality. Travelers would cross deserts to seek prayer or counsel, and the monks received them with compassion. They fed them, prayed with them, and listened to their sorrows. Why such generosity? Because they remembered death. They saw each visitor as a soul journeying toward eternity. They knew their time with that person was brief. They seized the opportunity to show love, to offer truth, to bear witness to the kingdom of God. Memento mori made them present. It made them attentive to the moment, alert to the needs of others, awake to grace.

This wakefulness is perhaps the most important fruit of the desert practice. To remember death is to remember reality. It is to step out of the fog of distraction into the clarity of truth. The monks believed that most sins arise from forgetfulness. Forgetfulness of God. Forgetfulness of judgment. Forgetfulness of the brevity of life. The remembrance of death heals this forgetfulness. It calls the soul back to its centre. It reorients desire. It strengthens the will. It brings the monk into that state the fathers called *nepsis*—watchfulness, vigilance, spiritual alertness. Nepsis is the opposite of acedia. It is the steady attentiveness that keeps a person grounded in God.

The fathers often compared the vigilant heart to a watchman standing on a city wall. The watchman must remain awake because danger can come at any moment. If he sleeps, the city falls. Similarly, if the monk falls into spiritual drowsiness, his heart becomes vulnerable. The remembrance of death keeps him awake. It keeps his vision clear. It makes him attentive to the movements of his thoughts, the stirrings of his passions, the whispers of temptation. The vigilant monk becomes a guardian of his own soul. He responds quickly when pride arises, when anger flares, when fear tightens its grip. He anchors his mind in the thought: "I will die, and I will meet Christ." This thought does not depress him. It strengthens him.

The Desert Fathers also understood that remembrance of death prepared them for judgment—not with dread, but with longing. They believed that the hour of death is the hour of truth, the moment when the soul stands before God and sees clearly. They called this moment the *telos*, the completion of the human journey. It was not a moment to fear because they had spent their lives preparing for it. Climacus observes that the monk who remembers death "awaits the hour of his departure as one awaits a feast." For him, death is not a thief but a herald. It announces the arrival of the Bridegroom. It signals the end of exile and the beginning of homecoming.

In their writings and stories, we find almost no trace of terror about death. The monks feared sin, not mortality. They feared losing vigilance, falling into acedia, drifting from God. Death itself they saw as a passage. Athanasius describes Antony's deathbed as a moment of serenity, a testament to a life lived awake. Surrounded by his disciples, Antony blessed them, exhorted them to perseverance, and then, with quiet confidence, commended his soul to God. Nothing dramatic. Nothing despairing. Just a man stepping into the presence of the One he had loved all his life.

This is the fruit of remembrance. Death becomes familiar, not foreign. Its arrival becomes expected, not feared. The heart becomes steady. The mind becomes clear. The soul becomes ready. This readiness is not resignation; it is hope. It is the hope born from centuries of Christian belief: that Christ has destroyed death, that the grave cannot contain the redeemed, that the body laid in dust will be raised in glory. The monks lived in the light of this hope, and it shaped everything they did.

The clarity the monks gained through remembering death did not make their lives smaller; it expanded them. Far from shrinking the world into a narrow corridor of fear or withdrawal, the remembrance of death opened the vast horizon of eternity before them. They saw their lives in the context of a divine story, a story stretching from creation to resurrection. They understood themselves not as isolated individuals but as pilgrims moving toward a final encounter with the God who made them. This vision gave their days weight and meaning. It made every task, every prayer, every moment of repentance significant. Nothing was wasted, because everything was ordered toward the hour they would stand before Christ.

The monks' insistence on remembrance of death often perplexes modern readers, who tend to associate any mention of death with morbidity or despair. The fathers saw the opposite. They believed that remembering death was the only way to truly live. A man who forgets his death forgets his purpose. He becomes scattered, distracted, restless. He chases after things that will not last. He allows trivial annoyances to dominate his heart. He postpones conversion. He refuses forgiveness. He succumbs to acedia. The monks understood this drift all too well. They had seen it in themselves. They knew that only the remembrance of death could anchor the soul in God, because only the remembrance of death dismantles the illusions that keep a person asleep.

In the *Apophthegmata*, a young monk once asked an elder how he might cultivate humility. The elder did not tell him to fast more or to take on heavier labours. Instead, he said, "Remember that you will die." This answer reveals the monastic logic: humility arises when a person sees his life truthfully. He is not the centre of the universe. He is a creature made from dust, sustained by grace, destined for judgment, and promised resurrection. When he remembers this, he becomes gentle, patient, and free. Humility is not self-hatred; it is self-knowledge. It is the fruit of seeing oneself in the light of God. Remembrance of death brings that light.

This truth also shaped how the monks approached virtue. They did not pursue virtue as a moral achievement or a spiritual résumé. They pursued it because they believed they would soon stand before God. Virtue was preparation for love. It was the cultivation of a heart capable of receiving God's presence. The remembrance of death gave urgency to this pursuit. It kept them attentive, deliberate, and sincere. They repented not because they were scrupulous, but because they were honest. They forgave not because they lacked boundaries, but because they understood the brevity of life. They prayed not to accumulate merit, but to deepen communion. Death kept this communion before their eyes.

One of the most tender sayings in the desert tradition comes from Abba Agathon, who, when asked what virtue requires the greatest effort, replied, "There is no labour greater than prayer to God." Why? "Because every time a man wants to pray, the demons want to prevent him, for they know that prayer is communion with God." The remembrance of death strengthened prayer because it kept the monk mindful of his need. It made him understand that prayer is not a duty but a lifeline. The man who remembers death knows he has nothing apart from God. This knowledge does not humiliate; it liberates. It leads him to pray with simplicity, confidence, and desire.

The remembrance of death also purified the monks' interpretation of Scripture. When they read the Gospels—especially Jesus' warnings to stay awake, to be ready, to prepare for the Master's return—they heard these words with the clarity that comes from living close to mortality. Christ's parables of vigilance were not abstract teachings. They were daily warnings. They understood the foolish virgins not as unfortunate characters but as portraits of the heart that delays conversion. They recognized themselves in the servant who says, "My master is delayed," and they fought that temptation by remembering their death. They saw in the parable of the talents the danger of spiritual sloth. They heard in the parable of the rich fool the tragedy of living a life without reference to the hour of judgment. The remembrance of death made them read Scripture with a sharpened awareness of its urgency.

For the monks, memento mori was not a practice confined to solitude. It shaped how they interacted with others, how they lived in community, how they faced conflict, and how they embraced joy. They knew that life was a gift and that it could vanish in an instant. This knowledge made them grateful. Gratitude permeated their spirituality. They thanked God constantly—for food, for water, for health, for the psalms on their lips, for the brothers beside them. They did not presume upon tomorrow. Each day was a grace. Each morning was a mercy. Their gratitude was not naïve; it was anchored in mortality. The man who remembers he will die learns to cherish the present moment. He sees God's goodness in everything.

It is here that the fruit of remembrance becomes unmistakably Christian. The monks did not meditate on death alone. They meditated on death in the light of the resurrection. They remembered their mortality in the presence of the God who had entered death and destroyed it. This is why their sobriety was radiant. They did not brood in shadows; they lived in hope. They longed for the moment when Christ would appear, when the veil would be lifted, when the heart's desire would be fulfilled. Antony, Macarius, Poemen, Moses, Climacus—they all remind us that remembering death only becomes wisdom when one remembers the One who conquered death. Without Christ, mortality would be despair. With Christ, mortality becomes a summons to love.

Their holiness testifies to what this remembrance produces. They lived in a constant state of preparation—not anxious preparation, but loving readiness. They acted as men who expected to see Christ soon. They spoke truthfully. They forgave readily. They prayed earnestly. They worked diligently. They loved deeply. Their lives were marked by urgency and tenderness, sobriety and joy, vigilance and peace. They prepared for death by living for God.

This is the lesson the desert offers the modern world. We do not need caves, skulls, or burial shrouds to practice memento mori. We need clarity, honesty, and faith. We need to remember that our days are numbered and that every day is a gift. We need to recognize that life is a pilgrimage, and death is its threshold. We need to look at our lives in the light of eternity and ask what will remain when we stand before God. The monks teach us that the remembrance of death is not a retreat from life but an entry into its deepest truth.

The desert fathers remind us that mortality is not a curse to dread but a compass to follow. It orients the soul toward God. It humbles pride, quiets fear, strengthens love, purifies desire, and awakens the heart to the presence of Christ. When remembered rightly, death becomes the doorway through which the Christian walks into the fullness of life promised by the resurrection.

The holy art of remembering death is not a relic of the ancient desert. It is a path for every Christian who longs to live awake.

4

When the Heart Awakens: Mortality as the Doorway to Christ's Warnings

never meant to remain an interior exercise. It presses outward. It demands a response. When a person begins to see life in the truthful light of mortality, something new awakens within him—a clarity that does not allow him to drift through his days as if they belonged to him. The psalmist's plea to "number our days," the dust and glory woven into the story of our creation, and the fierce sobriety of the monks all point toward the same revelation: human beings were made to live before the face of God. Mortality is not meant to shrink our world; it is meant to open our eyes.

Once this truth settles into the soul, the heart can no longer pretend it has endless time. The illusions that once softened sin begin to fall away. The excuses that once made delay seem harmless lose their persuasive power. The person who remembers that he will die becomes astonished at how casually he has treated the gift of life. He begins to ask questions that pierce deeper than sentiment: What am I living for? What am I clinging to? What have I postponed? What have I justified? These questions do not accuse; they illuminate. They reveal the distance between the life we live and the life we were made for.

Yet the human heart is fragile, and clarity alone cannot sustain it. Memory awakens desire, but desire needs to be guided. Mortality humbles the soul, but humility needs a teacher. If death reveals the truth about man, then the word of God reveals the truth about how man is meant to live. The remembrance of death brings us to the threshold of wisdom, but it is the voice of Christ that carries us across. For if the desert teaches us that life is short, Christ teaches us how to live it well. If the fathers show us that clarity begins with truth, Christ shows us that truth begins with obedience. The awakening that comes from remembering death must eventually meet the call that comes from the Lord.

In Scripture, that call is unmistakably urgent. The God who breathed life into dust does not speak with the tone of abstraction or gentle suggestion. He speaks with the authority of a Father who knows that His children stand on the edge of eternity. The prophets trembled at His word. The psalms cry out for His mercy. The early Christians lived with the expectation that His kingdom was near. But it is in Jesus that this urgency becomes most personal. He speaks as one who knows the human heart—its tendency to drift, its habit of delay, its vulnerability to spiritual drowsiness. He speaks not to frighten but to awaken, not to burden but to summon.

The remembrance of death prepares the soil for this summons. It softens the ground. It breaks the hardened clumps of presumption, pride, and procrastination. It allows the seed of Christ's word to take root. Without this preparation, the Lord's warnings sound severe, even unreasonable. But when the heart has seen the truth of its own fragility, these warnings become not threats but lifelines. Jesus does not shout because He is angry; He speaks urgently because He loves. The one who knows that life is short will hear His voice with clarity: *Stay awake. Be ready. Watch. Do not delay. Do not assume tomorrow belongs to you.*

The same wisdom that led Antony into the tombs, that taught Macarius to pray among bones, that humbled Poemen into mercy, becomes the wisdom that makes sense of Christ's teachings. Every parable of return, every image of a master arriving unexpectedly, every command to keep watch, flows from the same truth the desert fathers embraced: our lives unfold under the gaze of eternity. The Lord who conquered death calls us to live as people who believe it. His words are not burdens—they are the shape of freedom.

And this is the great turning of the Christian life: the remembrance of death awakens the soul to the reality that Christ's warnings are invitations. They are not meant to make us tremble but to make us alert. They do not shrink the heart; they expand it. They steady the will. They open the eyes. The person who has learned the first wisdom of mortality is finally able to hear the second wisdom: that God calls His disciples to vigilance not because He is distant, but because He is near.

The journey that begins with dust and breath, with the numbering of days, and with the fierce clarity of the desert fathers now moves toward the greater light of the Gospels. Here the Teacher Himself speaks. Here the Bridegroom calls. Here the One who will judge the living and the dead teaches us how to be ready—not in fear, but in love.

For mortality prepares the heart, but Christ instructs it.

Mortality awakens the soul, but Christ directs it.

Mortality humbles us, but Christ makes us watchful.

The wisdom born from remembering death finds its fulfillment in listening to the Lord who overcame it.

And now His words come into view with fresh sharpness, carrying the weight of eternity and the gentleness of a Shepherd who desires that none be lost.

II

THE WARNINGS OF THE LORD

5

"Stay Awake": Jesus' Full Teaching on Vigilance

When a person begins to see his mortality clearly, something remarkable happens when he turns to the Gospels. The words of Jesus, once familiar, suddenly blaze with a new urgency. Teachings that seemed cryptic or severe begin to make luminous sense. It is as though the Lord had been speaking to the heart all along, but the heart needed the sobriety of remembering death to hear Him rightly. Nowhere is this more evident than in His repeated call to stay awake. Among the many themes that flow through Jesus' preaching—the kingdom, mercy, forgiveness, the Father's love—none is delivered with greater insistence than vigilance. It is woven into parables, instructions, warnings, and even prayers. The Lord speaks often about love, but He speaks almost as often about readiness. Not because He delights in severity, but because He desires to bring His disciples into a life lived fully in the light of eternity.

Many Christians scarcely notice how often Jesus issues this command. It appears quietly, almost rhythmically, like a pulse beneath His words: *stay awake, be watchful, keep alert.* Yet this command is not an isolated line; it is a thread that binds together His entire vision of discipleship. In the Greek of the New Testament, the word He uses—*grēgoreite*—means more than avoiding sleep. It means to be spiritually animated, alive, attentive, sober, ready. It carries the sense of a watchman on the city wall who must guard against the unexpected, or a bride awaiting the arrival of her bridegroom, preparing herself for the joy of the wedding feast. Jesus speaks this word not as a taskmaster barking orders, but as the One who knows what lies ahead. He calls His disciples to vigilance because He loves them. He knows how easily the human heart is lulled into drowsiness, how swiftly distractions cloud the mind, how subtly sin persuades us that there will always be time later.

The first time many readers encounter the command "stay awake" is in Jesus' discourse about the coming of the Son of Man. In Matthew's Gospel, He speaks of a thief in the night—an image that startles precisely because it is so ordinary. Houses in ancient Palestine were simple structures, easily entered if the homeowner failed to secure the door. Jesus uses this image to expose a spiritual vulnerability: the danger of assuming that life will continue as it always has. He says, "If the householder had known at what part of the night the thief was coming, he would have watched." The point is not fear. The point is that a person who takes his life for granted is unready for the moment when everything will be revealed. Jesus concludes with the words that form the heartbeat of this chapter: "Therefore you also must be ready, for the Son of Man is coming at an hour you do not expect."

These words grow sharper when we remember our mortality. Death itself arrives like a thief. It is not predictable. It does not fit into our plans. It does not wait for our schedules to clear or our spiritual lives to finally settle. It comes in its own time. Jesus is not speaking only about His future return; He is speaking about the hour every soul will meet Him. That hour is not meant to terrify but to awaken. The disciple who remembers death hears Jesus' words not as a threat but as an invitation to live now in the truth of what is coming. The heart that has learned the wisdom of the desert recognizes the voice of a Shepherd calling His flock to vigilance because love demands preparation. No bride arrives at her wedding unprepared. No pilgrim reaches his destination by accident. Readiness is not fear—it is fidelity.

If the image of the thief reveals the unpredictability of the moment, the image of the returning master reveals its personal dimension. In Mark's Gospel, Jesus tells a brief yet powerful parable: a master departs, leaving his servants in charge, each with his task, and the doorkeeper with the responsibility to watch. "Watch therefore," Jesus says, "for you do not know when the master of the house will come—in the evening, or at midnight, or at cockcrow, or in the morning." These four times are not random. They mirror the watches of the night in the Roman world and correspond to the darkest hours of human vulnerability. Jesus evokes them to show that vigilance is required not occasionally but always. The disciples must live as though the master could return at any moment.

What is striking is not the unpredictability alone, but the affection behind the expectation. The servants are not told to fear the master; they are instructed to stay ready for him. Jesus presents His return not as the visit of a judge catching criminals unaware, but as the homecoming of the One to whom the household belongs. The call to vigilance is not the call of a tyrant—it is the call of a Lord who loves His household and expects His servants to share in His mission. The disciple stays awake not because he dreads punishment but because he desires communion. The one who loves Christ longs for His appearing.

The Gospel of Luke deepens this further. Jesus speaks of servants waiting for their master to return from a wedding feast. When he comes and finds them ready, Jesus says something astonishing: the master will gird himself, seat them at table, and serve them. This reversal is the key to understanding the entire theology of vigilance. Readiness is not primarily about avoiding disaster. It is about being counted among the faithful whom the Lord Himself delights to serve. The vigilant disciple is the one who expects not condemnation but communion. Vigilance is the posture of a heart trained in desire.

And yet, if this is so, why do so many Christians treat these passages with discomfort, even avoidance? Perhaps because vigilance feels demanding. It feels like spiritual intensity. It feels like resisting our natural inclination to drift. But Jesus does not call us to vigilance because He expects perfection; He calls us to vigilance because He knows our weakness. He knows how easily the heart falls asleep. He knows the power of distractions, the subtlety of temptations, the quiet slide into presumption. He knows that sin rarely erupts—it settles, slowly, like dust on the soul. Vigilance is the remedy.

Nowhere does this become clearer than in the garden of Gethsemane. In this moment of unfathomable intimacy, Jesus asks His closest friends for one thing: "Remain here and watch with Me." The Son of God, entering the agony of His passion, desires the companionship of His disciples in wakeful prayer. Yet they sleep. Jesus returns and asks with a piercing tenderness, "Could you not watch with Me one hour?" These words are not merely lament—they are revelation. They show that vigilance is not something we do for ourselves alone; it is something we do with Christ and for Christ. To stay awake is to keep Him company in His hour of sorrow, to join Him in the battle against temptation, to unite our frailty with His strength.

Here Jesus links vigilance with the deepest spiritual truth: "Watch and pray, that you may not enter into temptation; the spirit indeed is willing, but the flesh is weak." These words contain the entire theology of vigilance. The flesh is weak—our mortality, our passions, our limits. But the spirit is willing—our desire for God, our capacity for grace, our longing for holiness. Prayer is the meeting place of these two realities. Vigilance is the act of placing the whole person—flesh and spirit—before God in the present moment.

The disciple who remembers his death hears these words with particular clarity. To remember death is to remember weakness. To stay awake is to remember grace. And Jesus, the Lord of life, commands vigilance so that grace may triumph over weakness. His warnings are acts of mercy. His commands are expressions of love. He tells His disciples to stay awake because He knows that the hour will come when everything is unveiled, and He desires them to meet that hour with hearts alive.

The Gospels reveal something else that becomes clearer when read through the lens of mortality: Jesus does not simply warn the disciples that something will happen; He reveals that something is already happening. The Kingdom is breaking in. Judgment is drawing near. Eternity is approaching with every breath. His words about vigilance are not abstract predictions but present-tense realities. The Day of the Lord—so often spoken of by the prophets—has stepped into human history in His very person. When He says, "Stay awake," He is not speaking to an imaginary future event; He is speaking to the moment when God's presence stands before the human heart and demands a response.

This is why Jesus constantly draws on imagery from Israel's covenant story. The prophets had warned Israel for centuries to remain faithful, to keep watch, to guard the heart against idolatry. They spoke of the Day of the Lord as a moment of unveiling, when the truth of a person's life would stand before God's holiness. Jesus steps into this prophetic stream and intensifies its call. He does not reject the warnings of Isaiah, Ezekiel, Joel, or Zephaniah—He fulfills them. When He says, "Be ready," He speaks with the very authority that once thundered through the prophets. But now the warning carries a new tenderness, because the One who warns is the One who will save.

Jesus often compares His return to the days of Noah. People ate, drank, married, and went about their lives as though nothing were coming. It is not that these activities were sinful; they were simply thoughtless. Life carried on without reference to God, without awareness of judgment, without vigilance. Then the flood came. Jesus uses this ancient story not to frighten but to awaken. He calls His listeners to recognize that forgetfulness of God is the oldest temptation, the most persistent danger, and the easiest path to ruin. It is not wickedness that destroys the people in Noah's day—it is indifference. Jesus knows the human heart well enough to warn that the same indifference can take root anywhere, in any age, even among those who claim to follow Him.

In another moment of teaching, He speaks of servants waiting for their master. What is striking is how easily the servants fall into two groups: those who remain alert and those who assume the master's delay. The danger is not rebellion but presumption. The servant who believes the master is delayed begins to mistreat others, neglect his responsibilities, and live as if judgment will never come. Jesus exposes the logic of sin: it always begins with the quiet thought, "I have time." This is the core of acedia. Sin grows in the soil of postponement. Jesus' remedy is simple and profound: "Stay awake."

The weight of this command becomes clearer when one considers the Greek word *prosoche*, which appears throughout early Christian writings to describe vigilant attention. It means focus, alertness, carefulness of thought. Jesus does not merely tell His disciples to avoid sleep; He tells them to cultivate an inner attentiveness—a mind trained in spiritual perception. The fathers will later describe this as guarding the heart. Jesus gives the seed of this practice in His call to remain watchful. He wants His disciples to see reality as it is, not as they imagine it to be.

"STAY AWAKE": JESUS' FULL TEACHING ON VIGILANCE

One of the most revealing images Jesus uses to describe vigilance is the watchman on the walls. In ancient cities, watchmen were responsible for scanning the horizon for signs of danger. Their task required clarity, sobriety, and unbroken attention. They stood at their post through cold nights and long hours because the safety of the city depended on their alertness. Jesus adopts this imagery to describe the spiritual posture of every disciple. The Christian is not a passive recipient of grace; he is a watchman, entrusted with the care of his own heart. He guards against temptation, resists distraction, and keeps his attention fixed on the Lord's coming.

Yet Jesus' teaching on vigilance is not only defensive. It is profoundly relational. He does not call His disciples to stand guard against an enemy so much as He calls them to stand ready for a friend. He speaks of a wedding feast, of a bridegroom, of a joyful arrival. In these images, readiness becomes anticipation. The disciple does not stay awake because he fears what will happen if he sleeps; he stays awake because he desires to be present when the bridegroom arrives. Jesus' teachings on vigilance must be read through this lens of love. His warnings are not threats—they are invitations to intimacy.

This becomes especially clear when Jesus speaks of the blessings awaiting the vigilant. He says that the servant who is found awake when the master returns will be set over all his possessions. In Luke's Gospel, the master will even serve the servants. These images reveal the generosity of God. Vigilance is rewarded not with mere safety but with communion. To stay awake is to prepare the heart for joy. Jesus wants His disciples to remain in a state of readiness so they will not miss the moment of grace.

But vigilance is also necessary because Jesus acknowledges the weakness of the human heart. He knows our tendency to spiritual drowsiness. He knows how quickly we fall asleep to the things of God. He knows the distractions that cloud our minds, the desires that pull us in opposite directions, the anxieties that dull our perception. His command to stay awake is therefore an act of compassion. He does not want His disciples to be caught unaware, not because He delights in catching them unprepared, but because He knows that a prepared heart is a peaceful heart.

This is why the scene in Gethsemane is so central. It reveals what happens when vigilance fails. Jesus asks His disciples to watch with Him, but they cannot. They are overwhelmed by fatigue, sorrow, and confusion. Their bodies betray their intentions. Their weakness reveals the deep need for grace. Jesus' gentle rebuke—"Could you not watch with Me one hour?"—is not a condemnation but a diagnosis. He sees their weakness more clearly than they do. He knows they want to be faithful, yet He also knows how fragile their commitment is without prayer. "Watch and pray," He says, "that you may not enter into temptation." Vigilance without prayer becomes impossible. Prayer without vigilance becomes empty. The two form a single command.

The Gethsemane moment reveals a truth that runs through Jesus' entire ministry: the disciple's greatest danger is not persecution or suffering but spiritual sleep. Physical suffering can strengthen faith; external trials can purify love; opposition can deepen resolve. But spiritual sleep numbs the soul. It dulls the conscience. It makes the heart inattentive to God. Jesus warns His disciples again and again because He knows that the danger is real. He knows that the heart drifts when it stops watching. He knows that the path away from Him is gradual, imperceptible, and clothed in the illusion of normalcy.

This is where the remembrance of death meets the teachings of Christ with transformative power. The person who remembers his death recognizes the urgency behind Jesus' words. He hears the warnings not as exaggerated concern but as accurate diagnosis. He sees the wisdom of staying awake because he has glimpsed the fragility of life. The remembrance of death strips away the complacency that so often distorts the Christian life. It allows the disciple to hear Jesus clearly and respond with sincerity.

And the more the disciple meditates on Jesus' words, the more he realizes that vigilance is not a grim posture but a joyful one. To stay awake is to live a life entirely open to God. It is to see every moment as an opportunity for grace. It is to prepare oneself for the moment when Christ will appear—whether in glory or in the hour of death—and to welcome Him with love. This expectation changes everything. It makes prayer sincere, forgiveness urgent, holiness attractive. It gives shape to the entire Christian existence.

Vigilance becomes even clearer when considered in light of Jesus' teaching about the thief in the night. He says that if the master of the house had known at what hour the thief was coming, he would not have allowed his house to be broken into. The logic is simple, but the implication is profound. Jesus is not describing Himself as a thief; He is describing the attitude of the disciple who fails to watch. A thief does not announce his arrival. He comes when the household sleeps, when their guard is lowered, when they are least prepared. Jesus' point is not to frighten but to correct a deadly habit of the heart: the assumption that divine encounters—whether in grace or judgment—always give advance notice. Life does not offer such guarantees. Grace breaks in like dawn. Judgment arrives like evening. Death comes like a breath. The disciple who stays awake lives every hour ready for God.

This teaching shapes the early Church's understanding of time itself. Christians begin to see every moment as bearing an eschatological weight. Time is not neutral; it is charged with the presence of God. The Apostle Paul draws directly from Jesus' imagery when he writes, "The night is far gone; the day is at hand." He urges believers to wake from sleep, to cast off the works of darkness, and to live as children of light. Paul is not creating something new; he is interpreting the words of Christ. Jesus' teaching on vigilance becomes the Christian way of understanding the world. It becomes the lens through which believers see their lives, their decisions, and their destiny.

Mark's Gospel preserves one of the clearest exhortations Jesus gives regarding vigilance: "Be on guard, keep awake, for you do not know when the time will come." He then describes a man going on a journey, leaving his servants in charge, each with his own task, and placing the doorkeeper on watch. The image is striking for its simplicity. Each servant has work to do. Each servant is responsible for something entrusted to him. The doorkeeper stands watch not as an ornament but as a necessity. Jesus concludes with a universal command: "What I say to you, I say to all: Stay awake." The words are direct, encompassing, and unmistakable. They admit no exceptions. They apply to every disciple in every age.

The command to stay awake carries with it a quiet dignity. Jesus does not appeal to fear to motivate His disciples. He appeals to responsibility. Each disciple is entrusted with something sacred—his own soul, his vocation, his relationships, his gifts, his opportunities for love. To fall asleep spiritually is to neglect that trust. Jesus calls each believer to stand in the truth of his own accountability. He dignifies the human person by reminding him that his life matters, his choices matter, his attentiveness matters. Vigilance becomes an expression of human freedom rightly ordered toward God.

It is here that Jesus' warnings take on a fatherly tone. He knows the difficulty of remaining awake in a world that lulls the soul into complacency. He knows how the routines of life can erode spiritual sharpness. He knows how easily the mind drifts and how quickly the heart grows tired. He knows the temptations that whisper, "Later, tomorrow, not yet." His warnings are therefore not condemnations but mercies. They are the voice of a Father who wants His children alert to the dangers that threaten their joy.

Jesus' teaching reaches a kind of crescendo when He describes the sudden return of the Son of Man. He speaks not of a gradual event but of a moment that arrives like lightning. The shock is not meant to terrify but to awaken. It reminds believers that the end of the story is not a distant hope but a present certainty. Every day moves toward that encounter. Every heartbeat brings the disciple closer to the moment when Christ will come in glory or when the veil of death will open into eternity. Jesus teaches vigilance because He wants His disciples to live in the truth of this reality, not in the illusion of endless tomorrows.

One of the most striking features of Jesus' teaching on vigilance is how often it includes joy. The vigilant servants are blessed. The watchful steward is rewarded. The bridegroom's arrival is a feast. Jesus does not cast vigilance as a heavy burden. He casts it as the doorway to happiness. The vigilant heart lives with expectation. It looks toward the future with hope. It stands ready not only for accountability but for communion. Jesus wants His disciples to stay awake because He wants them to receive the fullness of the joy He promises.

This joyful dimension becomes clearer when one considers how Jesus connects vigilance with the readiness to receive the Holy Spirit. After the resurrection, He tells His disciples to wait in Jerusalem until they are "clothed with power from on high." They gather in the upper room, not knowing when the promise will be fulfilled, but remaining in prayer and watchfulness. Their vigilance becomes the condition for Pentecost. The same principle holds throughout the Christian life. Grace meets the heart that watches. God fills the soul that waits. The person who stays awake lives in a posture of receptivity, ready to welcome the movement of the Spirit.

The teachings of Jesus also reveal how vigilance protects the disciple from self-deception. He warns repeatedly that many will imagine themselves ready when they are not. The door closes on the foolish virgins not because they were wicked but because they were unprepared. The unfaithful servant is condemned not for rebellion but for negligence. Jesus exposes the danger of assuming that external association with Him is enough. Vigilance requires inward transformation. It requires a heart aligned with His will, not merely a life decorated with religious habits. The disciple who stays awake sees himself truthfully. He does not trust in appearances. He lives in humility, aware that he stands before God always.

This humility becomes essential because vigilance without humility hardens into anxiety or pride. Jesus guards against both. He warns His disciples not to be weighed down with the worries of life. He tells them not to be troubled. He calls them to trust in the Father's care. Vigilance rooted in fear becomes unbearable. Vigilance rooted in trust becomes peace. Jesus models this trust in His own life. He watches in Gethsemane with a heart surrendered to the Father. His vigilance is not frantic but faithful. He teaches His disciples to imitate this posture—a watchfulness grounded in love.

These teachings reveal a truth that sits at the centre of the Gospel: vigilance is the shape of Christian love. The person who loves stays awake. The person who desires communion with Christ keeps watch for Him. The person who longs for the Kingdom lives each day as if it could be the day of the Lord's arrival. Vigilance is not the tension of looking for danger but the anticipation of looking for the Beloved. Jesus tells His disciples to stay awake because He wants them to be present, ready, attentive when He comes—not as servants trembling before judgment but as friends waiting for a friend.

The heart of Jesus' teaching on vigilance comes into sharp focus when one listens to the rhythm of His parables. He tells stories of servants, stewards, bridesmaids, and householders—not to entertain, but to place the listener within a spiritual drama that unfolds every day. The parables grant access to the hidden movements of the soul. They expose the subtle ways in which a person can drift from God without noticing. They show how easily a life can be squandered when vigilance fades. They reveal the seriousness with which Jesus regards the present moment, the now in which salvation is offered and either embraced or postponed.

One of the most telling parables involves a master who goes on a journey and returns at an unexpected hour. The faithful servant remains attentive, fulfilling his responsibilities with integrity. The unfaithful servant, however, begins to act as though the master's delay grants him freedom to indulge his desires and ignore his duties. What is striking is that Jesus focuses not on the gravity of the servant's misconduct but on the root of it: the belief that the master is delayed. This belief—subtle, seemingly harmless—opens the door to moral collapse. The servant's behaviour unravels not because he hates the master but because he forgets the master. Jesus lays bare the psychology of sin: forgetfulness leads to presumption, presumption to negligence, negligence to disorder, disorder to judgment. The cure is vigilance.

In another teaching, Jesus describes a householder who remains watchful so that his home is not broken into. The implication is not merely that danger exists, but that danger exposes the need for constant attentiveness. A disciple who assumes that the spiritual life requires effort only in moments of crisis will be unprepared for the daily temptations that shape the soul. The true threat is rarely dramatic. It is the slow erosion of love, the quiet cooling of zeal, the subtle drift away from prayer. Jesus warns His listeners that the disciple who waits for an obvious threat before becoming watchful has already surrendered the battle. Vigilance must become habitual, woven into the fabric of ordinary life.

The ten virgins offer one of the clearest warnings Jesus gives. All ten fall asleep, yet the difference between the wise and the foolish is not the sleep itself but the preparation that came before it. The wise carry oil. The foolish assume there will be time to obtain it later. When the bridegroom arrives, the door shuts—not because he rejects them, but because they were unready. Jesus underscores a truth that resonates throughout Scripture: readiness cannot be improvised. Holiness cannot be borrowed. The life of virtue cannot be assembled at the last moment. Vigilance is not merely the alertness of the eyes but the orientation of the entire life toward God. It is the daily choosing of faithfulness, the steady accumulation of small obedience's that form the capacity to meet Christ with joy.

Jesus deepens this teaching when He speaks of the steward who must give an account of his management. The faithful steward acts in accordance with the master's will even when the master is absent. The unfaithful steward imagines that time grants immunity. Jesus does not focus on the gravity of the steward's wrongdoing but on the illusion that enabled it: the belief that the master's return is distant. This illusion breeds irresponsibility. Jesus exposes it so that His disciples may live with a different awareness—a holy readiness that understands every moment as lived in the presence of God.

The call to vigilance takes on yet another dimension when Jesus speaks of the end times. He describes cosmic signs, upheavals, and trials, but He repeatedly returns to a simple instruction: "Do not be led astray." The temptation during moments of crisis is to panic, to follow false voices, to abandon trust. Jesus' solution is not to provide a timetable but to cultivate discernment. He calls His disciples to remain steadfast, to recognize the signs of the times without being consumed by them, to lift their heads rather than lower their hearts. Vigilance here becomes the ability to remain anchored in truth while the world trembles. It is the refusal to let fear dictate one's response to suffering or uncertainty. It is fidelity under pressure.

This connection between vigilance and discernment reveals an essential truth: vigilance is not passive watching but active spiritual intelligence. The vigilant disciple does not merely avoid sin; he interprets the movements of his own heart. He recognizes temptation in its earliest stages. He perceives the subtle ways in which pride, anger, or sloth attempt to gain ground. He sees the difference between the promptings of the Spirit and the impulses of the flesh. Jesus' command to stay awake includes this interior attentiveness. It calls the disciple to live with a mind sharpened by truth, a heart anchored in prayer, and a will disposed to obedience.

Jesus makes this interior dimension explicit when He warns His disciples not to let their hearts be weighed down with dissipation, drunkenness, or the cares of this life. The danger is not only moral excess but spiritual heaviness. The heart becomes drowsy when burdened by anxiety, cluttered by distraction, or numbed by excess. Such a heart loses its capacity for watchfulness. Jesus, with pastoral tenderness, commands His disciples to avoid these burdens—not to restrict their lives but to safeguard their capacity to receive God. He wants their hearts light, clear, and responsive. Vigilance preserves the ability to encounter Him.

One finds this same theme in His teaching about prayer. He tells His disciples to pray at all times and not lose heart. The connection between prayer and vigilance is inseparable. Prayer awakens the heart, strengthens the will, and sharpens perception. It keeps the disciple attentive to God's presence and receptive to His grace. Jesus models this in His own life, retreating to deserted places to pray, rising early to commune with the Father, watching through the night when necessary. His vigilance flows from intimacy. He stays awake because He lives in the presence of the Father. He calls His disciples to the same way of life.

Vigilance also guards the disciple against complacency. Jesus warns that the path to destruction is wide and that many walk upon it. He cautions that the love of many will grow cold. He laments that some will honour God with their lips while their hearts remain far from Him. These warnings are not for the obviously wicked but for the seemingly devout. They expose the danger of external religiosity without internal transformation. A person may appear to be following Christ while drifting far from Him. Vigilance protects the heart from this deception by calling the disciple to sincerity, humility, and perseverance.

Throughout all these teachings, one thread remains constant: Jesus desires a people awake to His presence. He wants disciples who listen for His voice, respond to His grace, and live with an awareness that their lives are unfolding before the face of God. Vigilance becomes the posture of love. It is the expression of a heart that refuses to sleep through the hour of salvation, a heart that longs to be found faithful when the Lord appears.

The Gospels culminate this theme of vigilance in images that draw the entire Christian life into a single moment of decision. Jesus speaks of two men in a field, one taken and one left; two women grinding at the mill, one taken and one left. The suddenness of the separation is jarring, yet it serves a purpose. It reveals that the decisive moment does not wait for a dramatic context. It comes upon ordinary life—work, routine, daily tasks. The field and the millstone represent the quiet rhythms of existence. Jesus teaches that the moment of divine visitation arrives not in the extraordinary but in the ordinary. Vigilance, therefore, must be woven into the fabric of everyday life. It cannot be reserved for seasons of crisis. It is a daily readiness for God.

This ordinary readiness is what Jesus commends when He speaks of the faithful servant who remains watchful even when the master seems long delayed. The faithful servant does not lose heart because he lives with the constant awareness that his life is stewardship. Nothing he has belongs to him. Nothing he does is insignificant. Every act of fidelity prepares him for the moment when he will see the master again. Jesus portrays vigilance as a form of love's consistency—a long obedience that does not weaken when the visible signs of God's presence seem faint. It is faith expressed in perseverance.

Jesus also reveals that vigilance protects the disciple from surprise—not by removing the surprise of His coming, but by transforming the nature of the surprise. The moment of His arrival will astonish everyone. The difference is that for the vigilant, the astonishment becomes joy; for the negligent, it becomes dread. Jesus' teachings maintain this sober division without diminishing His mercy. He speaks truthfully because He wants His disciples to order their lives toward joy. His warnings carry the fullness of His love. A doctor speaks sternly not to frighten a patient but to save his life. Jesus' warnings function the same way. They serve the healing of the soul.

The parable of the talents captures this dynamic with particular clarity. The servants who invest their talents act with initiative, energy, and love. They do not need constant supervision because their hearts are aligned with the will of the master. They act not from fear but from devotion. Yet the servant who hides his talent betrays the logic of sloth. He imagines the master to be harsh, distant, demanding—a misunderstanding that reveals his lack of love. His failure is not caution but paralysis. He refuses to act because he refuses to trust. Jesus names his condition plainly: "You wicked and slothful servant." The severity of the judgment is not disproportionate; it is diagnostic. Sloth is not mere laziness. It is the refusal to engage the life God has given. Vigilance, then, is the remedy—a willingness to act, to respond, to risk love.

This truth becomes even sharper when Jesus speaks of the last day. He warns that many will call Him "Lord" but will not enter the Kingdom because they lacked obedience. They heard His words but did not act upon them. He compares them to a man who builds his house on sand. When storms come, the house collapses. The collapse is great because the foundation was never sound. This teaching exposes yet another dimension of vigilance: it is not merely waiting; it is living in a way that embodies readiness. Obedience becomes the structure that prevents collapse. The vigilant disciple does not separate hearing from doing. His life takes the shape of the Gospel. It is anchored in Christ.

Jesus' words in Luke 21 deepen this further. "Watch at all times, praying that you may have strength to escape all these things that will take place, and to stand before the Son of Man." The image is striking. To stand before the Son of Man requires strength—not the strength of physical effort but the strength of fidelity. Prayer becomes the lifeline that sustains vigilance. The disciple who prays remains attentive. His heart remains open. His spirit remains awake. Jesus does not leave vigilance to human effort. He ties it to grace. He commands His disciples to watch because He stands ready to strengthen those who seek Him.

One cannot overlook the tenderness that runs through Jesus' warnings. He does not speak as a distant judge but as a shepherd who knows the vulnerability of His sheep. He sees their fatigue, their confusion, their drifting hearts. He calls them to wakefulness because He wants them safe. When He speaks of the narrow gate, He does not intend to discourage but to protect. When He warns of wolves in sheep's clothing, He does so to guard the flock. When He tells His disciples that the road to destruction is broad, He reveals the cultural currents that lead hearts astray. Vigilance becomes the posture of the beloved who stays close to the shepherd.

This shepherding becomes most vivid in His post-resurrection encounters. The Risen Christ approaches His disciples in unexpected ways—walking beside them on the road, appearing in the midst of their fear, standing on the shore as they fish. Each encounter rewards a heart that remains open. Mary Magdalene recognizes Him when He speaks her name. The disciples on the road recognize Him in the breaking of the bread. Peter recognizes Him by the miraculous catch. Vigilance becomes recognition; recognition becomes communion. Jesus teaches vigilance not only for His future coming but for His present presence. The disciple who stays awake sees Him even now.

All of this reveals a simple but profound truth: vigilance is the atmosphere of Christian existence. It is the way a person lives when he knows that his life is being drawn toward an encounter with the living God. Jesus teaches vigilance repeatedly because the heart needs repeated awakening. The disciple is not asked to live in fear but in awareness. Not in anxiety but in expectation. Not in dread but in readiness.

The remembrance of death strengthens this awareness. It anchors vigilance in reality. It strips away the illusion of endless time. It brings the disciple into touch with the truth Jesus speaks: life is fragile, time is precious, and the hour of the Lord comes when it is not expected. Memento mori does not darken the Gospel; it illuminates it. It shows why Jesus speaks as He does. It reveals the love behind His warnings.

Vigilance becomes the shape of hope. It is the heart leaning forward toward the coming of the Lord, the mind attentive to His voice, the will aligned with His commands. Jesus' words, spoken across the Gospels with piercing clarity, gather into a single command that echoes through every age: "Stay awake."

The more one contemplates Jesus' words, the more it becomes clear that vigilance is not a spiritual hobby or an optional discipline reserved for the particularly devout. It is the very form of Christian life. It emerges wherever the Gospel is taken seriously. It shapes the way a believer thinks about time, grace, responsibility, and destiny. It draws the heart into a posture where God can be received at any moment, whether in a whisper of consolation, a summons to repentance, or the final call into eternity. Jesus teaches vigilance because He wants the soul to live with its eyes open.

This openness allows the disciple to see the world truthfully. Jesus often accuses the crowds of reading the weather but failing to read the signs of the times. Their problem is not ignorance but inattention. They see without perceiving, hear without understanding. Spiritual sleep blinds the heart to the reality unfolding around it. Vigilance restores sight. It enables the believer to discern God's presence in providence, in Scripture, in the sacraments, and in the unfolding of daily life. It awakens the soul to the sacredness of each moment. It reveals that nothing is ordinary when God is near.

Yet Jesus does not hide the cost of vigilance. He teaches that the watchful disciple must be prepared to endure misunderstanding, fatigue, and spiritual trial. He warns that the world will tempt the believer to distraction. He acknowledges that the heart grows weary. But He promises grace. He assures His disciples that the Father knows their needs. He reveals that the Spirit will strengthen them. He shows by His own example that watchfulness is possible even in sorrow, even in loneliness, even in the shadow of death. Vigilance does not demand superhuman effort; it calls for supernatural trust.

This trust takes shape in practices that form the vigilant heart. Prayer becomes a steady rhythm, not an occasional refuge. Scripture becomes nourishment, not mere information. Sacraments become the anchor points of a life lived before God. Charity becomes the natural expression of a heart awake to grace. Repentance becomes a daily cleansing that keeps the heart clear and free. Jesus' command to stay awake is not fulfilled by anxiety or strain but by faith expressed in these ordinary acts of fidelity. The vigilant life is simple, steady, and sincere.

What emerges from Jesus' teaching is a portrait of vigilance that is deeply hopeful. The command to stay awake is not a warning that God is eager to catch us off guard. It is a promise that He is coming to meet us. The disciple stays awake not because he fears judgment but because he longs for the Bridegroom. Vigilance becomes the posture of love that refuses to miss the moment of His arrival. It is the heart's anticipation of communion.

This is why the remembrance of death harmonizes so completely with Jesus' words. To remember one's mortality is to stand in the truth Jesus proclaims: the hour is unknown, the moment is near, the encounter is certain. The remembrance of death clarifies the meaning of vigilance. It strips away illusions and reveals the urgency of choosing God now. It draws the disciple into a deeper desire for holiness, a deeper longing for Christ, a deeper awareness of the Kingdom already pressing upon the present moment. Memento mori becomes the companion of every command to stay awake.

As Jesus' teachings accumulate across the Gospels—spoken on mountainsides, in parables, in private conversations, in the garden, at the temple, and along dusty roads—they form a single, unified call. It is the call to live lives that are transparent to eternity. It is the call to step out of spiritual lethargy and into the light. It is the call to live with the expectation that at any moment the Lord may appear—whether in grace that transforms the heart, in suffering that tests fidelity, or in the final summons that brings the soul before His face.

Jesus does not ask the impossible. He asks for attention. He asks for sincerity. He asks for a heart awake to the reality of God. Vigilance is simply faith that has opened its eyes. Hope that refuses to sleep. Love that listens for the footsteps of the One who comes.

The disciple who lives this way finds that vigilance becomes joy. The world no longer feels empty or meaningless. Every moment becomes charged with possibility. Every decision becomes an offering. Every passing hour becomes a preparation for the hour that truly matters. Vigilance reveals the Christian life as an adventure of expectancy—an ongoing readiness for God.

Jesus' words echo still, as clear now as when first spoken: "Stay awake." They are not burdens. They are invitations. They are the voice of a Lord who desires to find His servants waiting, watching, and filled with love when He comes.

6

Parables of Sloth, Delay, and Neglect

Jesus often teaches with images that seem familiar at first glance: lamps, vineyards, servants, feasts, seeds, doors, garments, barns. Yet beneath their simplicity lies a divine urgency. These parables do more than illustrate spiritual truths—they disclose the state of the human heart. They awaken the conscience. They expose the quiet patterns of delay, presumption, and negligence that shape a life without anyone noticing. Jesus uses these stories not to veil His meaning but to reveal it, separating the attentive from the distracted, the receptive from the indifferent. As Augustine observed, "Our Lord hides nothing from those who desire to hear, yet He hides everything from those who listen carelessly" (*Sermon 23*). The parables become mirrors: in hearing them, a person discovers whether he is awake or asleep.

Among all of Jesus' teachings, the parables that deal with sloth, delay, and neglect carry a particular weight. They gather the themes that have echoed since the prophets—the call to return, the danger of postponement, the urgency of repentance—and bring them to their fullest clarity. These parables show that the greatest threat to the soul is rarely rebellion, or scandal, or open defiance. The true danger lies in spiritual passivity: the quiet assumption that there will always be more time. If Satan's great temptation in the desert was "Turn stones into bread," his most effective temptation in the ordinary life of a believer is simply "Not today." Jesus confronts this temptation with parables that cut straight to the truth. They are stories of people who missed the moment of God's visitation not because they denied Him, but because they delayed Him.

Nowhere is this clearer than in the parable of the ten virgins. Jesus describes ten young women waiting for the bridegroom, each holding a lamp. Five are wise, five are foolish. The difference between them is not zeal, enthusiasm, or affection. It is preparation. All ten fall asleep. All ten hear the cry at midnight. All ten rise to greet the bridegroom. But only the wise have oil. What Jesus exposes is the difference between a life of superficial expectation and a life of true readiness. In the ancient world, lamps burned quickly. Without oil, a flame could not be sustained. The fathers interpret the oil as virtue, charity, and the inner disposition shaped through daily fidelity. Augustine says, "The oil is charity itself, which cannot be borrowed at the last hour" (*Sermon 93*). Chrysostom echoes this: "No one shall share another's virtue in that day" (*Homily on Matthew 78*). The foolish virgins are not condemned for sleeping—they are condemned for living as though there would always be time later to become holy.

Jesus intensifies the warning by describing the closed door. It is one of the most sobering images in the Gospel. The virgins arrive, breathless, anxious, pleading, but the bridegroom responds, "Truly, I do not know you." It is not ignorance but revelation. He reveals that their lives never took the shape of love. They desired the feast but not the preparation that makes the feast possible. The closed door is not an act of cruelty; it is the unveiling of a truth they ignored. They wanted the Kingdom without the cost, grace without transformation, arrival without readiness. Jesus uses this parable to show that holiness cannot be improvised. A soul cannot suddenly become what it refused to become over time. The hour reveals the truth; it does not create it.

The same theme appears in the parable of the talents, where Jesus describes a master entrusting his property to three servants. Two invest what they receive. One buries it. The first two act with initiative, trust, and love. The third acts with fear disguised as caution. His excuse is revealing: "I knew you to be a hard man." He imagines the master as harsh because he does not love him. Augustine interprets this fear as the root of sloth: "He feared to lose what he had, because he had no love to increase it" (*Sermon 25*). Sloth is rarely laziness in the bodily sense. It is resistance to the demands of love. It is the choice to avoid responsibility, to refuse engagement, to bury one's gifts so that nothing will be asked of one. The servant's judgment—"You wicked and slothful servant"—exposes the heart of acedia. He is not wicked because he committed grave crimes; he is wicked because he refused to move. The refusal to engage grace becomes a rejection of grace.

Jesus concludes the parable with an image that startles modern ears: the outer darkness. Yet this darkness is simply the natural consequence of the servant's choice. The one who refused to live in the light of his calling discovers the darkness he has already embraced. Judgment is the unveiling of a life's trajectory. Chrysostom comments that punishment is "nothing other than seeing clearly what one has become" (*Homily on Matthew 79*). Here again, Jesus shows that the greatest danger to the soul is not rebellion but inertia. The tragedy of the slothful servant is that he wasted the time he was given. He lived as though the master's return were irrelevant.

This same psychology of delay appears in the parable of the unfaithful servant, where Jesus exposes the most dangerous sentence a person can hold in the heart: "My master is delayed." This single assumption becomes the seed of corruption. The servant begins to mistreat others, indulge himself, and live without restraint—not because he intends evil, but because he believes there will always be more time to repent. The illusion of delay—*I will change later*—is the quiet ruin of the spiritual life. It gives sin room to grow and virtue no space to flourish. The fathers speak strongly of this temptation. Isaac the Syrian writes, "The devil rejoices in nothing so much as the word 'tomorrow'" (*Ascetical Homily 5*). Jesus unmasks the lie that time is guaranteed. He reveals that the heart that delays repentance will often delay it forever.

The unfaithful servant is judged not for unbelief but for presumption. He knows the master, but he lives as though the master's judgment will not come. Here Jesus diagnoses the subtle sin of half-discipleship—of belonging to God in word while reserving the heart for oneself. The parable's severity is mercy. Jesus shows the true consequences of a life that postpones conversion. He warns not to frighten but to awaken.

Jesus reinforces this warning through a story drawn from the life of every farmer in Israel: the barren fig tree. A man comes seeking fruit year after year and finds none. In the world of the prophets, Israel is often symbolized by a fig tree—planted, tended, and entrusted with every grace. When Jesus speaks this parable, He stands within that covenant imagery. The owner represents divine justice; the gardener, divine mercy. The owner says, "Cut it down," because fruitlessness is not a neutral condition. Time is not infinite; grace is not trivial. But the gardener intercedes: "Leave it one more year… if it bears fruit, well and good; if not…" The sentence remains unfinished, hanging over the tree like an unspoken truth. Chrysostom reads this pause as the echo of God's patience: "He delays the judgment that we might hasten our repentance" (*Homily on Luke 13*). Yet the delay itself becomes a warning. Mercy extended does not mean mercy presumed. A year of digging, watering, and tending implies a year of accountability. Jesus teaches that the refusal to grow becomes, in time, a refusal of God.

Fruitlessness is not merely inactivity. It is the slow exhaustion of opportunity, the withering of responsiveness. A barren fig tree still absorbs nutrients, water, air, and sunlight—but gives nothing back. It becomes an image of a life that receives the gifts of God but never cooperates with them. In the prophetic tradition, unfruitfulness is not merely unfortunate; it is tragic. Hosea cries out, "Ephraim is a trained heifer that loves to thresh, but I spared her fair neck" (Hos 10:11), lamenting how grace can be squandered. Jesus' parable sharpens this lament. He shows that fruitfulness is the natural response to grace; barrenness is the refusal of that response. The parable ends with mercy, but mercy that urges urgency. A year can be long or short—it depends on the heart. The gardener's intercession slows the judgment, but it does not suspend it. Jesus wants His listeners to feel the weight of grace: what one does with the present moment determines what the future moment will reveal.

This movement from grace to response appears again in Jesus' teaching on the vine and the branches. He says, "I am the true vine, and my Father is the vinedresser" (Jn 15:1). This declaration gathers the entire story of Israel—its vineyards, covenants, and prophetic warnings—into a single sentence. Israel was God's vineyard, planted with care (Isa 5). Yet it bore wild grapes. In Christ, God plants a new vine, the perfect vine, in whom fruitfulness is guaranteed. The only question is whether the branches will abide in Him. Jesus does not warn about enemies or persecutions. He warns about detachment. "Apart from Me you can do nothing." Detachment does not happen through dramatic rebellion. It happens through neglect, through the gradual drift of a branch that stops drawing life from the vine.

Basil the Great teaches, "To live without vigilance is already to be cut away" (*On the Holy Spirit, ch. 9*). Gregory the Great adds, "The branch that bears no fruit is cut because it no longer wishes to draw life from the vine" (*Homily on the Gospels 27*). Jesus speaks with similar clarity: fruitlessness leads to removal, and the branches that do bear fruit will be pruned. Pruning, though painful, is a mercy. It removes attachments that hinder life. It sharpens love. It awakens the soul to its purpose. The unfruitful branch, however, is cast into the fire—not because God desires destruction, but because the branch has ceased to bear the life it was created to carry. Fire becomes the natural end of what no longer participates in life.

Jesus then turns to another image of readiness that intensifies the call: the wedding feast. A king prepares a banquet for his son. Invitations go out. Those invited refuse. Some ignore the call. Others mistreat the messengers. So the king invites others—those from the highways and hedges—and the hall fills with guests. Yet Jesus adds a detail that changes the parable from a story about indifference to a judgment scene. One man enters without a wedding garment. The garment represents the transformation that accompanies entering the Kingdom—righteousness, repentance, the new life of grace. Origen says, "The garment is Christ Himself, in whom one must be clothed" (*Commentary on Matthew 22*). Augustine writes, "The garment is charity, without which even the good works avail nothing" (*Sermon 45*). When the king asks, "Friend, how did you come in here without a wedding garment?" the man is speechless. He has no defence because he has no transformation. He accepted the invitation but refused the conversion the invitation required.

This parable exposes one of the most dangerous illusions in the spiritual life: the belief that being in the right place—near the Church, near sacramental life, near religious activity—is itself enough. Jesus confronts this false security. Proximity is not fidelity. Association is not transformation. The garment of grace cannot be substituted with familiarity or convenience. The man's silence reveals the truth of his life. Judgment does not invent the verdict—it reveals it.

Jesus concludes the sequence of warnings with a story so direct that its force is impossible to evade: the parable of the rich fool. A man's land produces abundantly. He plans to tear down his barns and build larger ones. He speaks to his soul as though it were clay in his hands: "Soul, you have ample goods laid up for many years; relax, eat, drink, be merry." But God speaks into his illusion: "Fool! This night your soul is required of you." Basil the Great, in his famous homily, rebukes the man's logic: "The barns you build are the stomachs of the poor." Augustine reflects, "He counted his years but not his day" (*Sermon 36*). Jesus reveals the man's folly not because he was wealthy but because he lived as though death were irrelevant. He planned everything except the one moment guaranteed to arrive. The night claims him, and the barns remain. His soul is unprepared because his life had no reference to God.

This parable ties together the entire theme of vigilance and mortality. Jesus calls the man a fool because he forgot death. He mistook abundance for security. He mistook time for a possession. He mistook his soul for an object he could command. Jesus ends the parable with a stark line that resonates with every other warning: "So is the one who lays up treasure for himself and is not rich toward God." Riches are not condemned. Self-sufficiency is. Neglect of the soul is.

Through these parables—virgins without oil, servants without initiative, stewards presuming delay, trees without fruit, branches without life, guests without garments, a man with full barns but an empty soul—Jesus reveals the same truth from every angle: the spiritual life is lost not in rebellion but in postponement. Grace is wasted not in dramatic sin but in quiet neglect. Judgment arrives not to surprise but to disclose.

Taken together, these parables form a single, coherent revelation: the greatest spiritual danger is not hostility toward God, but indifference to Him. Jesus repeatedly directs His warnings not at those who openly reject Him, but at those who drift, delay, or live without urgency. His sharpest words are reserved for the unprepared, the unresponsive, the spiritually drowsy. In each parable, the crisis arrives suddenly, not because Jesus wants to alarm, but because He wants to awaken. He unveils the truth that eternity does not negotiate with procrastination. Time is a covenant gift, and like all gifts, it demands a response.

This truth becomes especially vivid when one notices how ordinary the settings of these parables are. Lamps, barns, fields, vineyards, feasts, household tasks—these are the fabric of everyday life. Jesus does not place vigilance against the backdrop of extraordinary trials or overwhelming temptations. He places it in the normal rhythms of existence. The foolish virgins were not engaged in scandalous behaviour. The slothful servant was not plotting wickedness. The unfaithful steward was not philosophizing about atheism. The fig tree simply absorbed nutrients while giving nothing back. The branch merely ceased to draw life. The man with the barns merely made long-term plans. Their failures were not dramatic—they were ordinary. Jesus reveals that the spiritual life is won or lost in the ordinary.

This is why the parables form the heart of His teaching on memento mori. Each story shows that death or judgment arrives unexpectedly, interrupting patterns of life that felt secure. What the characters assumed would continue indefinitely is suddenly brought to an end. Their lives are measured not by intentions but by reality. This is the theological weight of memento mori: remembering death brings clarity to life. The opposite is also true: forgetting death breeds delusion. When Jesus teaches about these sudden moments, He is not describing arbitrary divine decisions; He is describing the inherent structure of reality. A person who lives unprepared will be unprepared when the hour comes.

The fathers understood this with piercing insight. Gregory the Great writes, "A man should always fear the suddenness of the last day, because he is ignorant whether he is worthy of life or of condemnation" (*Homily 13 on the Gospels*). He does not mean a fear that paralyses, but a fear that disciplines. His point is that spiritual sleep is most dangerous when it feels most harmless. The sleep of the virgins without oil did not feel dangerous. The inactivity of the slothful servant felt safe. The unfaithful steward felt justified. The fig tree felt rooted and secure. The rich fool felt confident in his plans. Their downfall was not that they miscalculated—it was that they never calculated at all.

Acedia—the noonday demon, the temptation that whispers "later"—lurks beneath each parable. Evagrius describes acedia as "the paralysis of the heart, the refusal of the moment" (*Praktikos 12*). Cassian calls it "a weariness of the soul which drains away all desire for good" (*Institutes X*). Their descriptions could easily be applied to the foolish virgins, the slothful servant, or the barren fig tree. Acedia is the erosion of vigilance. It is the quiet deadening of spiritual attentiveness. Jesus, in His parables, reveals its consequences. He does not theorize about acedia. He dramatizes it.

In every story, time is the decisive element. The virgins had enough time before the bridegroom arrived—but they did not use it. The slothful servant had enough time to invest his talent—but he buried it. The unfaithful steward had enough time to serve faithfully—but he assumed delay. The fig tree had enough years to bear fruit—but they passed unused. The branch has time to abide—but it ceases to draw life. The invited guest had time to put on the garment—but arrived unprepared. The rich fool had years of harvest—but never considered the night. Jesus uses time as a spiritual x-ray. It reveals whether a person uses grace or wastes it.

Here, Jesus' teaching meets the realism of human psychology. People often imagine they will convert later, forgive later, pray later, grow later, repent later. The illusion of "someday" becomes a spiritual sedation. Yet Jesus reveals that *later* is the most dangerous word in the

Gospel. It lulls the soul into a false peace and blinds it to the fact that change becomes harder the longer it is delayed. Augustine confesses this in his own conversion: "I kept saying, 'Soon, tomorrow,' but my tomorrow never came" (*Confessions*, VIII.12). He realized that delay is not neutral—it shapes the soul. One does not remain the same while delaying repentance. One becomes less capable of it.

Jesus' parables make this truth unmistakable: the soul that delays readiness becomes unready by habit. Neglect forms a pattern. Acedia forms a disposition. The virgins without oil reveal what happens when a soul delays virtue. The slothful servant reveals what happens when a soul delays responsibility. The unfaithful steward reveals what happens when a soul delays conversion. The barren fig tree reveals what happens when a soul delays fruitfulness. The branch reveals what happens when a soul delays abiding. The guest without a garment reveals what happens when a soul delays transformation. The rich fool reveals what happens when a soul delays remembrance of death.

These are not separate teachings. They are facets of one diamond, one revelation, one message: the human heart is judged by how it uses the time it is given. Jesus presses this truth because He knows how fragile the heart is, how easily it drifts, how subtly it deceives itself. Augustine captures the heart of this teaching when he writes, "God has promised you forgiveness if you repent, but He has not promised you tomorrow" (*Sermon 169*). This is not severity—it is mercy. The warning is not meant to crush the soul but to awaken it before it is too late.

For Jesus, vigilance is not merely awareness—it is love. It is the refusal to let the heart grow numb, the refusal to postpone what is essential, the refusal to live as though the Bridegroom is irrelevant to the present moment. The virgins bring oil because they love Him. The faithful servants invest because they trust Him. The vigilant steward serves because he hopes in Him. The fruitful tree receives the gardener's care because it desires to bear fruit. The abiding branch clings because it knows its life depends on the vine. Every parable reveals the same truth: love stays awake.

What strikes the attentive reader is how Jesus uses these parables to reveal not merely human weakness but divine desire. God desires fruit. God desires readiness. God desires communion. Behind every warning stands a longing. The bridegroom longs to welcome the virgins. The master longs to reward his servants. The king longs to fill his banquet hall. The gardener longs to see fruit where there has been none. Judgment is not God's preference; communion is. Yet communion requires preparation, transformation, vigilance. Jesus' parables unveil the truth that God's generosity can be resisted, wasted, disregarded, or postponed—yet never without consequence. Grace is free, but it is not cheap.

This becomes particularly clear in the parable of the wedding feast. The joy of the king is evident: he has prepared a banquet, fattened the cattle, sent out invitations. He desires a full hall. Yet when the invited refuse, the urgency intensifies. The messengers are sent again. When even then the invitation is rejected, others are brought in—"both bad and good." The Father desires that His house be filled (cf. Lk 14:23). This divine generosity is so expansive that it gathers anyone willing to enter. But generosity does not erase the need for conversion. The man without a garment stands as a solemn reminder that one cannot accept the invitation while refusing the transformation that comes with it. As Origen notes, "The wedding is grace, but the garment is righteousness" (*Commentary on Matthew 22*). To enter without being changed is to reject the very heart of the feast.

Jesus' warnings, then, are invitations pressed into the form of stories. Each parable shows the human heart reaching a decisive moment where love must act. The virgins must carry oil. The servants must invest. The steward must remain faithful. The fig tree must bear fruit. The branch must abide. The guest must dress himself in righteousness. The rich man must remember death. These are not burdens but pathways into communion. Jesus does not warn to discourage; He warns to awaken desire. He calls His listeners to recognize the dignity of their choices—their capacity to shape eternity.

This becomes particularly evident when one reads these parables through the lens of covenant. Israel's story is woven into each image. The vineyard in Isaiah, the fig tree in Micah, the garments of righteousness in Isaiah 61, the lamps burning in Exodus, the banquet of the Messiah in Isaiah 25—all these background texts make the parables more than lessons. They are covenant indictments and covenant promises combined. Jesus, standing in the place of the prophets, confronts His people with the urgent question: Will you receive the Kingdom or refuse it? Will you prepare or postpone? Will you be awake or asleep? As Scott Hahn often emphasizes, the parables are covenant lawsuit and covenant renewal in one breath. They reveal whether the heart is aligned with God or drifting from Him.

If these parables feel severe, it is because Jesus teaches them near the end of His earthly ministry. Time itself is collapsing into the moment of His Passion. Judgment is at hand—not only the judgment upon Israel, but the judgment upon sin itself. Jesus speaks with urgency because the decisive hour is near. His listeners must choose. And so must we. These parables are not distant stories from a foreign world; they are examinations of conscience made visible. They reveal what a soul becomes when it delays conversion. They show what a life looks like when it forgets death. They expose the false security of "later." They reveal how easy it is to waste the time one is given, and how simple, beautiful, and necessary it is to use that time for love.

Acedia hides itself most successfully in outward stability. A life can appear religious while inwardly drifting. The foolish virgins stand with lamps in hand, yet they lack the one thing that matters. The slothful servant remains in the household, yet his heart is absent. The unfaithful steward still oversees the estate, yet he serves himself. The fig tree stands tall, yet bears no fruit. The branch remains connected, yet draws no life. The guest sits at the feast, yet has not clothed himself with righteousness. The rich man's barns are full, yet his soul is empty. Jesus reveals a pattern that echoes through every age: the soul can remain externally close to God while internally far from Him. Acedia does not shout; it sighs. It does not rebel; it drifts. It does not reject God; it delays Him.

The severity of the parables is therefore a mercy. Jesus speaks with such clarity not because He is eager to condemn but because He is unwilling to lose anyone to the quiet ruin of acedia. Augustine captures this tension perfectly when he writes, "He warns us as Judge, but He calls us as Father" (*Sermon 113*). The warnings carry the tenderness of a God who sees the danger more clearly than we do. They bear the tone of a lover who refuses to let the beloved sleep through the moment of visitation.

In each parable, the key movement is the arrival—the bridegroom comes, the master returns, the king enters, the gardener inspects, the hour arrives, the soul is required. These moments of arrival reveal the truth that was hidden in the passing of time. Jesus teaches that the decisive moment is always nearer than we think. The one who delays preparation discovers he has none. The one who postpones obedience finds he cannot give it. The one who assumes he has time discovers he has run out of it. As Augustine confesses of his own conversion, "I was late in loving You" (*Confessions*, X.27). Delay became a wound.

Yet here is the beauty of the parables: readiness is possible. Virtue can be cultivated. Fruit can be borne. Grace can be received. The lamps can be filled. The talents can be invested. The garment can be woven. The branch can abide. Jesus warns because He believes in the possibility of transformation. His severity is trust in our capacity, through grace, to become what we are called to be. He would not warn the soul if the soul were incapable of waking. He would not exhort vigilance if vigilance were beyond reach.

His parables reveal the structure of salvation: grace given, grace offered, grace invited—but never forced. The human heart must respond. Jesus' warnings dignify that response. They reveal that the soul is not a passive object swept along by fate. It is a participant in a divine drama. It stands at the crossroads of eternity. The parables become the scriptural echo of Moses' ancient words: "Choose life" (Deut 30:19). Jesus presses the urgency of that choice into the fabric of ordinary life.

If one listens closely, a subtle harmony runs through all these parables—a harmony both sobering and strangely hopeful. Jesus does not speak of vigilance as though it were a feat reserved for the strong. He speaks of it as though it were the natural posture of anyone who knows they are loved. The wise virgins bring oil not out of fear, but because they desire the bridegroom. The faithful servants invest because they trust the master's character. The fruitful tree grows because it welcomes the gardener's care. Jesus reveals that readiness is the fruit of relationship. It is not sheer discipline. It is desire awakened into action.

The tragedy of the foolish virgins is not simply negligence; it is forgetfulness of the bridegroom. They are not preparing for an inspection—they are preparing for a wedding. Yet somewhere along the way, the joy of that expectation faded, replaced by the assumption that there would always be time. This is the psychology of spiritual delay: when the love that first moved the heart grows distant, vigilance weakens. Passion cools. Faith becomes routine. Acedia slips in unnoticed, whispering that devotion can wait. Jesus teaches this parable not to scold but to draw the believer back to the love that first ignited faith. Readiness arises when memory is restored—when the heart remembers whom it waits for.

The same dynamic appears in the parable of the talents. The servants who invest boldly do so because they interpret the master's trust as an invitation to participate in his generosity. They understand that the gift given is meant to be used. They act out of communion. The slothful servant misinterprets the master. He sees Him as harsh, demanding, exacting—and so he hides the gift. His sloth is rooted in a distorted image of God. This is why Jesus' warning is so severe, because sloth is not merely passivity; it is a refusal of love's invitation. Augustine notes that the servant's fear "was the fear of a heart that does not love" (*Sermon 25*). When love fades, duty becomes unbearable. When trust is lost, obedience becomes impossible. Jesus teaches this parable to restore the truth: God entrusts His gifts because He desires our flourishing.

The parable of the unfaithful steward further deepens this insight. The steward does not become violent or indulgent because of malice. He becomes unfaithful because he stops expecting the master. The absence of the master creates a vacuum the steward fills with self-rule. Presumption thrives where presence is forgotten. Jesus reveals that vigilance is not merely a moral posture—it is relational awareness. The steward's downfall is not that he sinned, but that he lost sight of the master's nearness. Forgetfulness becomes the doorway to corruption. This is why the early fathers warned that the greatest temptation of the spiritual life is simply to forget God in the midst of daily responsibilities.

In the barren fig tree, Jesus introduces the mystery of time into this dynamic. The tree receives sunlight, water, and soil, yet gives nothing back. It lives without responsiveness. Fruitlessness in Scripture is always relational. It is not simply failure to produce; it is failure to return love for love. Grace comes; grace is resisted. Seasons pass;

change does not occur. The gardener intervenes not with accusation but with intercession—"Let it alone this year also." This intercession shows the gentleness of God, but it also reveals the urgency of human responsibility. The gardener's care can soften soil, clear thorns, and nourish roots, but it cannot bear fruit in place of the tree. Jesus is teaching that grace works with freedom, not instead of it. Failure to respond to grace becomes, over time, refusal.

In the vine and the branches, the relational dimension becomes unmistakable. Jesus does not speak of tasks, duties, or obligations. He speaks of *abiding*. Vigilance is rooted not in constant anxiety but in constant communion. The branch bears fruit because it draws life from the vine. Neglect is not primarily moral failure; it is severance from life. Basil the Great's comment strikes with force: "To live without vigilance is already to be cut away." Jesus makes this the central point: the branch that stops abiding does not die suddenly—it dies gradually, imperceptibly, like a soul drifting into acedia. The pruning that the Father performs becomes a mercy that protects life by removing what impedes it. Only one danger threatens the soul: drifting from the Source.

The wedding garment parable reveals another layer of relational truth. The man without the garment is not judged for ignorance, but for indifference. He accepted the invitation but refused the transformation it required. In covenant terms, he entered the feast without entering the relationship. The garment symbolizes not outward decorum but inward renewal. Isaiah speaks of "the garment of salvation" and "the robe of righteousness" (Isa 61:10). Paul speaks of "putting on Christ" (Gal 3:27). Augustine says, "The wedding garment is charity" (*Sermon 45*). Jesus teaches that readiness for the feast is not measured by presence but by love. Love clothes the soul for communion.

The rich fool stands apart from the others because he is not awaiting anything at all. His life has collapsed into the present moment, consumed by self-sufficiency. He speaks to his soul as though he owns it. He calculates years as though they are guaranteed. He builds barns as though he can secure his future with structures of his own making. Basil's homily cuts through the illusion: "The barns you build are the stomachs of the poor." Jesus' judgment—"Fool!"—is covenantal. In Scripture, a fool is one who lives without reference to God (Ps 14:1). The rich man is not evil. He is asleep. His plans are meticulous, yet his soul is neglected. Death does not come as punishment; it comes as revelation. The night exposes the truth: he lived for what he could not keep and ignored what he could not lose.

Across all these parables, a single pattern emerges: neglect is a relational failure. Neglect of preparation is neglect of the bridegroom. Neglect of the talent is neglect of the master's trust. Neglect of service is neglect of the master's nearness. Neglect of fruitfulness is neglect of the gardener's care. Neglect of abiding is neglect of the vine Himself. Neglect of the garment is neglect of the transformation offered. Neglect of the soul is neglect of the God who formed it.

Jesus warns not because He is harsh, but because He is relational. He does not desire servants who fear judgment but beloved sons and daughters who stay awake out of love.

Judgment in the parables is never arbitrary. It is the unveiling of a relationship either embraced or ignored.

The virgins cry out, "Lord, Lord, open to us," but they had never lived with Him in their hearts.

The slothful servant demands mercy from a master he never trusted.

The unfaithful steward appeals to authority he never respected.

The fig tree claims space in a vineyard whose life it never shared.

The branch claims attachment to a vine whose life it never drew.

The banquet guest claims entry into a feast he never adorned himself for.

The rich man claims years in a world he never treated as a gift.

Jesus' warnings are deeply theological because they reveal the structure of covenant relationship: grace given, response required.

And this response must be *now*.

Delay is the slow death of love.

If the parables unveil the dangers of delay, they also reveal the profound dignity of the present moment. Every warning Jesus gives assumes the same truth: the time to respond is now. Not later, not when life grows quieter, not when conditions improve. The present moment is the battleground of salvation. It is the place where grace is offered and where the heart either receives or resists. Jesus' parables do not frighten us with uncertainty; they dignify us with urgency. They declare that time is not an empty container to be filled but a sacrament in which God meets the soul.

This is why so many of the parables end with sudden arrival. The bridegroom comes at midnight. The master returns without warning. The king enters the feast unexpectedly. The gardener arrives after a set period. The hour in which the soul is required is never announced. Jesus is teaching something about the nature of grace: it does not conform to our schedules. God gives Himself when He wills, and the ready heart receives Him. The unready heart does not. Augustine reflects, "God comes to us, but we are often not in ourselves" (*Sermon 88*). The issue is not that God is absent but that the heart is inattentive.

The parables also show that judgment is not primarily a sentence pronounced from without, but a condition revealed from within. The foolish virgins did not suddenly become foolish when the door shut—they had been foolish for years without noticing. The slothful servant did not suddenly become slothful when the master returned—his whole life had been shaped by avoidance. The unfaithful steward did not suddenly become corrupt when he mistreated others—his corruption began when he stopped expecting the master. The fig tree was not suddenly barren when inspected—it had been barren through multiple seasons of wasted grace. The rich fool was not suddenly foolish after building barns—he had lived without reference to eternity long before the voice called him home.

This is why Jesus speaks so often of the heart. The heart is where delay becomes habit. It is where excuses collect. It is where love cools. It is where vigilance fades. The parables reveal that the human heart drifts not dramatically but gradually, like a boat untied from its mooring. Jesus calls His listeners to examine not the crises of life but the patterns of life. He wants His disciples to recognize how they rise in the morning, how they pray, how they forgive, how they handle time, how they respond to grace, how they speak, how they work, how they decide. Acedia hides in the unnoticed corners of ordinary days.

This is what makes these parables so pastoral. They confront the soul with truth, yet they do so with a clarity that awakens rather than crushes. Jesus does not mock the foolish virgins. He does not shame the slothful servant. He does not ridicule the unfaithful steward. He does not despise the barren fig tree. He does not scorn the branch. He does not condemn the poorly dressed guest until the moment of judgment reveals his refusal to change. He does not berate the rich fool for wealth. In every parable, Jesus teaches with a tone that combines gravity and gentleness. He speaks as one who desires the soul's salvation more deeply than the soul desires it for itself.

The severity of His warnings flows from the depth of His love. A physician warns strongly because he desires his patient to live. A shepherd calls loudly because he sees the wolf approaching. A father speaks urgently because he knows the danger his child cannot see. Jesus' warnings are no different. They are not the voice of a tyrant demanding submission but the voice of a Savior urging vigilance. Augustine says, "The mercy of God goes before the judgment of God"

(*Sermon 169*), meaning that every warning is itself an act of mercy—a chance to turn, to wake, to live.

Throughout these parables, there is another theme that runs quietly but powerfully beneath the surface: the finality of choices. The closed door, the outer darkness, the cut branch, the barren tree removed, the guest cast out—these images are not threats but truths. They reveal that the human heart has the capacity to define its own destiny. God respects human freedom with a seriousness that should humble us. He offers grace, invites conversion, extends mercy, sends prophets, tells parables, pleads for fruit, calls to repentance—but He will not force a response. Judgment reveals what the heart has chosen.

Yet Jesus never leaves the soul in despair. Behind every severe image stands a radiant promise: readiness leads to joy. When the bridegroom arrives, the wise virgins enter the feast. When the master returns, the faithful servants are set over many things. When the king inspects the banquet, those clothed in righteousness remain as honoured guests. When the gardener finds fruit, the tree remains in the vineyard. When the vine bears fruit, the Father prunes it so that it may bear more. Jesus warns of judgment, but He speaks far more often of the joy that awaits the prepared heart.

It is this joy that makes vigilance not only necessary but beautiful. The vigilant soul is not tense but hopeful. It is not anxious but attentive. It does not fear the bridegroom's arrival; it longs for it. It does not dread the master's return; it delights in it. It does not resent the king's invitation; it rejoices in it. Vigilance is not the posture of a servant who fears condemnation—it is the posture of a bride awaiting her bridegroom. When Jesus says, "Stay awake," He invites the heart into love's attentiveness.

The remembrance of death gives this invitation depth and clarity. Death reminds us that time is precious, that the soul is eternal, that grace is not an abstraction, that every day is a gift, that every moment is an opportunity to love. Death turns the parables from stories into lifelines. It shows that Jesus was not speaking about distant eschatology but about the structure of the spiritual life right now. The fool of Luke 12 is every soul that forgets death. The wise virgins are every soul that prepares for it. The slothful servant is every soul that postpones its own conversion. The prepared servant is every soul that sees death as the doorway into communion with God.

Thus the parables do not simply warn—they orient. They shape a way of being. They summon the heart to awake. They teach that salvation is not mechanical nor automatic nor casual. It is relational, covenantal, and urgent. God offers Himself, and the soul responds— or does not. Jesus' parables unveil this truth with a clarity that pierces complacency and ignites desire. They reveal that heaven is given to those who are ready, and readiness is nothing other than love lived in vigilance.

These parables gather into a single revelation: the greatest danger to the soul is not dramatic rebellion but quiet delay. Jesus never presents sin chiefly as a spectacular collapse. He presents it as neglect. As forgetfulness. As postponement. As the slow cooling of desire. His images are ordinary because the danger is ordinary. Lamps without oil, talents left unused, a fig tree left untended, a servant who shrugs at the passing days, a guest who arrives without preparation, a man who plans for every contingency except the one certainty. The kingdom is lost not through extraordinary wickedness but through habitual indifference.

This is why the parables strike us so deeply. They describe the spiritual life as it actually unfolds. Most people do not consciously reject God. They drift. They intend to pray later. They assume there will be time to forgive later. They imagine holiness will come naturally later. They treat vigilance as a task for the devout few rather than the vocation of every Christian. Jesus names this drift as the true spiritual crisis. He sees what we overlook: delay has a shape, a momentum, a spiritual weight. It forms a character. A soul becomes what it repeatedly postpones.

In this way, the parables uncover the anatomy of acedia. Acedia is not merely laziness; it is a refusal of the present moment in which God wishes to act. It is the soul's resistance to grace now. The slothful servant who buries the talent does not reject the master outright; he simply sets aside the responsibility entrusted to him. The foolish virgins do not despise the bridegroom; they merely fail to prepare for him. The unfaithful steward does not deny the master's authority; he behaves as if the master will not return today. The rich fool does not hate God; he simply ignores Him. Acedia is always mild in its beginnings and tragic in its end.

The parables also reveal something essential about divine judgment. Judgment is not arbitrary. Judgment is the soul coming to terms with what it has become. The closed door in the parable of the virgins is not divine cruelty; it is the necessary boundary that reveals the truth of preparedness. The outer darkness into which the slothful servant is cast is not a punishment unrelated to his choices; it is the consequence of a life that refused the joy of responsibility. The removal of the barren fig tree reflects the seriousness of grace wasted season after season. Jesus teaches that judgment confirms, rather than contradicts, the shape a soul has chosen.

Yet woven through every parable is the unmistakable tenderness of God. He warns because He loves. He awakens because He desires us to live. He unsettles because He refuses to let us settle for mediocrity. Even the hardest images carry hope. The door that closes reminds us that time is a gift and that every hour is charged with divine possibility. The slothful servant's condemnation reveals the dignity of the tasks God entrusts to His children. The removal of the fig tree underscores the gardener's patient search for fruit—year after year, offer after offer. The rich fool's shock becomes an invitation to reorient our lives while time remains.

The heart of these parables is not fear but longing. Jesus calls His disciples to stay awake because He desires their joy. He urges preparation not because He wishes to burden them but because He wishes to share His glory with them. The wise virgins enter the feast. The faithful servants hear the words every Christian longs for: "Well done… enter into the joy of your master." The branches that abide in the vine bear fruit beyond measure. The fig tree that responds to the gardener's care stands renewed. The guests who clothe themselves in righteousness share in the banquet. The soul that remembers death becomes rich toward God.

Memento mori makes these parables luminous. When the remembrance of death enters the heart, the parables cease to feel distant. They become descriptions of our own spiritual condition. They become mirrors in which we see our desires, our fears, our delays, our hopes. They become invitations to order our lives toward eternity. The remembrance of death sharpens the urgency Jesus teaches. It exposes the illusion of "later." It reveals that time is not a guarantee but a grace. It shows that every day is a gift extended by the One who desires our readiness.

In the end, these parables reveal that vigilance is nothing other than love that stays awake. The wise virgins keep oil because they desire the bridegroom. The faithful servants work because they love the master. The branches bear fruit because they draw life from the vine. The prepared guest dresses because he honours the king. The soul that is ready lives not in fear of judgment but in expectation of joy.

Jesus does not warn us because He wishes us to tremble. He warns us because He wishes us to hope; He wishes us to live awake; He wishes us to desire Him as He desires us.

Every parable points toward the same truth: the Christian life is

preparation for the moment we meet the Lord.
   The soul that remembers this lives wisely.
   The soul that forgets it lives in illusion.
   The soul that prepares enters joy.

7

Lukewarmness: "I Will Spit You Out"

There are moments in Scripture when the voice of Jesus reaches us with a clarity that feels almost overwhelming. The Gospels speak through parables and stories, through gestures of mercy and signs of power, through the rhythms of His earthly life. Yet in one place, the voice of Christ sounds with a directness so unfiltered that it leaves no room for misunderstanding. It is the risen Lord, standing not within the dusty roads of Galilee but within the blazing vision of Revelation, speaking to His own Church with the authority of One whose eyes are "like flames of fire" and whose word divides truth from illusion. His message to the community of Laodicea stands as one of the most arresting statements in all of Scripture: "I know your works: you are neither cold nor hot. Would that you were cold or hot! So, because you are lukewarm, and neither cold nor hot, I will spit you out of my mouth" (Rev 3:15–16). The shock of those words has echoed through the centuries. They are spoken not to unbelievers or persecutors but to the baptized, to those who gather in His name, to those who profess faith yet allow their hearts to drift into a comfortable indifference. Jesus directs His severest warning toward those who treat the life of grace as something optional, negotiable, respectable, manageable. He addresses those who do not deny Him, yet do not love Him; those who do not rebel, yet do not respond.

The Christians of Laodicea had become spiritually tepid without realizing it. They said, "I am rich, I have prospered, and I need nothing," but the Lord responds with devastating clarity: "You do not know that you are wretched, pitiable, poor, blind, and naked" (Rev 3:17). The problem is not that they were weak or struggling or wounded. The Lord never rejects weakness. He draws near to the struggling sinner with tenderness. The problem is self-deception—an imagined sufficiency that blinds the heart to grace. The Laodiceans believed they were spiritually well, when in truth they were spiritually numb. Tertullian once remarked, "Security is the mother of carelessness," and Laodicea had become the image of that carelessness. Their city, prosperous and self-assured, had no sense of its vulnerability. Their water supply, neither refreshing nor boiling, arrived tepid through long aqueducts—a physical reality that Christ transforms into a spiritual diagnosis. Lukewarm water leaves no one revived; neither does a lukewarm soul.

What disturbs Jesus is not struggle but indifference. Not fear, but complacency. Not the sinner who collapses under temptation, but the believer who lives without urgency, without desire, without fire. Lukewarmness is not the rejection of God; it is something far more subtle: the refusal to give Him one's whole heart. Gregory the Great explains that lukewarmness is the state of one who "does not renounce God, yet is also not moved to fervour; who keeps a semblance of devotion but lacks its power" (*Moralia in Job*, 31.45). It is the condition in which the soul settles into a plateau, where prayer becomes occasional, repentance becomes postponed, charity becomes selective, and discipleship becomes respectable. The lukewarm Christian lives with the vocabulary of faith but not its vitality. He believes but does not burn. He hears the Gospel but is no longer pierced by it. He approaches the sacraments but without hunger.

This is the illness Jesus confronts with such severity because it is the most spiritually lethal condition a Christian can endure. Sin often awakens the soul; failure can shock the heart back into truth. But lukewarmness numbs. It produces the quiet satisfaction of a life that feels spiritually adequate. Augustine observed that "the lukewarm man fears to fall but is unwilling to rise" (*Sermon 169*). He remains in a middle place, comfortable with mediocrity, unwilling to take the risks of love. Tepidity is the death of desire, and desire is the engine of holiness. When desire cools, the soul drifts, and the drift becomes a story told over years rather than hours.

The imagery Jesus uses—"I will spit you out of my mouth"—is not cruel, though its force is startling. It expresses the incompatibility between divine love and half-hearted faith. Lukewarmness provokes revulsion because it misrepresents the covenant. God is not indifferent, nor is His love partial, nor is His mercy casual. He gives His whole heart. He gives His whole self. He gives His Son. A half-hearted response distorts the very relationship for which we were made. Thomas Aquinas describes tepidity as "the resistance of the will to the fervour of charity," meaning that God's fire is offered, yet the soul holds itself back, content with minimal love (*Summa Theologiae*, II-II, q.30). This withholding grieves the Lord not because He is offended, but because He desires to share His life fully with His people.

Lukewarmness blinds the soul to its own condition. It whispers, "You are fine. You pray enough. You give enough. You love enough. There is no urgency to change." It replaces repentance with mild regret, holiness with vague aspiration, and discipleship with religious routine. It is possible to attend liturgy, receive the sacraments, avoid scandalous sin, and yet remain spiritually asleep. Cassian saw this clearly in the desert, noting that the lukewarm monk is one who "keeps the form of monastic life but not its power; who is still, but not watchful; who reads, but not with hunger; who prays, but not with expectation" (*Conferences*, 10.8). The same diagnosis fits countless Christians who avoid grave sin yet avoid great love.

What Jesus opposes in lukewarmness is not weakness but refusal. He sees a heart that could burn, yet chooses dimness. He sees a soul invited to intimacy, yet content with distance. He sees disciples who have lost the urgency of love, who no longer watch for the Bridegroom, who have settled for a faith that costs little and asks little. This is why the lukewarm are worse off than the cold. At least coldness recognizes its lack; lukewarmness masks it. Coldness can awaken through shock; lukewarmness drifts in a haze of illusion. The lukewarm person thinks he sees, but does not; thinks he is clothed, but is naked; thinks he is secure, but stands at the edge of spiritual collapse.

Jesus' words are an act of mercy. He tears away the illusion that destroys the soul from within. He forces the Laodiceans to see what they cannot see. Revelation is unveiling—not merely of the end times but of the present spiritual condition of the heart. When Christ speaks with such severity, it is because He desires to rescue. These words are like a surgeon's incision—sharp, painful, necessary, healing. The wound is opened so that life may begin anew.

Lukewarmness reveals itself most clearly in its relationship to time. The lukewarm soul is not rebellious—it is delayed. It does not reject the call to prayer; it postpones it. It does not refuse conversion; it simply waits for a more convenient season. It does not say "no" to God; it says "soon." In this way, tepidity resembles the mindset Jesus condemned in the servant who said, "My master is delayed" (Lk 12:45). The servant does not deny the master's existence; he merely assumes the master will not arrive today. That assumption becomes the seed of corruption. When Jesus exposes lukewarmness, He exposes the soul's hidden confidence that there will always be more time, more chances, more tomorrows. But the life of grace does not grow in the soil of postponement. Love thrives only in the present moment, the moment where God speaks, where grace acts, where the heart must choose.

This is why Jesus' warnings throughout the Gospels prepare us for the severity of His words to Laodicea. Every command to "stay awake," every parable of delay, every image of sudden arrival teaches that the life of discipleship cannot be half-lived. The God who is a consuming fire cannot be answered with embers. Jesus desires friendship, intimacy, communion—real communion, not polite acknowledgment. Tepidity is an insult to divine generosity. The lukewarm heart demands nothing and offers nothing; it is content with a spiritual life in which nothing substantial ever changes. It is the spiritual equivalent of drifting through marriage without love or effort, maintaining the appearance of fidelity while the interior covenant decays. Christ refuses to pretend such a relationship is life-giving.

The Fathers understood lukewarmness as the corruption of desire. Basil the Great wrote that the lukewarm believer "does not entirely forsake the Lord, yet he does not serve Him with his whole heart; he lives between two realms and belongs to neither" (*Homily on Psalm 1*). That image—the soul suspended in a spiritual middle place—captures the essence of tepidity. It clings to just enough religion to soothe the conscience but not enough to transform it. It keeps Christ close enough to feel safe but far enough to avoid surrender. Lukewarmness is the refusal to let grace do what grace intends to do: make the soul holy.

The tragedy of lukewarmness is that it feels safe. It feels stable. It feels moderate. It rarely feels sinful. The lukewarm believer does not experience the violent tremors of a guilty conscience that accompany grave sin. He experiences instead the spiritual equivalent of numbness.

A person in this state may mistake the absence of conflict for spiritual peace. He may interpret the dull quiet of his interior life as maturity rather than stagnation. Yet Jesus' words remind us that this state is not peaceful—it is perilous. Augustine once confessed, "I feared to be without God, yet I feared to be fully with Him" (*Confessions*, VIII), revealing a tension every lukewarm heart knows. Tepidity fears the demands of holiness more than the consequences of mediocrity.

The imagery of Revelation intensifies this truth through its covenantal symbolism. The language of being "spit out" echoes the Old Testament's warnings about Israel being "vomited out" of the land when the covenant was betrayed (Lev 18:28). The connection is unsettling yet illuminating. Lukewarmness is covenantal infidelity—not through dramatic rebellion, but through the slow erosion of love. It is the spiritual equivalent of a marriage in which one partner remains physically present but emotionally absent. The Lord desires a bride whose heart burns for Him. Tepidity insults the nuptial mystery by offering apathy where love is meant to dwell.

The Laodiceans believed their wealth made them secure. Yet Christ describes them in terms of absolute vulnerability: poor, naked, blind. Their spiritual blindness prevents them from recognizing their condition, and the blindness itself is part of the judgment. The danger of lukewarmness is precisely that it convinces the soul nothing is wrong. Chrysostom explained that "none are so in danger as those who do not know they are sick" (*Homily on Matthew* 25), for their very ignorance prevents them from seeking a cure. The lukewarm Christian is spiritually ill yet spiritually unaware—alive, but barely; awake, but not truly watchful.

What then is Christ's remedy? He does not condemn in order to destroy; He diagnoses in order to heal. "Those whom I love, I reprove and chasten; so be zealous and repent" (Rev 3:19). The severity of His earlier words blossoms into tenderness. He stands at the door and knocks, not at the gates of unbelief but at the threshold of apathy. He pleads not with rebels but with those who have forgotten how to love. This is a Jesus who refuses to settle for half of the heart. He wants the whole thing.

His counsel is astonishingly personal. He calls the lukewarm to buy "gold refined by fire"—the gold of purified desire, love refined through trial. He offers "white garments" to cover their nakedness—the robe of righteousness that comes from repentance and grace. He gives "salve to anoint your eyes"—the illumination that comes when the heart awakens from self-deception. These are the gifts of a Bridegroom restoring His bride. They are the very opposite of apathy. They are symbols of renewed passion, renewed clarity, renewed intimacy. Christ's solution to lukewarmness is not punishment but rekindling.

Lukewarmness dies when love grows. Tepidity evaporates in the presence of desire. What Jesus seeks is not fear-driven vigilance but love-driven wakefulness. The earlier parables taught us that the wise virgins kept oil because they longed for the Bridegroom. The faithful servants worked because they loved their master. Lukewarmness breaks this link between vigilance and love by hollowing out desire. It leaves the lamp without oil, the servant without purpose, the disciple without fire. This is why Jesus speaks so sharply—He is fighting not against His people, but for them.

And then, into the midst of this severe diagnosis, comes one of the most tender promises in all of Scripture: "Behold, I stand at the door and knock; if anyone hears my voice and opens the door, I will come in to him and eat with him, and he with me" (Rev 3:20). This is covenant language of intimacy restored. The Bridegroom seeks His bride. The Lord seeks His people. The desire of God for the human soul does not diminish because the soul has cooled. He knocks even at the door of tepidity. He knocks at the door of forgetfulness. He knocks at the door of delay. His goal is not to shame the lukewarm

Christian but to wake him.

Lukewarmness reveals its full danger when seen against the mystery of divine love. God does not love moderately. He does not save cautiously. He does not redeem half-heartedly. Every movement of salvation history is marked by the extravagance of divine charity. From the burning bush to the Incarnation, from the Cross to the empty tomb, from Pentecost to the Eucharist, God's actions are entirely wholehearted. He holds nothing back. Augustine captured this when he said, "God loves each of us as if there were only one of us," a line that speaks of a love so complete, so personal, that anything less than a full response from the human heart is a kind of dissonance in the symphony of grace. Lukewarmness is the soul responding to divine fire with a dampened matchstick. It is the heart hearing the call of eternity yet rolling over to sleep a little longer.

This contrast—between God's wholehearted gift and our half-hearted response—becomes unbearable once it is seen clearly. It is why Jesus speaks with such force to the Church in Laodicea. Tepidity is not merely a spiritual weakness; it is an incongruity in the covenant. In the Old Testament, God describes His love in the fiery terms of a spouse. "I will betroth you to me forever," He promises through Hosea, "in steadfast love and mercy" (Hos 2:19). This nuptial vision reaches its fulfillment in the New Testament, where Paul declares that Christ loved the Church and "gave himself up for her" (Eph 5:25). A covenant made through total self-gift cannot be answered with polite religiosity. A love that dies on a Cross cannot be reciprocated with mild interest. Tepidity is the failure to recognize the cost of love.

Yet lukewarmness rarely appears in dramatic form. It is subtle. It begins in small concessions—a shorter prayer, a half-hearted act of charity, a convenient omission of truth. It grows through distractions that multiply, responsibilities that claim the time once reserved for God, comforts that expand until sacrifice feels burdensome. Like rust on metal, it corrodes slowly but relentlessly. Isaac the Syrian warned that "the lukewarm soul does not notice its own sickness," because tepidity creates a fog over the spiritual senses. The soul no longer feels hunger for holiness, nor thirst for righteousness, nor joy in sacrifice. It settles into a grey neutrality that confuses stillness with peace and apathy with maturity.

This interior dullness explains why lukewarmness appears so often in Scripture through the imagery of sleep. Jesus speaks of servants who fall asleep instead of keeping watch, of virgins who slumber while the bridegroom approaches, of disciples who sleep in the Garden while He cries out in agony. Sleep is morally neutral for the body but spiritually dangerous for the soul. It symbolizes inattention—the heart's failure to remain awake to the movements of grace. Paul intensifies this imagery when he exhorts the Romans, "It is full time now for you to wake from sleep. For salvation is nearer to us now than when we first believed" (Rom 13:11). Lukewarmness is spiritual drowsiness made permanent.

The terrifying element of lukewarmness is not that it damns through dramatic sin, but that it quietly forms a character incapable of love. Heaven is a communion of burning charity, a life of unending desire for God. A soul that resists love on earth cannot suddenly love in eternity. Bernard of Clairvaux wrote that "hell is truth seen too late," meaning that the soul discovers in the end that the love it refused is the very love for which it was created. The lukewarm man becomes incapable of joy because he has trained his soul in half-heartedness. He stands before the Beloved unable to receive what he has never desired.

This is why Jesus' voice in Revelation contains both thunder and invitation. After declaring that He will spit the lukewarm out of His mouth, He immediately reveals the motive behind the warning: "Those whom I love, I reprove and chasten" (Rev 3:19). Divine correction is always an act of divine affection. The harshness of the words reflects the urgency of the danger. A parent does not speak softly when a child reaches toward fire. Mercy sometimes wounds in order to heal. Christ's reproof cuts only to remove what kills.

Yet the invitation that follows is astonishingly tender: "Behold, I stand at the door and knock." This image is one of the most intimate in Scripture. The Lord does not shout through the window or force the door open. He knocks. He waits. He desires to enter but respects freedom. This gesture is directed not toward pagans but toward the baptized who have let their love grow cold. Hans Urs von Balthasar once reflected that God's knock is "the sound of love seeking room," a line that captures both the patience and the urgency of Christ. The Bridegroom who once carried the Cross now stands at the door of a sleepy Church, asking to be welcomed with renewed desire.

The tragedy is that lukewarmness often makes the soul too numb to hear the knock. The desires that once rose readily toward God fall flat. The prayers that once carried fire become perfunctory. The sacraments that once exhilarated now feel routine. This dullness is not the absence of faith but the cooling of love. Thomas Aquinas insisted that charity is meant to burn continuously: "Fervour belongs to charity as brightness belongs to fire" (*Summa*, II-II, q.28). Where fervour dies, love dims. Lukewarmness is therefore not a minor vice—it is the dimming of the very flame of divine life within the soul.

Yet Christ's promise is astonishing. "If anyone hears my voice and opens the door," He says, "I will come in to him and eat with him, and he with me" (Rev 3:20). This is covenant table fellowship, the intimacy God has desired since Eden. The one who awakens from lukewarmness does not receive reproach but communion. The coldness of the heart becomes the place where Christ brings warmth. The emptiness becomes the place where He brings fullness. The indifference becomes the place where He ignites desire. The Lord who knocks is the Lord who enters, and the Lord who enters is the Lord who transforms.

The severity of Jesus' warning is therefore the severity of divine longing. He does not want half of the heart because half of the heart cannot hold His love. He does not want moderate devotion because moderate devotion cannot receive the fire of the Spirit. He desires us to burn because He Himself is burning. John of the Cross described God's love as a flame that seeks to consume the soul not in destruction but in union. Lukewarmness cannot endure such fire; only a heart stirred awake can.

The image of Christ knocking at the door reveals something essential about the nature of the Christian life: love must be awakened. It cannot be coerced. It cannot be automated. It cannot be assumed. The lukewarm soul is not condemned because it feels little—feelings rise and fall like wind over water—but because it refuses to awaken love through repentance. The danger is not emotional coldness but spiritual inertia. Jesus does not command His disciples to feel more, but to love more, to choose more, to respond more. Lukewarmness settles for a life in which nothing is deeply wrong yet nothing is deeply right. It builds its security on the illusion that a mild devotion is enough for the God who has given everything.

This is why Jesus exposes lukewarmness through the language of disgust. "I will spit you out of my mouth" is startling precisely because it reveals a relationship fractured not through rebellion but through mediocrity. The Lord who welcomed tax collectors and sinners refuses to accept tepidity. It is not the magnitude of sin that provokes His severity but the refusal of passionate love. A soul in grave sin may yet rise again through repentance; a soul that thinks it needs nothing cannot be healed. The lukewarm man is satisfied with being spiritually "good enough," which means he has ceased to desire God Himself. Augustine taught that the entire Christian life is "a holy longing," and that "the whole life of a good Christian is a desire to see God" (*Tractates on the Gospel of John*, 4). Where longing dies, the Christian life collapses inward into mere habit.

The imagery of desire becomes even more striking when read alongside the Song of Songs, that great poem of divine and human love. The bride cries, "I slept, but my heart was awake" (Song 5:2). She hears her beloved knocking, and she rises to meet him. The early Fathers saw this passage as a mirror of Revelation 3: the Bridegroom knocking at the door of the soul, calling His beloved into deeper communion. In the Song, the failure to respond quickly leads to sorrow; the lover departs, and the bride must seek him with renewed longing. When the Church becomes lukewarm, she mirrors the bride who delays. Christ still knocks—but she hesitates. This hesitancy is the essence of tepidity: not denial, not refusal, but delay.

Delay is spiritually deadly because it reshapes the interior world of the heart. Every postponed confession, every deferred act of charity, every quiet surrender to distraction slowly forms a habit of indifference. The will becomes accustomed to passivity. The heart becomes accustomed to comfort. Blaise Pascal once wrote that the great tragedy of the human condition is that we can grow accustomed even to misery; the same is true spiritually. The soul can grow accustomed to mediocrity until it no longer recognizes its own poverty. Jesus' terrifying words to Laodicea—"You do not know"—strike at this blindness. The lukewarm Christian feels spiritually fine precisely because he is spiritually ill.

Revelation adds another layer of meaning by situating this warning within the larger narrative of judgment. Christ's severe words to Laodicea appear just before the vision of the heavenly throne room, where the Lamb is revealed as the One who alone is worthy to open the scroll of history. The placement is deliberate. Lukewarmness is not merely a personal struggle; it is a cosmic danger. It renders the Church impotent in the drama of salvation. A faith without fire cannot bear witness in a world needing light. A Church content with comfort cannot confront the powers that enslave the human heart. Tepidity is not a private vice—it is a failure of mission.

The early martyrs understood this intuitively. To follow Christ meant to stake everything on Him. There was no middle place between Caesar and the Cross. Polycarp could declare, "Eighty-six years I have served Him, and He has done me no wrong," because his heart burned with a love that could not be extinguished by threat or flame. Lukewarmness would have been inconceivable to such believers, not because they were naturally fervent, but because they recognized the urgency of the covenant. They knew that to belong to Christ was to live with a love that was worth dying for. What is worth dying for is worth living for with fervour.

It is precisely this fervour that lukewarmness extinguishes. Tepidity drains the Christian life of its joy. It turns the sacraments into duties. It turns prayer into obligation. It turns Scripture into information. It turns the moral life into a negotiation. Love fades into formality. The lukewarm Christian may keep the structure of faith intact while losing its soul. This is the state Jesus condemns—not because He despises the believer, but because He desires to restore the fire. Throughout Revelation, Christ appears as the One whose eyes are flames, whose feet glow like bronze in a furnace, whose voice thunders like many waters. There is nothing lukewarm about Him. To encounter Him is to be set aflame.

Yet even in the face of such fervour, the lukewarm soul often resists the vulnerability required to change. Tepidity often springs from a fear of surrender. To grow in holiness requires letting go of control, comfort, self-protection. The lukewarm Christian fears that if he gives God everything, God may ask for more than he wants to give. He fears the loss of idols he secretly cherishes. He fears the suffering that accompanies sanctification. He fears the unknown. So he keeps a safe distance—near enough to feel religious, far enough to avoid transformation. But love cannot grow at a distance. The narrow gate that Jesus speaks of is narrow precisely because it leaves no room for excess baggage. Tepidity attempts to pass through the narrow gate carrying comfort, fear, and self-will. It cannot fit.

This narrowness is not cruelty but clarity. Christ invites the believer to shed everything that constricts love. The martyr's path is narrow, but so is the path of the saint, the mother, the monk, the priest, the ordinary Christian who chooses humility over pride, forgiveness over resentment, prayer over distraction. Lukewarmness resists this path because it requires a decision—an interior act of the will to choose the fire of charity over the dullness of habit. Jesus calls His followers to choose the narrow gate daily, not because He delights in difficulty but because He delights in love.

Here the words of Christ reveal their deepest purpose. When He says, "Be zealous and repent," He is not demanding performance; He is inviting the rebirth of desire. The Greek word for "zealous" (ζήλευε) carries the sense of "burn with longing." Jesus asks the lukewarm to burn again—not with emotional enthusiasm, but with the steady flame of love that chooses Him above all else. Repentance is simply the act of clearing away the ash that has smothered the flame. Gregory the Great described repentance as "the re-igniting of the extinguished lamp," a line that captures the heart of this chapter. Jesus does not want lukewarm Christians to despise themselves; He wants them to light their lamps.

The flame that Christ desires to kindle in the lukewarm heart is not a flash of momentary emotion but the steady, purifying fire of the Holy Spirit. When Jesus speaks of buying "gold refined by fire," He is speaking of a love tested, strengthened, and made radiant. Fire in Scripture is never merely destructive; it is illuminating, transforming, sanctifying. The pillar of fire that led Israel, the fire that consumed Elijah's sacrifice, the fire that fell upon the Apostles at Pentecost—each reveals a God who burns away illusion and ignites a new creation. Lukewarmness fears this fire because it fears what must be given up: comfort, complacency, mediocrity. But the purified gold that emerges is nothing less than the likeness of Christ Himself formed in the soul.

The white garments offered to the Laodiceans reveal another dimension of the cure. Clothing in Scripture signifies identity, dignity, and mission. Adam and Eve's nakedness is a symbol of their lost glory; the prodigal son's robe signifies restoration; the baptismal garment signifies new life. The lukewarm believer is spiritually naked not because he lacks religious habits but because he lacks the radiance of love. He is clothed in routine but not in holiness. Christ offers a garment woven from grace—the renewed purity that arises when the soul turns wholeheartedly back to God. Augustine preached that the white garment is "the garment of charity," without which even the most impressive deeds are empty. Jesus does not simply ask the lukewarm to try harder; He offers them a new identity.

The eye salve that Christ prescribes completes the triad. Blindness is one of the dominant images in Revelation. The lukewarm soul is blind precisely because it believes it sees. Spiritual blindness is not ignorance but misperception: the inability to recognize one's own poverty, the inability to perceive the urgency of grace, the inability to see the beauty of holiness. Jesus restores sight not by flattery but by truth. His diagnosis is the first act of healing. Chrysostom taught that Christ's harsh words are "the bitter medicine that restores sight to the blind," because they tear away the veil of self-deception. When the lukewarm Christian hears the truth and accepts it, his spiritual vision begins to clear. He sees again the greatness of God, the shortness of life, the beauty of holiness, the urgency of love.

At the core of all of this lies the mystery of divine condescension.

The Lord who thunders from His cosmic throne is the same Lord who stands gently at the door of the human heart. He does not storm the house; He knocks. He does not demand entry; He requests it. He does not shame; He invites. The One whose voice shakes creation lowers His voice to a whisper so that the lukewarm soul may hear without fear. The same divine majesty that judges the nations stoops to ask for fellowship with the heart that has forgotten Him. There is no greater humiliation of God's love—nor any greater hope for the soul—than this image of Christ waiting outside a door that should belong to Him by right.

The tragedy, then, is not divine distance but human indifference. Jesus does not abandon the lukewarm; the lukewarm abandon desire. They treat God as a distant figure rather than an intimate presence. They approach prayer as an obligation rather than a relationship. They receive the sacraments as rituals rather than encounters. They live a life in which nothing is overtly wrong, yet the deepest thing is missing: love. The deepest tragedy of lukewarmness is not that it sins too boldly but that it loves too weakly. A soul may avoid serious faults and still fail in the great commandment—to love the Lord with all one's heart, soul, mind, and strength. Tepidity shrinks this commandment until it fits comfortably within the life the believer already lives.

But no one drifts into holiness. No one coasts into sanctity. Grace requires cooperation; love requires choice. Jesus' warnings in Revelation 3 are therefore not simply corrective but vocational. He calls the lukewarm Christian back to the fundamental decision of discipleship: to choose the Lord above all, again and again. He calls the soul to become intentional rather than accidental, fervent rather than passive, decisive rather than drifting. Gregory the Great observed that "the lukewarm are those who begin well but do not persevere," and perseverance is always a decision renewed in the present moment. Tepidity dies the moment the heart chooses to love God fully.

This is why Christ's promise to the victorious believer is so astonishing: "To him who conquers I will grant to sit with me on my throne" (Rev 3:21). The same Church that risked being spit out of His mouth is invited to sit beside Him in glory. The contrast is overwhelming: from divine disgust to divine enthronement. This is the gospel in miniature. Christ confronts our mediocrity not to condemn us but to exalt us. He warns us not to shame us but to awaken us. The divine severity is always in service of divine generosity. He speaks hard words because He longs to give unimaginable gifts.

This promise reveals what lukewarmness ultimately steals. It robs the soul not merely of fervour but of destiny. A lukewarm Christian is not simply a weak Christian; he is a Christian who lives beneath his calling. He is a son who has forgotten his inheritance, a bride who has forgotten her Bridegroom, a pilgrim who has forgotten his destination. Jesus does not call him to intensity for intensity's sake; He calls him to become what he is. Tepidity is therefore not merely morally deficient but ontologically tragic—it prevents the soul from becoming its true self in Christ.

Here the narrow gate returns, not as a threat but as a path to fullness. Jesus speaks of the gate as narrow because it leads to life. Lukewarmness chooses the wide gate—the gate of ease, of delayed repentance, of diluted love. But the wide gate does not lead to joy; it leads to a life in which nothing matters intensely, nothing burns, nothing transforms. The narrow gate is the gate of desire—the choice to press deeper, to surrender more, to give one's whole self in response to the God who gives His whole self. The lukewarm soul avoids the narrow gate because it fears the cost, yet the cost is precisely what opens the soul to the joy Christ promises.

In this light, Jesus' words in Revelation are revealed not as condamnation but as invitation. He is not rejecting the lukewarm; He is calling them back to love. He is summoning them to awaken, to repent, to burn. He is inviting them to open the door, not merely to avoid judgment but to receive friendship. The goal is not fear but communion. The warning is the prelude to the feast. Christ does not merely wish His people to avoid hell; He wishes them to taste heaven.

The call to awaken from lukewarmness becomes even clearer when placed in the wider sweep of salvation history. God has always formed His people not through comfort but through encounter. Abraham left Ur because he heard a voice. Moses approached a burning bush and removed his sandals. Israel followed pillars of fire and cloud. The prophets cried out because the word of the Lord burned within their bones. Holiness never emerged from indifference. Whenever the people of God drifted into complacency, the Lord sent a prophet—not to terrify but to rekindle. The voice of Christ in Revelation belongs to this same pattern. It is the prophetic voice of a God who refuses to let His beloved settle for less than the fullness of divine life. Tepidity is dangerous not simply because it leads to judgment, but because it abandons the joy of covenant intimacy.

This is why Jesus speaks so fiercely. Lukewarmness is the quiet suffocation of the spiritual life. It strangles vocation. It blinds the conscience. It drains the sacraments of their transformative power. It leaves the soul alive but languid, breathing but barely awake. It is a half-life masquerading as the fullness of faith. John Cassian warned that tepidity is "the most destructive of the vices because it disguises itself as moderation," and his insight remains piercing. Tepidity rarely shocks. It rarely scandalizes. It simply settles—like dust on a sacred object, slowly obscuring its beauty.

Yet Christ, in His mercy, keeps disturbing the dust. His knock at the door is not a polite tap but a summons of love. He is the Bridegroom who will not give up on His bride, even when her heart has grown dull. He is the Shepherd who goes searching even for the sheep that has not run away, but has merely lain down in the grass and refused to move. He is the Physician who wounds in order to heal, who exposes the sickness so that the cure may begin. His severity is tenderness in disguise. His warning is the final barrier before ruin, placed there not to frighten but to save.

The path forward is therefore not complicated, though it is costly. Jesus gives the remedy within the rebuke: "Be zealous and repent." These two movements—zeal and repentance—are the twin engines of the awakened Christian life. Repentance clears the ash; zeal ignites the flame. Repentance reveals where love has cooled; zeal rekindles love's fire. Repentance breaks the inertia of the will; zeal directs the will toward God with renewed intensity. Together, they restore the soul's capacity to receive the grace it has long resisted.

And when this grace is received, something remarkable happens: the lukewarm soul becomes a soul of fire not through emotional fervour but through fidelity. The awakened Christian does not live in perpetual ecstasy; he lives in perpetual surrender. Lukewarmness dies when the heart begins to say yes to God in small, immediate, concrete acts. The yes to prayer in the morning. The yes to forgiveness when wronged. The yes to silence instead of distraction. The yes to generosity when tempted by comfort. These small decisions accumulate into a life that gradually becomes incapable of tepidity because it is continually returning to the flame.

Christ's final promise crowns the chapter with unimaginable dignity: "He who conquers, I will grant him to sit with me on my throne, as I myself conquered and sat down with my Father on his throne." To sit with Christ on His throne—this is the destiny from which lukewarmness tries to lull us. Tepidity is the enemy of glory not because it is dramatic, but because it is small. It shrinks the Christian life into something manageable, forgetful of its cosmic purpose. The lukewarm Christian lives as though he is meant to survive life; Christ calls him to reign.

Here the remembrance of death returns with clarifying force. If lukewarmness dilutes the urgency of the spiritual life, memento mori restores it. The memory of death burns through complacency. It refuses to let the heart drift. It exposes the illusion of endless tomorrows. It reminds the soul that every moment is an opportunity either to welcome the Bridegroom or to delay Him. When death is remembered, the knock at the door sounds louder, clearer, truer. Lukewarmness thrives in forgetfulness; vigilance thrives in remembrance.

To remember death is to awaken desire. It is to see clearly that life is short, eternity is near, love is urgent, and Christ stands waiting. It is to understand that the mediocrity we tolerate today becomes the character we carry into judgment. It is to hear, beneath the sternness of Revelation, the tenderness of a God who calls His people back to fervour because He longs to share His glory with them.

The risen Christ ends His message to Laodicea with a final declaration: "He who has an ear, let him hear what the Spirit says to the churches." The Spirit still speaks this word. The knock still sounds. The door still waits. Lukewarmness still threatens. And grace still burns for those willing to open.

The soul awakened from tepidity does not live in fear of being spat out. It lives in the hope of being taken in. It hears the Bridegroom's voice and rises. It feels the flame of divine love and answers it. It chooses the narrow gate, not because it must, but because it desires the Life waiting on the other side. It prepares, it watches, it burns.

And the One who once warned, "You are lukewarm," will one day say to that soul, "Enter into My joy."

8

When Death Becomes Desire: From Holy Fear to the Longing for the Bridegroom

There is a moment, after hearing the voice of the risen Christ thunder through Revelation, when the soul finds itself standing in a kind of holy stillness. His words have cut through excuses and shattered illusions. They have exposed the quiet dangers of delay, the hidden poison of complacency, the sleep that settles over the heart when desire grows weak. The warnings of the Lord do not leave the disciple crushed; they leave him awake. They do not weigh the heart down with fear; they clear the fog of spiritual drowsiness so that the call of God can be heard again with clarity. What remains, after the thunder of His voice subsides, is the simple truth that the Christian life must be lived with intention. Nothing in the Gospel is casual. Nothing in the kingdom is lukewarm.

This awakening is not meant to be temporary—an emotional stirring that fades after the shock of hearing Christ name our condition. It is meant to drive us into a new way of living, a way marked by watchfulness of heart. The warnings of Jesus are not merely revelations of danger; they are invitations into a deeper vigilance. They press the believer to ask not only, "Am I ready?"

but, "How do I stay ready?" Love must be guarded. Desire must be protected. The flame of the Spirit must be tended. A heart awakened by Christ must learn to remain awake.

This is where the ancient wisdom of the Christian tradition becomes indispensable. The early monks understood what few in our age are willing to admit: that the greatest battles of the spiritual life are not fought in moments of crisis, but in the slow hours of the ordinary day. They grasped that the enemy of the soul rarely appears with dramatic temptations but whispers through distraction, weariness, restlessness, and the subtle pull toward ease. They saw with piercing clarity that the threats Jesus Himself named—sloth, delay, forgetfulness, lukewarmness—do not vanish simply because one has heard the warning. These threats must be confronted, resisted, exposed, and overcome.

For the awakened Christian, the question becomes: how does one live out the vigilance Christ commands? How does a disciple keep his lamp lit while the hours of the night stretch on? How does a servant remain ready when the master delays? How does a heart that has tasted truth avoid drifting back into the habits that once dulled its love? The warnings of Jesus create the urgency. The monastic tradition offers the strategy.

There is a strange mercy in realizing that the danger Christ names is not unique to us. The softening of desire, the slippage into apathy, the slow decay of fervour—these were known intimately by the men and women who fled into deserts seeking God alone. They described this inner resistance with a precision that feels startlingly modern. They named the heaviness that settles over the soul at the hour of prayer. They diagnosed the boredom that corrodes spiritual discipline. They identified the subtle self-deception that convinces a believer that "later" will be soon enough. They saw within themselves the very lukewarmness Christ condemned in Laodicea, and they refused to make peace with it.

The saints who withdrew into solitude did not do so to escape the world but to confront the worldliness within themselves—the worldliness that makes the soul sluggish, inattentive, divided. They knew that forgetting death leads to forgetting God, and forgetting God leads to forgetting oneself. They learned that vigilance is not a posture of anxiety but a form of love: the beloved watching for the presence of the Bridegroom. Their lives became laboratories of spiritual clarity, places where the warnings of Jesus were not merely heard but practiced, tested, fought for, and lived.

Their witness shows us that the warning of Christ is only the beginning of the journey. Awakening precedes battle. Clarity precedes struggle. The voice of Jesus shakes the heart so that it may see the enemy it must now resist: the slow, creeping force that turns fervour into habit, habit into indifference, and indifference into spiritual death. If the warnings of the Lord reveal the danger, the monastic path reveals the remedy.

Yet this remedy is not a technique. It is a way of life. It is the cultivation of an inner stance—a readiness of heart that does not come naturally but is shaped through discipline, prayer, humility, and the remembrance of death. The monks understood that the soul drifts toward sleep unless it chooses watchfulness. They also understood that the remembrance of death is not morbid but liberating. It frees the heart from illusions. It restores priorities. It anchors vigilance in truth. It keeps desire awake.

As the disciple steps from the stern warnings of Jesus into the landscape of the spiritual struggle, he discovers that the battle is not fought with fear but with focus. Christ does not awaken us so that we may tremble; He awakens us so that we may love. His warnings are not the end of the Christian life—they are the threshold of the deeper life He desires to give.

The Bridegroom has spoken. The heart has awakened. Now comes the work of staying awake, guarding the flame, resisting the drift, and learning the holy art of a vigilant heart.

This is where the wisdom of the desert begins.

III

THE MONASTIC BATTLE WITH SLOTH

9

Acedia: The Noonday Demon

There is something almost startling about the honesty of the desert tradition. For all our modern psychological vocabulary, for all our attempts to explain why the human heart grows weary, why it loses focus, why it drifts from God even after being awakened by grace, no language matches the clarity of those early monks who withdrew into the burning silence of Egypt and Palestine. They were not naïve men, nor were they spiritual escapists. They were realists. They entered the desert not because they believed holiness was easier there, but because they knew the greatest battles would follow them wherever they went. They sought a place where they could finally see themselves without distraction. And what they found in that quiet, stripped of noise and comfort, was an adversary the modern world barely acknowledges— an interior force that resists love, dulls desire, erodes resolve, and turns the awakened heart sluggish. They named it with a word as sharp as a blade: acedia.

Acedia is not simply laziness, though laziness is one of its children. It is not mere boredom, though boredom is its frequent companion. It is not sadness, though Cassian calls it a "weariness of the heart." Acedia is something deeper, something more elemental. It is the refusal of the present moment, the impulse to flee the very place where God is waiting. It is the strange heaviness that descends when the soul wishes to pray. It is the restlessness that makes every other task suddenly attractive except the one that leads to holiness. It is the whisper that says, "Not now. Later. Soon. Tomorrow." Acedia interrupts the awakened soul and gently presses it back toward sleep.

None described this enemy with more precision than Evagrius Ponticus, the fourth-century monk whose spiritual psychology shaped the entire ascetical tradition. He wrote that acedia is "the most oppressive of all the demons," the one that attacks the monk "at the fourth hour," when the day seems endless and the heart grows weary of the struggle. It makes the sun appear to move slowly or not at all. It convinces the monk that the cell is prison rather than refuge. It stirs agitation, restlessness, a longing to escape one's commitments. It whispers that holiness is possible—but not here, not now, not in this task, not in this body, not in this place. Under its influence, Evagrius says, the monk becomes "slothful in all things," unable to remain present to prayer, charity, or the labour assigned for the salvation of his soul. The desert fathers knew that acedia is not an exhaustion of the body but an exhaustion of desire.

John Cassian, who translated the wisdom of the East for the Latin West, presses this diagnosis even further. He calls acedia "a tedium or weariness of the heart," a heaviness that settles upon the soul precisely at the hour of prayer. It causes the monk to glance repeatedly at the sun, longing for the day to end. It tempts him to leave his cell under the guise of some virtuous task. It floods the mind with thoughts of other places, other people, other responsibilities, until the silence once embraced becomes unbearable. "It makes one sluggish and immobile," Cassian writes, "whispering that holiness will be easier elsewhere." Prayer becomes a burden. Work feels meaningless. Even the Scriptures lose their sweetness. Nothing is attractive except escape.

What is striking in Cassian's account is how acedia disguises itself. It rarely presents as rebellion. It does not urge the monk to abandon God. Instead, it whispers that he will pray better later, after he rests, after he eats, after he visits a brother, after he clears his mind—later, always later. The monk is not tempted to sin boldly; he is tempted to delay quietly. It is the same logic Christ condemned in the servant who said, "My master is delayed," and so failed to remain vigilant. Acedia is spiritual procrastination baptized in the language of good intentions. It has the shape of repentance but none of its substance.

And the more the soul listens, the more the will weakens. Evagrius described this paralysis with chilling accuracy: the monk under acedia "is like one sick with fever," unable to remain still yet unable to act with purpose. He wants to pray, yet resists praying. He wants to stay, yet longs to flee. He desires holiness, yet this desire flickers like a dying flame. The demon of acedia "makes the monk idle and useless," not by dramatic temptations but by suffocating his energy for love. It is the demon of the middle of the day, Evagrius says, because it attacks when the early enthusiasm of morning has faded and the evening consolation is far away. It is the demon of the long stretch—the part of the spiritual life where perseverance is most needed and most difficult.

John Climacus later echoed this diagnosis in *The Ladder of Divine Ascent*, calling acedia "the paralysis of the soul," "the laziness of the heart," and "the fog that blinds its vision." Climacus saw that acedia does not merely impede action; it suffocates desire itself. The lukewarmness Christ condemned in Revelation is the offspring of acedia. The two differ in intensity, not kind. Climacus observed that the acedic man becomes "incapable of prayer," not because he denies God, but because he can no longer sustain the interior attention that prayer requires. He is present physically but absent spiritually. He lives in the world, but not in the moment. He becomes a wanderer without moving, a drifter without traveling.

Yet what alarmed the monks most was not acedia's emotional symptoms but its spiritual consequences. Acedia kills the desire to seek God. It creates an interior resistance to grace. It convinces the heart that nothing urgent is at stake, that holiness can be postponed, that the danger Jesus warns about is real but distant. Over time, a soul that once burned with zeal becomes content with mild devotion. The flame dims not because it is extinguished violently but because it is suffocated slowly. And like the lukewarmness Christ condemns, acedia blinds the soul to its own condition. It numbs the spiritual senses until the believer is no longer troubled by the absence of fervour.

This is why the monks fought acedia with such seriousness. They understood that the battle for vigilance is not fought in moments of ecstasy but in moments of dryness. They knew that the danger Jesus addressed is not abstract; it is psychological, emotional, and deeply human. They knew that staying awake requires learning to remain present in the very moment acedia urges us to avoid. The desert did not produce acedia; it revealed it. And the same demon that visited the cell of an Egyptian monk now visits the living room illuminated by a smartphone. The spiritual struggle has not changed; only its context has.

The more one studies the desert tradition, the clearer it becomes that acedia is not merely an ancient monastic problem. It is a universal human crisis intensified by modern life. The monks saw with terrifying clarity what we disguise with constant motion: the inability to remain where God has placed us. They fled the distractions of the cities only to discover that distraction follows the human heart. They removed themselves from noise only to uncover the noise within. They abandoned earthly attachments only to find a deeper interior attachment to self. Acedia is the refusal of stability, the resistance to staying put in the will of God. The desert made this visible. Our age makes it invisible.

Evagrius described acedia as a kind of interior flight, a dragging of the feet combined with a desire to run. The monk wants to be anywhere except where he is; he wants to do anything except what is required. This is not simply laziness; it is a protest against the constraints of love. It is the reluctance to give oneself fully to the present task, the present moment, the present grace. Cassian recounts that the acedic monk will "leave his cell under pious pretences," eager to visit another brother, to inquire about the sick, to help with a charitable task—anything, so long as he avoids remaining still. And the irony is that each of these acts is good in itself. Acedia does not lure the monk into obvious vice but into restless virtue. It turns him into a man who would do anything except the one thing God is asking now.

This insight from Cassian reveals why acedia is so difficult to diagnose in our own century. We have built an entire culture upon restless virtue. We pride ourselves on being constantly occupied, constantly moving, constantly connected, constantly achieving. We rarely sit still, not because we are zealous, but because stillness threatens to expose the emptiness within. Our distractions are socially approved. Our hyperactivity looks like productivity. Our constant scrolling looks like engagement with the world. Yet beneath all this movement is a silent refusal to give our heart wholly to God. We are present everywhere except where we are. We do everything except what matters.

The monks feared acedia not because it made them inefficient but because it made them faithless. Acedia corrodes the capacity for covenant fidelity. It weakens perseverance in prayer. It dulls obedience. It makes commitment feel oppressive. It makes holiness appear monotonous. The monk suffering under acedia does not deny his vocation; he simply stops loving it. The marriage between his soul and God becomes strained not by dramatic infidelity but by emotional withdrawal. He remains in the relationship physically but absent interiorly. Climacus describes this paralysis with painful precision: "Acedia dries up the tears of repentance, dulls the edges of zeal, and makes the heart heavy with forgetfulness."

Forgetfulness is one of acedia's most potent weapons. Under its influence, the soul forgets why it began the spiritual life, forgets the sweetness of early grace, forgets the urgency of Christ's call, forgets the danger of delay. Acedia encourages amnesia. It invites the soul to live without memory—memory of death, memory of judgment, memory of the love that awakened it. The practice of memento mori confronted acedia directly because remembering one's death revives memory of one's purpose. Mortality sharpens attention. Acedia dissolves it.

The desert fathers responded to acedia with remedies that remain startlingly relevant. They insisted on stability, on staying in one's cell, on faithfulness to the present task. They regarded monotony not as a threat but as medicine. Cassian writes that "perseverance in the cell" is the hammer that shatters acedia's illusions. Evagrius taught that the monk must remain unmoved by the desires that pull him outward. "Sit in your cell," he said, "and the cell will teach you all things." This was not a romantic claim about solitude. It was a recognition that the only place a man can truly meet God is where he actually is. The cell becomes a mirror. It shows him the truth of his heart. And until that truth is faced, no movement will bring peace.

Yet the fathers were not Stoics. They did not advise mere white-knuckled endurance. They understood that acedia must be met with spiritual warmth, not just mechanical perseverance. Isaac the Syrian taught that "a heart enflamed with love cannot know acedia," because love makes even difficult tasks sweet. The aim is not to force the soul through weariness but to rekindle desire. Seraphim of Sarov echoed this centuries later when he said, "Acquire the Spirit of peace, and thousands around you will be saved." Acedia is defeated not only by staying put but by staying present to the Holy Spirit, whose fire renews zeal and whose grace restores interior energy. The battle is won when the soul learns to love again.

Prayer itself becomes both the battleground and the remedy. The fathers observed that the demon of acedia attacks most fiercely at the hour of prayer because prayer is the place where we confront reality—the reality of God, the reality of ourselves, the reality of our need. Acedia resists this confrontation. It prefers noise to silence, distraction to truth. Cassian says that the monk must "force himself to prayer" when acedia strikes, not because prayer is effective only when felt, but because prayer strengthens the will to love. "When you feel nothing," he writes, "pray doubly." Climacus calls this persistence "the courage of the steadfast." It is the refusal to surrender the love of God to interior turbulence.

Modern forms of acedia multiply endlessly. The desert fathers warned against wandering from cell to cell; we wander from app to app. They feared the urge to visit their brothers out of restlessness; we fill our hours with digital visits that leave us more fragmented than before. They struggled with the temptation to look repeatedly at the sun; we struggle with the temptation to look repeatedly at a glowing screen. Our distractions are more attractive, more constant, more engineered for addiction. Yet the spiritual dynamic remains the same. Acedia is still the refusal of the present moment, the inability to remain where love is calling.

The fathers also observed a paradox: acedia often intensifies when the soul is on the verge of breakthrough. The monk begins to taste dryness precisely when his heart is drawing near to God, because acedia is the resistance of the old self to the demands of new life. This is why Evagrius said that acedia is "most fierce before noon," the hour when the day's heat becomes strongest. The demon attacks most violently when the will is poised for perseverance. If the monk endures this internal storm, he emerges with new clarity and grace. If he yields, he sinks into a torpor from which it is difficult to rise.

All of this reveals why acedia became known as "the noonday demon." It is the demon that attacks when the day is brightest, when the sunlight exposes everything, when illusions crumble and the soul is left face-to-face with its calling. Morning zeal has faded; evening rest is far away. In this middle place, the monk must choose: to remain faithful or to flee inwardly. Acedia thrives in this middle space—in the fatigue of perseverance, in the ordinariness of daily holiness, in the long stretch of fidelity where no dramatic consolations appear. The battle is not glamorous. It is steady, hidden, and interior. Which is why the fathers took it so seriously.

To understand how deeply acedia wounds the spiritual life, one must grasp its relationship to time. Acedia reshapes the soul's experience of time in two devastating ways. It makes the present moment unbearable and the future endlessly appealing. The now becomes too difficult, too demanding, too exposed. The later becomes filled with imaginary ease. Evagrius observed that the acedic monk dreams constantly of leaving his cell: of better monasteries, gentler elders, more suitable conditions for prayer. The temptation is always toward an imagined future where holiness will be easier. The present, with its concrete imperfections, becomes intolerable.

This temporal illusion is identical to the sin Jesus exposes in His parables. The slothful servant imagines that vigilance will be easier later. The virgins without oil assume the Bridegroom will be delayed. The rich fool imagines years of ease stretching ahead, unaware that the present hour holds his judgment. Acedia is this imagination baptized into spiritual life. It is the quiet belief that "later" belongs to us. It is the presumption that time will bend to our convenience. It is, in its essence, a rebellion against the truth that salvation happens now. "Now is the acceptable time," Paul writes. Acedia sneers at this urgency and whispers, "Tomorrow."

Cassian warns that this temptation toward "tomorrow" is particularly deadly because it feels pious. The monk under acedia is not openly rebellious. He remains outwardly obedient. He continues to speak reverently of God. Yet his heart has withdrawn from the immediacy of grace. He convinces himself that the spiritual life will flourish when circumstances improve. He waits for inspiration, for clarity, for energy, for the perfect emotional climate. Holiness becomes a project deferred. Fidelity becomes a dream rather than a decision. Acedia delays love until love loses its edge.

This is why Benedict in the *Rule* treats acedia with pastoral severity. Though his language is gentler than Evagrius, his wisdom is the same. The monk must persevere in the community, persevere in his tasks, persevere in the ordinary rhythm of prayer and labour. Stability is the antidote to acedia because it prevents the soul from living in imaginary futures. Benedict understood that holiness is forged through constancy. The acedic man wants a life without endurance, a discipleship without steadfastness, a vocation without the slow work of fidelity. Benedict insists the monk remain rooted where he is planted, because roots deepen only through weathering seasons.

The Philokalia echoes this insistence with a nearly unanimous voice. Hesychios the Priest writes that the heart must be guarded with vigilance, because acedia enters through small cracks—through minor distractions, through subtle neglect, through the refusal to resist early movements of boredom. "Attention," he writes, "is the path to the kingdom." But attention requires effort, and effort is precisely what acedia undermines. Acedia does not ask the soul to commit grave sin; it asks the soul to stop trying. It convinces the believer that the small acts of fidelity are meaningless. Yet Scripture and tradition agree that the kingdom is built on small acts—mustard seeds, widow's mites, daily crosses. Acedia despises smallness.

Isaac the Syrian offers one of the most beautiful correctives to this contempt for smallness. "If you cannot yet bear the heavy cross," he writes, "bear the small one that lies before you." For Isaac, the way out of acedia is not through grand resolutions but through humble endurance in the task at hand. God meets the soul in the present moment, not the imagined future. The holy act is the immediate one. The grace available is the grace given now. Isaac teaches that when the soul returns to simplicity—one prayer, one act of charity, one moment of stillness—it finds again the sweetness of God's presence. Acedia cannot endure simplicity. It thrives on complex fantasies; it withers before concrete obedience.

This wisdom reveals a striking truth: acedia is fundamentally a failure of love. Not emotional love, but covenant love—love that chooses, love that commits, love that stays. The monk under acedia does not cease to believe in God; he ceases to love God with the attention love requires. He becomes, in the words of Climacus, "a corpse with a heartbeat." He is alive but dormant. He prays with his lips while his heart wanders. He moves through the day half-awake. Christ warns of this condition not to condemn but to awaken. "Blessed are those servants," He says, "whom the master finds awake." Acedia is the force that puts them to sleep.

Seraphim of Sarov, writing in a very different age yet with the same spiritual clarity, saw acedia as a drying of the soul. He taught that the presence of the Holy Spirit brings warmth, joy, and energy, while acedia brings coldness, heaviness, and inertia. "When the Spirit is present," he said, "the heart burns with love." When the heart grows cold, acedia is often near. Seraphim's remedy was not merely ascetical but sacramental: participation in the life of the Church, confession of sins, the Eucharist as fire for the soul. The Spirit ignites what acedia darkens. The sacraments restore what the demon drains.

And yet, even with these remedies, the fight remains daily. The fathers knew that acedia returns as persistently as Israel's forgetfulness. It has many disguises: fatigue, irritation, oversleeping, compulsive busyness, avoidance of silence, resistance to prayer, an unexplained heaviness that makes every spiritual duty feel burdensome. Climacus describes it as "a paralysis that spreads to the entire soul," making even the thought of holiness exhausting. The danger is not that acedia will tempt the believer into dramatic evil, but that it will tempt him into nothing at all. A life of vague good intentions replaces a life of concrete obedience. Acedia tempts us to drift gently away from God without noticing the distance.

Yet the fathers insist that this battle, though fierce, is fruitful. Evagrius observes that when a monk perseveres through the assault of acedia, he experiences a clarity afterward "as bright as the noonday sun that once oppressed him." The very hour of greatest temptation becomes the hour of greatest grace. The demon that sought to suffocate the soul becomes the occasion for deeper purity of heart. Perseverance in dryness becomes the seed of genuine love. The trial becomes the teacher.

This is the paradox the desert tradition offers the modern world: the very demon that seems most destructive becomes, when resisted, the instrument of sanctity. Acedia reveals the weakness of the human heart, but also the strength of God's fidelity. It strips away illusions, exposes self-deception, and forces the soul to decide whether it seeks God or comfort. Climacus writes that "he who conquers acedia has conquered the world," because acedia is the spiritual form of worldly attachment—the desire to escape the narrow path of the cross for an easier road.

The victory over acedia is not dramatic. It is quiet, almost hidden. It looks like perseverance in small duties. It looks like showing up to prayer when the heart is dry. It looks like resisting the urge to flee the present moment. It looks like choosing fidelity when nothing in the soul feels inspired. It is the slow refining of the will by grace. It is the cultivation of love in its purest form: love without reward, without consolation, without applause.

The more deeply one immerses oneself in the monastic witness, the more one realizes that acedia appears whenever the soul confronts the cost of fidelity. It is the temptation that rises not at the beginning of the spiritual journey, when grace feels new, nor at its heights, when consolation is strong, but in the long middle stretch where holiness is forged through repetition. Acedia is the enemy of the middle distance—the long obedience where nothing dramatic occurs, where no crisis forces us to cling to God and no ecstasy sweeps us upward. It preys on the ordinary. It clouds the everyday. It drains the sweetness from prayer, the meaning from work, the zeal from charity. It makes the steady path appear pointless.

For this reason, the fathers judged acedia to be among the gravest threats to salvation. Not because it provokes scandalous sin, but because it erodes love. Augustine understood this dynamic intuitively when he warned that sin begins in the "aversion of the will," the soul turning away in subtle movements long before it turns away in outward actions. Acedia is this aversion in its infancy—a refusal to remain where grace is calling, a coolness toward the demands of love. Augustine wrote in *Confessions* that the heart becomes "curved in on itself" when it ceases to delight in God. Acedia is the bending of the heart inward, the quiet collapse of its outward reach toward the Divine.

This is also why the fathers link acedia so closely to pride. Pride does not always manifest as arrogance; sometimes it shows itself as resistance to the ordinary means of sanctification. Acedia whispers that our vocation is too small, our tasks too mundane, our circumstances too confining. It suggests that God should have arranged things differently: a different marriage, a different job, a different community, a different body, a different season of life. It whispers that holiness would be possible if only the conditions were changed. Pride is the refusal of the present moment as God's gift. Acedia is its emotional echo.

Macarius of Egypt, whose homilies radiate the warmth of experiential wisdom, wrote that the soul must "descend into its own heart and there do battle." He understood that the greatest spiritual struggles occur not in external circumstances but within the interior chamber where the will is shaped. Macarius taught that the heart becomes a battlefield where the Spirit and the old self contend. Acedia is the heaviness that drags the soul downward in this struggle, making the labour of prayer feel oppressive. Yet Macarius promises that when the soul perseveres, "the heart is filled with light, and the demons who troubled it flee." For him, the victory over acedia is the victory of the heart opened to the Spirit's fire.

It is notable that the fathers did not treat acedia as a purely emotional condition. They observed its psychological effects—restlessness, irritability, heaviness, inattention—but they understood it primarily as a spiritual distortion. Its root is not sadness but resistance. It is the soul recoiling from communion. Climacus goes so far as to call acedia "the paralysis of the soul" because it immobilizes the very faculty by which we respond to God. Acedia is not solved by entertainment, distraction, or self-care; these merely thicken the fog. Its remedy lies in renewed love, which awakens the will to choose again what the soul was made for.

And yet, love in the biblical sense is forged precisely through endurance. Charity is tested and strengthened in the crucible of faithfulness. This is why Evagrius insists that the monk who battles acedia "should not abandon the cell, even if every passion assaults him." The temptation to flee must be resisted not by gritting teeth but by leaning into grace. Evagrius teaches that once the monk endures the storm, "a state of peace follows, and the mind begins to taste the joy of God." This promise does not minimize the difficulty; it reveals the pattern of sanctification. God permits the dryness so that fidelity can deepen beyond emotion. The noonday demon exposes our dependence on feelings; the victory over it teaches us dependence on grace.

The modern world, perhaps unknowingly, has constructed a culture that magnifies acedia's reach. Our devices, our pace of life, our fixation on novelty, our allergy to silence—all of these form a perfect breeding ground for spiritual sloth. We are assaulted by images, notifications, and options. We are conditioned to avoid stillness and to treat boredom as a problem requiring technological medication. We move from entertainment to entertainment not because we love pleasure but because we fear facing ourselves. Acedia thrives in this environment because modern life trains the soul to abandon the present moment. The desert father fled the world to fight acedia; we carry the world in our pockets.

Yet the antidote remains the same. Fidelity. Prayer. Stability. Honesty. Presence. These are the ancient weapons forged by the fathers and handed down to every generation. Benedict's call to stability teaches us to stop seeking a different life and to start learning how to love the one God has given. Isaac's call to simplicity teaches us to quiet the imagination so we can perceive the grace before us. Cassian's insistence on perseverance teaches us that the storm does not last forever. And Evagrius' clarity helps us recognize the enemy early enough to resist him.

One of the most beautiful insights from the monastic tradition is that acedia's defeat makes possible a new kind of joy. Climacus describes it as "the joy that arises from patience." It is not emotional exuberance but the deep peace that comes when the soul stops running. The monk who remains in his cell, who prays in dryness, who accepts the present moment as grace, discovers that God is found not in dramatic experiences but in quiet fidelity. The noonday demon, once conquered, becomes the hour in which the soul learns to see God in the ordinary.

This insight prepares the ground for understanding why the remembrance of death became such a central practice in the desert. Memento mori is not morbid fascination; it is the antidote to acedia's illusion. If acedia tempts the soul to believe that time is endless and holiness can be postponed, memento mori reveals the truth: time is short, and the present moment matters. If acedia convinces us that another life would be easier, memento mori anchors us in the truth that this life is the only arena in which we will ever learn to love God. Mortality strips away fantasies. It dissolves imaginary futures. It returns us to the now where grace is found.

The monks kept skulls not to frighten themselves but to remain awake. They slept near tombs not out of morbidity but to remember that death is the doorway to the Bridegroom. They recited the hours not to fill time but to sanctify it. In their struggle with acedia, memory of death became an anchor. It reminded them that the battle is brief, that the stakes are eternal, and that the One who calls them to fidelity is the same One who conquered death for them. Acedia dulls the heart; memento mori sharpens it.

Thus the monastic tradition teaches something the modern world desperately needs to recover: the awareness of death is not an obstacle to joy but the path to it. When the soul remembers that life is short, love becomes urgent. Forgiveness becomes possible. Prayer becomes necessary. Fidelity becomes meaningful. The duties of the day become sacraments of God's presence. Acedia loses its grip when the soul sees the truth: to live awake is to live ready for the Lord.

What the desert fathers grasped with haunting clarity is that acedia is not finally a matter of temperament but of love. It is a crisis of desire. When the heart's longing for God is faint, the pressures of the present moment feel unbearable. When that longing is strong, the same circumstances become occasions of grace. This is why the fathers insist that the cure for acedia is not simply discipline but renewed affection for God. The monk must not only endure; he must rediscover the sweetness of the One who calls him. Evagrius taught that the remembrance of God—mindfulness of His presence, His mercy, His nearness—is the fire that drives away the noonday demon. "A mind occupied with God," he wrote, "cannot be seized by acedia." The more the soul turns toward Him, the less room remains for the heaviness that drags it downward.

This dynamic reveals why acedia is fundamentally incompatible with hope. Hope is the theological virtue that fixes the heart on God's promises, making the future luminous. Acedia darkens the future, convincing the soul that nothing truly matters. Hope strengthens the will to pursue holiness; acedia robs the will of energy. Hope sees the Christian life as pilgrimage; acedia sees it as monotony. Hope endures dryness because it trusts in God's fidelity; acedia interprets dryness as futility. Hope moves the soul forward; acedia immobilizes it. The fathers warn that acedia is not merely discouragement but despair in embryonic form—a spiritual sadness that drains the courage to seek God.

And yet, it is precisely here that the mercy of God reveals itself. For what the monks discovered is that God does not abandon the soul in acedia. On the contrary, He uses it as a teacher. When Evagrius speaks of the clarity that follows the battle, when Cassian speaks of the fruit that emerges after perseverance, when Climacus speaks of joy arising from endurance, they are describing the same mystery: God allows the soul to confront its weakness so that it may learn where its strength truly lies. Acedia becomes the occasion for deeper humility. It exposes the limits of natural zeal. It reminds the soul that holiness is not achieved by human enthusiasm but by grace. In resisting acedia, the soul is drawn from superficial fervour into mature love.

This transformation is evident in the witness of the saints. Many who battled acedia later became radiant examples of spiritual joy. Their joy was not naive or sentimental; it was hard-won, the product of fidelity forged in dryness. They discovered that when the fog of acedia lifts, the heart sees with new purity. Prayer becomes less about emotion and more about communion. Work becomes less about achievement and more about offering. Daily life becomes less about escaping monotony and more about encountering God in small things. The battle with acedia transforms the soul into a vessel of stability—what Benedict calls *stabilitas cordis*, stability of heart. This stability is not rigidity; it is rootedness in God's unwavering love.

The fathers also teach that victory over acedia requires community. Though the demon often isolates the soul, the remedy frequently comes through brothers. Cassian recounts conversations with elders whose words pierced through his fog of weariness. Benedict insists on communal prayer precisely because the support of others sustains the weary monk. Climacus warns that acedia thrives in isolation but weakens in the sound of the psalms. Even Evagrius, often associated with solitary asceticism, acknowledges that counsel and confession expose acedia's lies. The modern world, which isolates while pretending to connect, needs this monastic wisdom desperately. Friends who pray together, communities that worship together, families that persevere together—these become safe harbors where hope is rekindled.

Perhaps the most striking dimension of the monastic teaching is its refusal to romanticize the spiritual life. The fathers do not promise that acedia will vanish completely. They accept that it returns in waves. They do not portray holiness as effortless. They do not present the saints as men immune to struggle. Instead, they speak with sober hope. They teach that the heart becomes strong by being tested, that perseverance produces character, and that God uses even the periods of dryness to purify desire. The victory over acedia is not a single moment but a lifelong pattern of choosing God again and again, especially when the soul feels nothing.

This realism gives the tradition its enduring power. When modern people speak of burnout, numbness, distraction, emotional exhaustion, or spiritual dryness, they are naming symptoms the fathers diagnosed centuries ago. Acedia is not a medieval eccentricity; it is the spiritual condition of an age overwhelmed by comfort and starved of meaning. Our culture's frantic pace masks a deep interior weariness. Our endless entertainment numbs the soul rather than nourishing it. Our constant connectivity fragments attention until prayer feels impossible. Acedia hides beneath all of this, quietly draining the capacity to love.

What the fathers offer is not condemnation but healing. They remind us that God is not shocked by our weakness. They remind us that perseverance matters more than intensity. They remind us that holiness begins with showing up—showing up to prayer, showing up to charity, showing up to the life God has given us. They teach that fidelity in dryness is more precious than zeal in consolation. They teach that the Spirit works powerfully in hidden endurance. They teach that remembering death—remembering that time is not endless—revives seriousness, humility, and gratitude.

For the desert fathers, the remembrance of death was not a way of escaping life but of entering it more fully. It made them attentive to grace. It made them eager for repentance. It purified their motives. It sharpened their vigilance. It revealed the beauty of each moment and the sacredness of each decision. Acedia thrives where life feels endless; it dies where the soul knows the hour is short. Memento mori became their shield not because it frightened them but because it awakened them. It broke open the illusion that tomorrow is guaranteed. It returned them to the present moment where God dwells.

This is why the monks could say, without morbidity, that the remembrance of death gives birth to spiritual joy. It focuses the heart on what matters. It cuts through distraction. It strengthens prayer. It humbles pride. It ignites charity. It turns life into preparation for the Bridegroom. Acedia loses its power when the soul sees the truth: life is short, God is near, and the time to love is now.

In the end, the fathers knew that the battle with acedia is not won by willpower alone but by a heart anchored in the reality of God. The noonday demon thrives when the soul believes itself alone, when prayer becomes a monologue, when fidelity feels like self-reliance. Its power dissolves the moment the soul remembers that God is present in the very moment acedia urges us to abandon. Cassian insists that perseverance in prayer is sustained not by human resilience but by divine companionship. Climacus says that the one who endures acedia "is being held by God even when he feels nothing." Evagrius promises that clarity dawns not because the monk finally musters strength but because grace breaks through in the silence. The desert is never empty. The cell is never abandoned. The heart is never left to battle unaided.

This assurance becomes the bedrock of hope, for acedia, at its root, is a distrust of God's nearness. It is the suspicion that the present moment is devoid of grace, that prayer is fruitless, that effort is meaningless, that holiness is out of reach. The fathers respond by revealing the truth hidden beneath the dryness: God is closer in those moments than we imagine. The Lord who cried out in His own desolation, "My God, why have You forsaken Me?", sanctified every experience of spiritual heaviness. He entered the silence so that no believer would ever walk through it alone. The Christian does not face acedia as an isolated soldier but as one united to the Crucified, whose fidelity in abandonment becomes the pattern and power of our own.

And when this truth sinks into the soul, acedia's fog begins to lift. The present moment, once unbearable, becomes bearable again. Prayer, once suffocating, becomes possible. Work, once tedious, becomes meaningful. Fidelity, once oppressive, becomes freedom. The monk discovers that holiness is not waiting in some distant future but rising from the very tasks he resisted. He sees that God has been shaping him precisely through the dryness he feared. The cell that felt like prison becomes sanctuary. The silence that felt empty becomes communion. The struggle that felt pointless becomes fruitful. What once appeared as darkness reveals itself to be the dawn of maturity.

This transformation is not dramatic; it is quiet, steady, and real. It produces a kind of joy unknown to the world—the joy of a heart that has stopped running from itself. The soul, once dispersed by distraction, becomes gathered. Its attention, once scattered, becomes focused. Its desire, once faint, becomes firm. Climacus calls this the "resurrection of the soul before the resurrection of the body," a rising from spiritual slumber into awakened life. The one who endures acedia becomes capable of deeper prayer, deeper charity, deeper communion. He becomes a man who can remain—remain in love, remain in truth, remain awake.

This is the wisdom the world has forgotten. Acedia has not disappeared; it has become the air we breathe. It hides behind endless entertainment, behind compulsive busyness, behind the myth of constant productivity, behind the fear of silence, behind the restless search for novelty. We are a civilization allergic to stillness and terrified of interiority. The desert fathers, speaking across seventeen centuries, offer a diagnosis sharper than any modern analysis: a restless age is an acedic age. We are forever moving because we do not know how to remain with God.

Yet the remedy they offer is timeless. Persevere in prayer. Guard the heart. Embrace silence. Love the present moment. Attend to the tasks given by God. Seek the Spirit's fire. Remember death. These are not monastic relics but Christian weapons. They break through the fog of acedia and awaken the soul to the reality of God's love. They reveal that holiness is not found by escaping life but by entering it faithfully. They teach that spiritual strength grows through endurance, that joy is born from perseverance, and that every moment of dryness can become an altar where love is renewed.

The noonday demon still walks among us, restless and subtle. Yet the wisdom of the fathers still stands firm. Acedia is not stronger than grace. Weariness is not deeper than God's mercy. Distraction is not louder than His voice. Forgetfulness is not final when the soul chooses to remember. The battle is real, but so is the victory. And the remembrance of death—memento mori—remains the sharpest sword in this ancient combat, because it calls the soul back to what matters, back to the present, back to fidelity, back to the Lord who will one day call us home.

For when a Christian remembers that life is short and God is near, acedia loses its power. The heavy heart becomes watchful again. The wandering mind becomes anchored. The lukewarm soul begins to burn. And the believer learns to live with the urgency, the steadiness, and the joy of one who is already standing in the light of eternity.

10

Nepsis: Watchfulness of Heart and Mind

There is an old story the desert fathers loved to tell, simple enough for a child yet sharp enough to pierce the complacency of the most seasoned monk. A young disciple once asked his elder why vigilance mattered so much in the spiritual life. The elder said nothing at first. Instead, he led the young man to the monastery's outer wall as dusk was falling. In the fading light, a lone watchman stood above them, scanning the horizon with unwavering attention. The elder pointed upward and said, "If he sleeps, we lose the whole city. If he stays awake, we remain safe." Then he placed his hand on the disciple's chest and added softly, "You are the city. Your heart is the gate. Someone must keep watch."

The image is striking in its simplicity: a lone sentinel guarding the frontier between safety and danger. Yet that is exactly how Scripture portrays the life of the soul. The heart is the inner Jerusalem, the dwelling place of God, and the enemy presses against its walls not with armies but with thoughts—subtle, persistent, often disguised. Jesus' words in Gethsemane carry this same seriousness: "Watch and pray, that you may not enter into temptation." The command is not anxious; it is covenantal. It is the vigilance of love. It is the alertness of a bride awaiting the Bridegroom. It is the wakefulness of a people who know the stakes of the spiritual battle.

The Greek fathers called this watchfulness *nepsis*. The word means sobriety, clarity, attention, wakefulness of mind and heart. It is the opposite of spiritual drowsiness, the antidote to acedia, the posture Jesus commands again and again. The vigilant heart is not tense but awake. Not fearful but alert. Not suspicious but receptive. It stands at the gate of the inner life, examining the thoughts that approach, discerning which lead to God and which lead away. Proverbs captures this in its ancient wisdom: "Above all else, guard your heart, for from it flow the issues of life." The fathers took this command literally. To guard the heart is to guard everything.

Nepsis emerges most clearly in the tradition of hesychasm, the spiritual stream flowing through Athos, Sinai, Palestine, and the Egyptian desert. Hesychasm is often described as the spirituality of stillness, yet stillness in their sense is not mere quietude. It is the interior posture in which the mind ceases its scattered wandering and descends into the heart to meet God. Hesychios the Priest in the *Philokalia* describes nepsis as the "unceasing practice of attention"—a vigilance that watches the movements of the mind the way a shepherd watches his flock, or a soldier watches for the first sign of an approaching enemy. Without this attention, he says, "the heart is easily plundered."

The fathers understood something modern psychology rediscovers in fragments but cannot fully explain: the human mind is porous. Thoughts come uninvited. Images rise without intention. Memories flash unexpectedly. The monk's task is not to prevent thoughts but to discern them. Maximos the Confessor teaches that the passions begin not in the body but in the heart's unguarded consent to a suggestion. A thought appears—an irritation, a memory, a desire, a fantasy—and if the heart remains awake, the thought fades like smoke. But if the heart is inattentive, the thought takes root, becomes a movement, becomes an impulse, becomes a habit, becomes a vice. "The warfare begins in the first moment," Maximos says. "He who is watchful sees the enemy while it is still far off."

This is why nepsis is not simply a spiritual discipline but a form of wisdom. It teaches the soul to perceive its own interior landscape with honesty. It trains the mind to recognize the first stirrings of sin long before they manifest externally. Dorotheos of Gaza states the principle bluntly: "The beginning of sin is negligence." Negligence of thought. Negligence of desire. Negligence of the heart's movement. A man does not fall into great sins by accident; he drifts into them by neglecting small moments of watchfulness. The soul that stops guarding its thoughts soon finds itself surprised by temptations it once recognized easily. Vigilance is not paranoia; it is spiritual maturity.

And yet nepsis is not opposed to peace; it is the path to it. The fathers insist that watchfulness produces freedom, because a guarded heart is a heart that cannot be ruled by passing impulses. A watched mind is not carried away by every distraction. A vigilant soul is not at the mercy of moods. When the fathers speak of guarding the heart, they are not advocating suspicion toward oneself; they are advocating custody of the inner sanctuary where God dwells. Paul speaks of this in Philippians: "The peace of God, which surpasses all understanding, will guard your hearts and minds in Christ Jesus." Peace becomes the guardian when the heart becomes the temple.

This is the mystery that Hesychasm seeks to protect—the meeting of the mind and heart in the presence of God. Theophan the Recluse, perhaps the most articulate guide in the modern era, writes that the entire spiritual life can be summed up in one phrase: "Bring your mind into your heart and keep it there before God." The mind that scatters across a thousand trivial thoughts cannot pray. The heart that drifts through the day half-awake cannot love. Theophan teaches that stillness is the gathering of the dispersed person—the recollection of oneself in God's presence. Vigilance protects this recollection. It prevents the soul from dissolving into distractions. It trains the believer to return again and again to the remembrance of God.

Theophan saw clearly what the desert fathers saw: distraction is not a minor inconvenience but a spiritual wound. A mind that never rests in God cannot heal. A heart that never grows still cannot perceive the movements of grace. Watchfulness is therefore not optional; it is essential. It is the means by which the believer remains awake to the presence of Christ in ordinary life. It is the disciplined refusal to drift. It is the posture of one who knows that the greatest battles are fought not against flesh and blood but against forgetfulness.

The fathers often compared the unwatchful soul to a house with its doors left unlatched. Even if the owner intends no harm, even if the household is peaceful and orderly, even if no crime has yet occurred, the vulnerability is fatal. One intruder can overturn the entire home. So it is with the movements of thought. The unguarded mind is open to every influence that passes by—memories that wound, fantasies that inflame, anxieties that paralyse, judgments that cool charity. Nepsis is the locking of the door, not in fear, but in wisdom. It is the refusal to let the heart be shaped by whatever thought happens to enter. It is the discipline of choosing what one meditates on, what one allows to rest in the imagination, what one consents to with the will.

The fathers never separate watchfulness from freedom. A soul that does not guard its thoughts is not free; it is reactive, driven by impulses it scarcely recognizes. Maximos the Confessor teaches that the passions are strengthened through unexamined thoughts and weakened through vigilant discernment. "When the mind is watchful," he writes, "the passions wither before they grow." He describes the spiritual battle in stages: a thought appears, the soul is aware of it, the will deliberates, the will consents or rejects. Sin occurs not in the appearance of the thought but in the consent. Watchfulness is the discipline of interrupting this process early, before the soul has surrendered itself. It is the spiritual equivalent of catching a spark before it ignites a fire.

But nepsis is not simply defensive. It is not the soul's attempt to swat away every passing distraction. It is attentiveness to God. The watchman on the wall does not stare only at the horizon; he also watches for the arrival of the king. The heart that is vigilant is not merely cautious; it is expectant. It lives in anticipation of grace. It becomes attuned to the subtle movements of the Spirit—the warmth that stirs in prayer, the humility that rises in repentance, the sudden clarity that comes through Scripture, the quiet consolation that appears without explanation. Watchfulness is the posture of a soul that knows God is near and wishes not to miss His approach.

This is why nepsis and prayer are inseparable. Hesychios says, "Watchfulness is the foundation of prayer." The scattered mind cannot pray. The heart drowned in distractions cannot listen. Nepsis prepares the soul to enter communion; it clears the inner room where the Lord will speak. Climacus says that the vigilant man has "eyes that see God," not because God suddenly appears, but because the fog of distraction has lifted. When Jesus commands, "Watch and pray," He gives not two commands but one—watchfulness that becomes prayerfulness.

Theophan the Recluse speaks with a kind of quiet boldness when he says that the Christian must "become all attention." This does not mean constant strain; it means constant openness. Attention in the spiritual sense is readiness, receptivity, availability to God. The one who practices nepsis becomes like the watchman in the psalm: "My soul waits for the Lord more than watchmen for the morning." Vigilance becomes desire; desire becomes love.

Dorotheos of Gaza, the great physician of the soul, roots this watchfulness in humility. A man watches because he knows he is weak. He guards his heart because he knows it is fragile. He discerns his thoughts because he knows he is vulnerable to deception. Dorotheos warns that pride is the enemy of nepsis because pride falsely assures the soul that it cannot fall. Negligence follows pride. Sin follows negligence. "The beginning of sin is negligence," he says, meaning not carelessness in action alone but carelessness in interior life—carelessness with thoughts, intentions, memories, and motives. Without vigilance, even a devout person slowly becomes inattentive to grace.

This teaching harmonizes perfectly with the remembrance of death. Memento mori awakens the soul, but nepsis keeps it awake. Remembering death shocks the heart into truth; watchfulness guards that truth throughout the day. One reveals the stakes; the other sustains the effort. One cries out, "Stay awake!" and the other answers, "Here I am, Lord." The two practices are twins in the spiritual life. Without memento mori, nepsis becomes harsh and anxious. Without nepsis, memento mori becomes sentimental and fleeting. Together they produce the sober joy of a soul that lives each hour in the light of eternity.

The fathers knew that such vigilance must be gentle. Harsh watchfulness collapses under its own weight. True nepsis is firm yet peaceful, attentive yet untroubled. It is like standing by a quiet lake, watching the ripples on the surface—nothing forced, nothing frantic. Hesychios teaches that the vigilant soul "observes thoughts with detachment," not wrestling with them immediately but allowing the Spirit to illuminate their origin. The soul becomes a kind of inner sanctuary where the movements of the mind can be discerned without fear. Vigilance does not crush the heart; it steadies it.

Watchfulness also teaches the believer to identify the sources of thoughts. The fathers speak of three kinds: from God, from the self, and from the enemy. Thoughts that bring peace, humility, repentance, or clarity are usually born of grace. Thoughts that arise from memory, emotion, or imagination are natural and require discernment but not alarm. Thoughts that inflame pride, fear, lust, resentment, or despair must be rejected early, before they settle in. Maximos says, "Discernment is greater than all the other virtues," because without it, even prayer can become a snare, and zeal can become pride. Nepsis trains the soul in this discernment—not analytically, but intuitively, through habitual attentiveness to God.

Modern culture, however, is almost designed to destroy this watchfulness. It fragments attention, multiplies distractions, assaults the mind with images and noise. The average person lives in a state of chronic interior scattering, which the fathers describe as the very opposite of nepsis. The scattered person cannot pray deeply. He cannot listen. He cannot perceive his own motivations. He cannot repent effectively because he cannot see clearly. He is constantly reacting, never remaining. In such a world, the ancient call to watchfulness becomes not only relevant but urgent.

And yet, the human heart—even the modern heart—remains capable of nepsis. The soul was made for attention. The mind was made for truth. The heart was made for God. When the believer begins to practice even a small measure of vigilance—pausing before reacting, noticing interior movements, returning the mind to the presence of God—the fog begins to thin. Distractions lose some of their power. Temptations slow their pace. Prayer gains depth. Scripture begins to speak more clearly. The heart becomes more responsive to grace. The soul begins to awaken.

The fathers insist that watchfulness grows through small, repeated choices rather than dramatic gestures. Nepsis is formed not in rare moments of ecstasy but in the steady discipline of returning—

returning the mind to God when it wanders, returning the heart to humility when it swells with pride, returning the imagination to purity when it drifts toward desire, returning the will to obedience when it inclines toward self. The entire spiritual life, as Theophan teaches, is a continual turning of the interior gaze toward the Lord. "If you fall a thousand times a day," he writes, "rise a thousand times and return your mind into your heart." Watchfulness is the stubborn refusal to give up on attention.

This returns us to one of the most important insights in the hesychast tradition: the mind is healed not through effort alone but through quiet. Hesychasm does not mean withdrawal from the world in a geographical sense; it means interior stillness—the silence of heart in which thoughts lose their power and the presence of God becomes perceivable. Hesychios compares the vigilant mind to a calm sea: when the waters are still, even small disturbances can be detected; when they are turbulent, nothing can be seen. The modern soul, tossed by endless stimulation, often confuses turbulence for vitality. In truth, turbulence is blindness. Only stillness sees.

Yet the fathers were realistic. They understood that the mind does not become still all at once. It must be trained, gently and persistently. The first stage of nepsis is simply noticing the noise—recognizing how scattered the mind has become. The second stage is learning to interrupt that scattering—pausing before opening another app, pausing before responding in anger, pausing before indulging a fantasy. The third stage is redirecting—offering a short prayer, breathing slowly, letting the heart remember God. The final stage is the grace-filled awareness that begins to arise naturally over time, the spiritual taste that discerns movements of thought almost effortlessly. This is not a technique but a transformation. The Spirit Himself cultivates this vigilance in the willing soul.

The heart plays a decisive role here. In biblical language, the heart is not the seat of emotion alone but the centre of the person—the place where desire, understanding, and will converge. When Jesus says, "Where your treasure is, there will your heart be also," He speaks of the deep interior orientation of life. Watchfulness, therefore, is not merely cognitive; it is affective. It trains the heart to desire God above all distractions. It awakens love. This is why Theophan insists that the mind must descend into the heart, because the divided person—the one whose thoughts go one way and whose desires go another—cannot maintain vigilance. Unity of heart begins where attention and desire meet.

St. Maximos adds an essential dimension: the purification of thoughts. He warns that the passions are not merely emotional disturbances but disordered movements of the soul that arise from distorted thoughts. Greed begins with a thought of possession. Lust begins with a thought of beauty detached from charity. Anger begins with a thought of injury magnified by pride. Despair begins with a thought that forgets providence. Watchfulness is therefore a sacrificial attentiveness: the willingness to let go of thoughts that feel pleasurable or justified but lead the soul away from God. Maximos teaches that this interior combat is itself an offering to the Lord. "If you wish to be free," he writes, "do not allow your mind to linger over thoughts that give birth to passion." Holiness begins in the imagination.

Dorotheos of Gaza, with characteristic pastoral candour, reminds us that neglect always begins small. A moment of unguarded thinking becomes an indulgence of resentment. A small fantasy becomes a habit of desire. A minor distraction becomes a daily escape. A brief lapse becomes a disposition. "The enemy enters through the small door," he writes. Nepsis closes that door. It watches the hinges and the latch. It is not suspicious of the world but cautious regarding the unredeemed impulses that stir within us. Dorotheos teaches that the spiritually mature do not fear temptation; they recognize it early.

They greet it not with panic but with clarity.

This clarity is one of the great fruits of watchfulness. When the soul practices nepsis, it begins to see the motives behind its actions. Pride is recognized early and humbled. Envy is detected before it poisons charity. Fear is named before it stiffens the will. This interior honesty is not self-obsession but self-awareness in the presence of God. Maximos calls it "the eye of the heart," and Jesus calls it the lamp of the body. When the heart is clear, the whole life becomes luminous. When the heart is dim, even good things become sources of stumbling.

Such vigilance is impossible without grace. The fathers insist on this continually. Nepsis is cooperation with God's work, not a self-made purification. Evagrius says that the vigilant mind is like a fisherman sitting quietly by the water; he watches the surface not because he can control the fish, but because he must be attentive to what appears. Grace reveals the movements of the heart; vigilance responds. Grace convicts; vigilance yields. Grace strengthens; vigilance chooses. Without the Holy Spirit, watchfulness becomes anxiety. But with the Spirit, watchfulness becomes peace.

This is why nepsis is deeply joyful. The vigilant soul is not perpetually tense; it is perpetually available. It listens easily. It prays simply. It forgives quickly. It notices beauty. It becomes gentle because it has learned to recognize the stirrings of anger before they erupt. It becomes pure because it has learned to starve impure thoughts before they grow. It becomes humble because it has learned to detect pride at its roots. Watchfulness makes the soul light, not heavy. It unburdens the heart from the tyranny of unexamined impulses.

But perhaps the most beautiful fruit of nepsis is love. When the soul is attentive, it becomes capable of real charity. It notices the needs of others. It listens without distraction. It responds without irritation.

It speaks with intention. Distraction is the enemy of love; attention is its servant. Dorotheos observed that many sins in community arise not from malice but from lack of awareness—words spoken carelessly, gestures misinterpreted, duties forgotten. Watchfulness repairs this. It makes the believer sensitive to the presence of God in others. It trains the heart to see Christ in the unexpected. Love requires vigilance.

A vital dimension of nepsis appears when the fathers describe what happens to a soul that loses watchfulness. They do not portray an immediate collapse into grave sin—though that is always possible. Instead, they describe a gradual dulling of the spiritual senses, a slow erosion of clarity. The unwatchful soul becomes like a man walking through a dim room without realizing the light is fading. Little by little, the world inside grows hazy. The voice of God becomes softer. Prayer becomes distracted. Scripture becomes opaque. Conscience becomes dull. The soul begins to live by instinct rather than by discernment. Dorotheos calls this "the sleep of negligence," a spiritual torpor that creeps in unnoticed.

This dullness leads inevitably to confusion. Without vigilance, the soul struggles to recognize the difference between temptation and desire, between inspiration and impulse, between holy zeal and anger disguised as righteousness. Maximos warns that a person without watchfulness "calls darkness light and light darkness," not because he intends deception, but because he lacks clarity. A soul that does not examine its thoughts cannot discern their origin. It becomes vulnerable to subtle distortions, where virtues become vices in disguise. Courage becomes recklessness. Prudence becomes fear. Charity becomes enabling. Humility becomes passivity. Without nepsis, even good intentions become tangled.

The fathers insist that this confusion is not merely psychological but spiritual. The enemy delights in the unguarded mind, for the mind without vigilance is like a field without a fence. Thoughts wander freely. Temptations grow unchecked. The heart—created to be a sanctuary—becomes a crossroads of impulses. Hesychios describes this with stark realism: "A mind without watchfulness is devoured as easily as a lamb among wolves." This image reveals why Jesus commands vigilance with such urgency. Watchfulness is not about self-perfection; it is about spiritual survival.

Yet this vigilance is always grounded in hope. The fathers do not speak as pessimists. They believe deeply in the transformative power of grace. The unwatchful soul can awaken. The scattered mind can gather itself. The heart lost in distraction can return to simplicity. The hesychast tradition insists that the Spirit is always calling the soul back, gently restoring attention, illuminating the thoughts that must be rejected and the ones that must be cherished. "The Spirit prays within us," Paul says. Vigilance is the act of cooperating with this interior prayer.

This cooperation becomes especially powerful when joined to the remembrance of death. Memento mori breaks the spell of distraction; nepsis builds the habit of attention needed to remain awake. The two disciplines reinforce one another. Remembering death exposes the urgency of holiness; watchfulness protects that urgency from being drowned by daily noise. Remembering death humbles the soul; watchfulness protects that humility from pride. Remembering death awakens fear of losing salvation; watchfulness converts that fear into love for God's will. Together, the two practices form a rhythm: awaken, guard; awaken, guard; awaken, guard. This is the rhythm of the vigilant Christian.

The fathers describe this vigilance not as an abstract idea but as a way of living every hour. It begins when the believer rises in the morning, calling to mind the presence of God before any other thought. It continues through the day in small acts of recollection—

short prayers, gentle pauses, deliberate choices to quiet the heart. It intensifies during temptation, when the soul detects a harmful thought early and rejects it by invoking the name of Christ. It returns in moments of silence, when the believer allows the heart to rest in God without words. It concludes at night, when the soul reviews the day with gratitude and repentance, guarding against spiritual drift. In this way, watchfulness becomes a posture, not an event.

Theophan the Recluse offers a vivid metaphor: the Christian must act like a man carrying a bowl filled to the brim with oil. Every step must be taken with care; every movement must be intentional. This is not anxiety but reverence—the reverence of a soul entrusted with grace. The bowl is the heart; the oil is the presence of the Spirit. Watchfulness is the disciplined effort to prevent the bowl from tipping, not out of fear of punishment but out of love for the treasure it contains. When this reverence becomes habitual, the believer moves through life with quiet dignity and spiritual confidence.

This interior posture produces a remarkable effect: the vigilant person becomes less reactive. He no longer lives at the mercy of his moods. He is not pulled violently by irritation, nor steered by sudden impulses, nor drowned by passing fears. He notices these movements early and hands them to God. The vigilant soul becomes spacious inside. It becomes capable of hospitality, of patience, of generosity. Love has room to grow. The Fathers teach that clarity of heart leads to clarity of action; nepsis purifies not only the interior life but the exterior one as well.

Modern Christians often believe that spiritual growth requires dramatic resolutions. The fathers propose something humbler: attention. Attention is the soil in which grace grows. Attention is the shield against temptation. Attention is the birthplace of prayer. Attention is the expression of love. When a husband listens attentively to his wife, he communicates love. When a parent watches attentively over a child, he communicates care. When the soul attends to God, it communicates devotion. Nepsis, then, is not merely an ascetic discipline—it is the language of love spoken from the heart to God.

But vigilance will always feel costly. It demands energy. It requires effort. It is resisted by the ego, which prefers comfort to conversion. Dorotheos says that negligence enters when the soul is unwilling to exert "a little hardship." That phrase—*a little hardship*—is the key. Watchfulness is not heroic suffering; it is small, daily effort: resisting a distracting thought, guarding speech, noticing an impulse toward anger, choosing stillness instead of noise. The fathers assure us that God meets the soul precisely in these small fidelities. "He who is faithful in little," Jesus says, "is faithful in much." Nepsis is the faithfulness of little things.

And this leads to a final insight: watchfulness is not merely a personal discipline but a communal gift. A vigilant soul becomes a source of peace for others. Its clarity becomes contagious. Its steadiness becomes supportive. Its attentiveness becomes love lived visibly. Dorotheos observed that the brother who guards his heart ends up guarding the hearts of those around him. Vigilance is not self-absorption; it is the foundation of charity. The man who watches his thoughts speaks gently. The woman who guards her heart forgives easily. The believer who practices nepsis becomes a vessel of God's presence in a distracted world.

The fathers often stress that true watchfulness is learned not in extraordinary moments of inspiration but in the ordinary texture of life. It is shaped in the quiet hours when nothing dramatic happens, when the soul simply chooses to stay awake. Climacus says that God often hides Himself slightly from the beginner, not to discourage him but to train his desire. Love deepens through seeking. Fidelity strengthens through perseverance. A man learns to guard his heart the way he learns to play an instrument—through practice, patience, and many small corrections. The watchful Christian becomes a craftsman of the interior life, shaping his soul with gentle strokes, attentive always to the movements within.

This craftsmanship becomes especially important in an age where attention itself has become one of the rarest human capacities. Our culture is structured not around contemplation but consumption. It fragments the mind with infinite stimuli, splintering the heart into shallow impressions. We live in a constant posture of reaction. Instant notifications, perpetual news cycles, streaming entertainment, endless scrolling—each trains the mind to skim, never to dwell. The fathers would see this not merely as a cultural shift but as a spiritual emergency. A soul that never dwells on anything cannot dwell in God.

Yet nepsis offers a path through this turbulence. It teaches the believer to reclaim attention as a spiritual discipline. A moment of silence in the morning. A brief prayer before entering a task. A pause to examine a sudden emotion. A decision to put the phone aside. A quiet remembrance of death before bed. These small acts of recollection form a habit—a rhythm—an interior liturgy that gradually reorders the entire life. The vigilant soul becomes intentional. It becomes centred. It becomes awake.

Watchfulness also alters the way the believer interprets suffering. Without nepsis, suffering provokes confusion, anger, or despair. But with vigilance, suffering becomes a moment of revelation—an unveiling of the heart's attachments, fears, and desires. The watchful Christian is able to say with the psalmist, "Search me, O God, and know my heart," because he has already been searching his own heart in prayer. Climacus writes that suffering can become a spiritual furnace not because it is desirable but because it exposes what lies hidden. The vigilant soul reads its own reactions and sees where healing is needed. Suffering becomes not meaningless but instructive, a teacher sent by the God who desires our sanctification.

The fathers also emphasize that nepsis is bound intimately to humility. Pride blinds the soul; humility opens its eyes. The proud man does not watch his heart because he believes it is strong. The humble man watches because he knows he is weak. Theophan insists that humility is the root of attention: the soul cannot descend into the heart unless it first bows low before God. The humble man becomes vigilant not out of fear but reverence. He recognizes that grace must be guarded. He knows how easily distraction can steal communion. He sees his own vulnerability and rests in the mercy of God.

One of the greatest paradoxes in the fathers is that watchfulness produces rest. The vigilant man is not agitated; he is peaceful. He is not exhausted; he is composed. He is not burdened; he is freed. Vigilance saves the soul from being tossed by every impulse. It simplifies life. It clarifies priorities. It silences unnecessary desires. It exposes the futility of so many anxieties. Nepsis does not add weight to the heart; it releases weight. The mind becomes quiet not because nothing happens but because everything is placed under the gaze of God.

This peaceful vigilance is perfectly illustrated in the hesychast prayer tradition. The constant invocation of the name of Jesus—"Lord Jesus Christ, Son of God, have mercy on me"—becomes the anchor that steadies attention. At first the prayer is recited, then whispered, then held in the mind, then settles into the heart as rhythm. The fathers describe this not as technique but as grace, a gift given to the soul that practices watchfulness. The prayer becomes a stream flowing beneath all thoughts. It companions the believer in work, in rest, in temptation, in joy. The name of Jesus becomes the hedge that guards the heart.

Modern Christians often misunderstand this practice, imagining it belongs only to monks or mystics. But the fathers insist that watchfulness is for all believers. Dorotheos writes, "Everyone has a cell within the heart." Even in the midst of a busy life, one can remain attentive to God. The mother caring for her children, the worker labouring in the city, the elderly man alone in a quiet room—all can practice vigilance. It requires not isolation but intention. The heart becomes a monastery when attention becomes prayer.

This universality explains why watchfulness is indispensable for the remembrance of death. Without vigilance, memento mori becomes distressing or abstract. But when the heart is watchful, the remembrance of death becomes clarifying. It dispels illusions. It awakens gratitude. It strengthens repentance. It focuses the soul on what is eternal. Death remembered in a watchful heart does not produce fear; it produces readiness. It becomes a light shining into every choice, revealing what leads to God and what leads away.

The father's wisdom here is profound: the vigilant heart becomes the free heart. It is not dragged by compulsions. It is not ruled by reactions. It is not enslaved to images. It is not swayed by every emotional gust. It is steady because it is rooted in the presence of God. As Theophan writes, "Attention is the key to the spiritual life, and the spiritual life is nothing other than life in God." Watchfulness is what keeps the door unlocked to grace and locked against confusion.

We must not overlook the Christological foundation beneath all of this. The call to nepsis is not merely a monastic ideal; it is a command from the Lord Himself. Jesus warns again and again, "Stay awake." "Be ready." "Watch and pray." These imperatives do not arise from fear of a tyrant but from the love of a Bridegroom who desires a prepared bride. Jesus calls His disciples to vigilance because He wants them to remain close to His heart. Watchfulness is the posture of discipleship. It is how the Christian abides in Christ moment by moment.

Nepsis, then, becomes not only a discipline but a way of seeing. The vigilant Christian sees the world differently. He notices grace.

He perceives temptations early. He interprets suffering in the light of eternity. He recognizes God's presence in small things. He reads Scripture with a listening heart. He encounters others with compassion rather than irritation. He sees his own weaknesses without despair. Watchfulness becomes a lens through which the whole life becomes sacramental.

The fathers often speak of nepsis as a kind of inner light—not a physical light, nor even an emotional one, but the clear, steady brightness of a soul that refuses to live in the fog. A man who practices watchfulness discovers that much of life's confusion comes not from circumstances but from inattention. He suffers not because God is distant, but because his own heart has wandered. When he becomes attentive, the same world appears different. What was once chaotic becomes coherent. What was once heavy becomes bearable. What was once random becomes providential. He begins to see what the saints mean when they speak of life as a pilgrimage illuminated from ahead by the presence of God.

This inner light reveals another dimension of watchfulness: the capacity to discern spirits. The vigilant Christian becomes skilled at recognizing the tone of a thought, the direction of a desire, the weight of an impulse. Is it leading him toward humility or toward pride? Toward charity or resentment? Toward prayer or distraction? Nepsis trains the soul to hear the difference. Evagrius says that the demons are subtle, but they rely on the unguarded heart. They cannot force entry; they require a door left ajar. Watchfulness is the vigilance that keeps that door closed. It is not fear-driven but truth-driven, grounded in the confidence that the Holy Spirit already dwells within and equips the believer for battle.

The heart, when guarded, gradually becomes a sanctuary. Theophan insists that the goal is not simply to watch thoughts but to dwell in the presence of Jesus. "When the mind is in the heart and stands there before the Lord," he writes, "then the spiritual life has begun." This is the meaning of hesychia, the quiet dwelling of the soul in God. It is not silence as emptiness but silence as fullness—where the noise of unnecessary desires fades and the voice of the Lord becomes unmistakable. The vigilant heart becomes a resting place for the name of Jesus.

Yet the fathers are equally clear: vigilance without love becomes harsh. Nepsis is not suspicion of oneself; it is reverence for God. It is not self-condemnation; it is self-knowledge. It is not the anxious tracking of faults; it is the attentive waiting for grace. The watchful Christian does not stare at himself; he keeps the eyes of his heart fixed on Christ. This outward gaze prevents vigilance from becoming scrupulosity or self-preoccupation. It transforms it into relational fidelity, the attentiveness of a lover who does not wish to miss the footsteps of the Beloved.

This explains why memento mori and nepsis belong together. The remembrance of death provides the horizon; watchfulness provides the posture. Death tells us what matters; vigilance teaches us how to live in light of it. Death humbles us; vigilance steadies us. Death awakens urgency; vigilance gives that urgency direction. The fathers saw these two disciplines as inseparable gifts for the Christian life. Without watchfulness, the remembrance of death becomes heavy. Without the remembrance of death, watchfulness loses its sharpness. Together they create a soul that is both grounded and alert, sober and joyful, humbled and inflamed with love.

The effect of this union is profound. The believer begins to desire God with a purified longing. The distractions that once dominated lose their hold. The anxieties that once consumed fade into proportion. The temptations that once overcame reveal their emptiness. The vigilant Christian does not become superhuman; he becomes truly human, restored to the image of the One who created him. The fathers repeatedly emphasize that vigilance is not a burden placed on human strength but a cooperation with divine grace. God does the heavy lifting; man simply stays awake.

Maximos the Confessor offers the most luminous summary: "The one who watches over his heart preserves the kingdom of God within." This is the goal—not simply to notice thoughts, not simply to resist sin, but to guard the kingdom within, the place where Christ dwells by grace. Nepsis becomes the architecture of that kingdom. It builds walls against despair, gates against temptation, windows that let in divine light, and an altar upon which the heart offers itself to God.

When this interior kingdom is guarded, the believer becomes capable of love. True love requires attention. It requires presence. It requires a heart that is not scattered. The man who guards his heart becomes the man who can give his heart. Vigilance makes fidelity possible. It prepares the soul for prayer. It prepares it for repentance. It prepares it for obedience. Above all it prepares it for Christ, who comes to the heart with the same suddenness with which He will come at the end of history.

This is why watchfulness is not optional for the Christian life. Jesus commands it. The apostles echo it. The fathers build entire spiritual traditions upon it. It is the posture of those who understand that every moment carries eternal weight. It is the readiness of the soul that knows God can speak at any time, call at any time, purify at any time, and come at any time. Watchfulness is not about living on edge; it is about living in love—a love that refuses to sleep when the Bridegroom is near.

Nepsis, then, stands at the centre of the Christian way. It gathers Scripture, tradition, ascetic wisdom, and daily experience into a single imperative: awaken the heart. Guard the mind. Remember the end. Attend to the presence of God. The Christian who embraces this path discovers that what the fathers promised is true: the vigilant heart becomes a radiant heart, a heart in which Christ reigns even now, long before the day when we see Him face to face.

11

"My Master Is Delayed": The Lie That Damns Souls

There is a particular kind of lie that rarely sounds like rebellion. It does not announce itself with defiance or blasphemy. It does not shake a fist at heaven or challenge the authority of God. It whispers instead. It settles into the heart like a gentle fog. It tells a man that he can take his time. It assures him that conversion can wait, that discipleship can wait, that obedience can wait, that love can wait. This lie is quiet enough to feel harmless and familiar enough to feel true. Yet in the teaching of Jesus Christ, no lie is more dangerous, more spiritually destructive, or more consistently condemned. It is the lie that begins with a single thought: *"My master is delayed."*

When Jesus first speaks these words in the Gospel of Matthew, He places them on the lips of a servant who has grown accustomed to the absence of his lord. The servant has not rejected his master; he has simply forgotten him. He has begun to live as though the master's return is unlikely or irrelevant. What begins as forgetfulness quickly becomes presumption, and presumption becomes license. "The wicked servant says in his heart, 'My master is delayed,' and he begins to beat his fellow servants and eat and drink with drunkards"

(Mt 24:48–49). The spiral is startling: delay breeds indulgence, indulgence breeds cruelty, and cruelty breeds judgment. Jesus is describing not a rare pathology but the ordinary trajectory of a heart that postpones fidelity. Delay does not remain passive; it becomes destructive.

This is the logic Jesus traces again and again. In His parables, delay is never neutral. It is the breeding ground of unfaithfulness. It is the hidden root of negligence and spiritual sloth. It is the soil in which acedia grows. Whenever a character in Jesus' parables delays, the outcome is catastrophic. The five foolish virgins delay purchasing oil. The slothful servant delays investing his talent. The unfaithful steward delays preparing for his master's return. The barren fig tree delays bearing fruit. The man invited to the wedding feast delays clothing himself properly. In each case, delay reveals the heart's reluctance to love, its unwillingness to respond, its refusal to take God seriously.

In the world of the New Testament, delay is not a scheduling problem; it is a theological statement. It says to God, "Not yet." It says, "Your call is real, but not urgent." It says, "Your grace matters, but not today." The fathers of the Church understood this with penetrating clarity. Origen calls delay "the quiet refusal of the will," a resistance masked as indecision. John Chrysostom warns that there is "nothing colder than a Christian who postpones obedience," for coldness is not the absence of heat but the evidence that the heart has stopped responding to love. Dorotheos of Gaza names delay as "the beginning of negligence," and negligence as "the mother of every sin." The demons, Cassian observes, do not need to provoke open rebellion when a man can be lulled into indefinite postponement. "Tomorrow," the fathers say, "is the devil's favourite word," because tomorrow never arrives. Only today belongs to God.

This is woven deeply into the biblical story. When Israel delays repentance, the prophets cry out. When the kings delay justice, the covenant trembles. When the disciples delay prayer in Gethsemane, Jesus finds them asleep and warns them that temptation comes not with banners but with fatigue. The drama of salvation is always fought in the present moment. Paul expresses this with unmistakable force: "Now is the acceptable time; now is the day of salvation" (2 Cor 6:2). The entire Christian life stands or collapses on the word *now*. Grace does not live in the imagined future. Grace meets us in the moment God gives—the moment that carries eternal weight, the moment that asks for trust, obedience, and love.

The human heart resists this. Delay is appealing precisely because it feels safe. It allows a person to affirm the truth without obeying it. It gives the illusion of reverence without the cost of discipleship. It lets the conscience remain theoretically aligned with God while practically drifting from Him. Many believers fall not by outright denial of faith but by gradual postponement of fidelity. They do not say "no" to God; they say "later." They do not reject holiness; they defer it. They do not despise prayer; they avoid it. They do not abandon the Church; they simply fail to return. Their intentions remain intact even as their souls become numb.

Augustine understood this inner struggle with piercing honesty. His famous plea—"Lord, make me chaste, but not yet"—captures the psychology of delay better than any modern analysis. Augustine was not mocking God; he was exposing the divided will. He wanted God, but he also wanted his excuses. He wanted conversion, but he also wanted time. His conversion came only when he realized that delay was not caution but bondage. "I was wasting away," he writes, "in the postponement of my decision." Delay slowly emptied his freedom until he could no longer trust himself to respond to grace. His liberation came when he surrendered the illusion of "later."

Jesus does not allow His disciples the luxury of "later." His words cut through the fog with unmistakable clarity: "Watch therefore, for you know neither the day nor the hour" (Mt 25:13). The warning is not theoretical. It is not about fear. It is about reality. Human life is fragile. The timing of death is unknown. The opportunities for repentance are finite. The master's return is certain, but its timing is hidden. Jesus speaks plainly because the stakes are eternal. He does not soften His tone because He knows how subtle and seductive delay can be. The danger is not that a person will openly rebel against God but that he will quietly drift away from Him while assuming he has plenty of time to return.

The tragedy of delay is that it prevents love from maturing. Love requires response. It must be chosen in the moment offered. A bride who continually postpones her "yes" never becomes a bride. A disciple who delays obedience never becomes a disciple. A servant who assumes he has time to put his household in order never does so. Jesus' parables reveal this over and over: the door closes, the master returns, the reckoning arrives, and those who delayed discover that time was not theirs to command. The closed door of the wedding feast is one of the most haunting images in Scripture—not because Christ is cruel, but because the virgins assumed they had time to spare. Their exclusion is not arbitrary; it is the consequence of delay elevated into habit.

Delay is the silent destroyer of discipleship because it slowly dissolves the sense of accountability. When a man tells himself that the master is delayed, he begins to believe that the master may never return at all. His conscience shifts. His priorities drift. His actions become shaped not by the certainty of the master's return but by the convenience of the present moment. In Jesus' parable, the servant does not become wicked overnight. His cruelty is the fruit of a deeper failure: he stopped living as though the master's will mattered. He did not deny the master's authority; he simply neglected it. He did not rage against the master's commands; he quietly postponed them. And in that postponement, the heart that once served began to harden.

The same dynamic appears in the parable of the talents. The slothful servant does not reject his master. He does not squander the talent on immoral pleasures. He does not rebel or run away. He simply buries what he was given. His sin is not extravagance but inertia. When confronted, he speaks in the language of delay: "I was afraid, and I hid your talent in the ground." Fear becomes his excuse for inaction, and inaction becomes his justification for disobedience. He tells himself that safeguarding the talent is safer than risking it. What he really means is that obedience can wait. The master's demand can wait. Fruitfulness can wait. His life becomes one long postponement. And the judgment he receives is the most severe in the parable: "Cast the worthless servant into the outer darkness." Jesus does not offer this as a dramatic flourish. He is revealing the spiritual consequence of a soul that chooses inaction over faith.

The parable of the ten virgins exposes the same pattern with striking clarity. All ten know the bridegroom is coming. All ten have lamps. All ten fall asleep. The difference is not fatigue but preparation. Five have oil; five do not. The foolish virgins are not immoral, rebellious, or malicious. They simply delay. They intend to acquire oil—just not yet. Their delay is quiet and undramatic, and it proves fatal. When the cry goes out, "Behold, the bridegroom! Come out to meet him!" they are unprepared. Their request for oil is sincere, even urgent, but sincerity cannot replace readiness. By the time they seek to prepare, the moment for preparation has passed. "And the door was shut." The words are as solemn as Scripture ever speaks. Judgment is not cruelty; judgment is consequence. A lifetime of postponement meets the moment where postponement is no longer possible.

Jesus returns to this pattern repeatedly because He knows how deeply rooted delay is in the human heart. The barren fig tree stands for years without fruit, living on borrowed time. The vineyard owner grants one more year, an act of mercy that reveals the patience of God. But mercy is not permission. The extra year is given for repentance, not avoidance. The tree that refuses to bear fruit is cut down not out of anger but out of truth: a life that will not respond to grace will not bear fruit simply by existing longer. Time does not convert a soul; grace does. And grace can only work where it is welcomed.

In the Gospel of Luke, Jesus intensifies the warning. "Stay dressed for action and keep your lamps burning," He says, "and be like men who are waiting for their master to come home" (Lk 12:35–36). The image is deliberate. Servants who love their master live in readiness, not because they fear punishment but because they desire to be found faithful. Readiness is the posture of love. Delay is the posture of indifference. When Peter asks if this teaching is for the disciples or for everyone, Jesus answers by describing the faithful steward and the unfaithful one. The faithful steward tends to the household as if the master's return were imminent. The unfaithful steward behaves as though the master will not come at all. He says in his heart, "My master is delayed," and that single thought unravels his vocation.

Jesus does not soften His words. "The master of that servant will come on a day when he does not expect him, and at an hour he does not know, and will cut him in pieces and put him with the unfaithful" (Lk 12:46). These are not metaphors for mild disappointment. They are the Lord's own description of what it means for a soul to meet judgment while living in deliberate delay. Jesus uses the language of separation, exclusion, and loss because delay has eternal consequences. A heart that will not give itself to God in life will not find itself able to do so in death. The problem is not that God refuses the soul. The problem is that the soul has trained itself not to respond.

The fathers saw this with apocalyptic clarity. Basil the Great warns, "Do not say, 'Tomorrow I will repent,' for you do not know whether you will have a tomorrow." His point is not despair but urgency.

Repentance belongs to the moment God gives, and that moment is always the present. Chrysostom echoes this when he says, "There is nothing so cold as a Christian who does not seek the salvation of his own soul." Coldness, for Chrysostom, is not emotional detachment but spiritual paralysis—an inability to move toward God because one has become accustomed to postponing everything that matters. Isaac the Syrian goes further still: "To every sin is joined the thought, 'Not yet.'" The root of every fall is delay.

One of the most striking observations in the monastic tradition comes from the sayings of the Desert Fathers: "The devil does not say, 'There is no God.' He says, 'There is no hurry.'" The fathers are not engaging in exaggeration. They are naming the strategy by which the enemy drains the soul of vigilance. If he can convince a man that there is time, he never needs to convince him to reject God. The man will drift far enough on delay alone.

Delay becomes especially dangerous because it does not feel like sin. It does not provoke guilt the way anger or impurity might. It rarely alarms the conscience. It disguises itself as prudence, caution, emotional fatigue, or simply the desire for a more convenient time. It is a parasite that thrives on good intentions. A man says, "I will pray when life is calmer." "I will repent when I feel more sincere." "I will forgive when the hurt is less sharp." "I will return to the sacraments when I am more prepared." He speaks in the future tense as though grace belongs to some later version of himself. What he forgets is that grace belongs to God, and God gives it in the present. Delay places one's hope not in God but in a hypothetical future that may never exist.

This is why Jesus repeatedly binds the call to vigilance with the reality of mortality. Human life is limited, and its limits are not negotiable. Jesus does not frighten His disciples with this truth; He frees them with it. He teaches them to measure time not by the illusion of human control but by the gift of divine opportunity. When He says, "You know neither the day nor the hour," He is not speaking only of His Second Coming. He is speaking of the hour a soul will meet Him in death. The two events share a theological logic: both arrive suddenly, both reveal the truth of the heart, both expose whether a man has lived in readiness or in postponement. Delay, therefore, is not merely imprudent—it is a gamble with eternity.

Nowhere is this clearer than in Jesus' parable of the wedding feast. The man who enters without a wedding garment is not a villain. He is not immoral. He is unprepared. He shows up, but he has not clothed himself with what the king requires. The garment represents righteousness—grace received, virtue cultivated, love practiced. To arrive without it is to live as though the moment of encounter will tolerate postponement. The king's question is devastating in its simplicity: "Friend, how did you get in here without a wedding garment?" There is no accusation, no anger—only truth. The man is speechless because the truth reveals not a mistake but a lifetime of delay. He assumed there would be time to prepare later. The king's judgment is swift because the issue is not the absence of a garment but the absence of readiness.

Paul speaks in the same key. He urges believers to awaken from sleep because "the night is far gone; the day is at hand" (Rom 13:12). He is not appealing to fear or social pressure. He is appealing to covenant identity. Believers are children of the day, and children of the day live in the light. They do not postpone fidelity. They do not drift into the shadows of "later." Paul's language is not mild. He insists that delay belongs to darkness. Readiness belongs to light. The present moment is the battlefield on which the Christian life is won or lost.

Modern psychology describes procrastination as avoidance of discomfort. Scripture describes it as avoidance of truth. The Gospel does not speak merely to patterns of behaviour but to the posture of the heart before God. The man who delays repentance is not avoiding an unpleasant task; he is avoiding the presence of the One who calls him to life. The woman who postpones forgiveness is not waiting for a better emotional climate; she is resisting the grace that would make forgiveness possible. The believer who sets aside prayer because of fatigue or distraction is not lacking discipline; he is failing to understand that prayer is where the heart learns to love. Delay weakens love because it trains the soul to expect nothing of itself.

The tragedy is that every postponement makes the next one easier. Once the soul becomes accustomed to delay, it loses the capacity for decisive response. This spiritual paralysis is what the fathers meant by the word acedia. Acedia is not simply laziness; it is the loss of the will's elasticity—the ability to leap toward God when He calls. The soul becomes stiff. It becomes slow. It becomes resistant to movement, not because it rejects God but because it no longer remembers how to respond to Him. Acedia thrives where delay is habitual. It is the hardening of the heart through countless neglected opportunities.

And yet, Jesus never reveals the danger of delay without simultaneously revealing its antidote. The antidote is not panic. It is not fear-driven activism. It is not frantic attempts to earn God's favour. The antidote is readiness—watchfulness grounded in love, vigilance grounded in relationship. Jesus calls His disciples to be ready because He is with them. He urges them to stay awake because He is near. Vigilance is not a burden placed upon a lonely soul; it is the posture of a heart that knows it is loved and refuses to drift away from that love. Readiness is simply love in motion.

This truth becomes clearest in Gethsemane. Jesus asks Peter, James, and John to watch with Him. Not to perform. Not to strategize. Not to prove themselves. To watch. To be present. To respond to the moment given. Their failure is not the failure of wickedness but the failure of delay. They allow sleep to claim the moment grace offered. Jesus' question—"Could you not watch with me one hour?"—reveals the tragedy of delay at its most intimate. It is a missed moment of love.

Delay always feels reasonable in the moment, which is why it is so spiritually lethal. When Jesus warns, "Be ready," delay answers, "I will be." When Jesus says, "Repent," delay says, "I will, soon." When Jesus calls a man to take up his cross, delay replies, "When life settles." It masks itself as calmness, as emotional prudence, even as the desire to "do things properly." But beneath these disguises lies a refusal to surrender. Delay is the soul's attempt to remain in control. It offers God eventual obedience rather than immediate trust. It treats conversion as a negotiation rather than a response to love. This is why Jesus confronts delay with such uncompromising clarity: the soul that delays today will find it even harder to respond tomorrow.

The pattern appears throughout the Old Testament. Israel delays repentance again and again, and the prophets cry out not because God is impatient but because the people have grown numb. Hosea speaks of a people who "hesitate like a deceitful bow." Their intentions aim at God, but their actions fall short. Isaiah laments that Israel "honours God with their lips while their hearts are far from Him," a distance created not by rebellion but by delay. Jeremiah describes a people who say, "Peace, peace," while their souls drift toward destruction. Delay becomes a spiritual narcotic: it numbs judgment, dulls conscience, and convinces the heart that there will always be more time.

Jesus enters this history not to soften the prophets but to fulfil them. He speaks with the same urgency because He sees the same danger. When He says, "Strive to enter by the narrow gate," He is not describing a future decision but a present one. The gate is narrow because the moment is narrow. It demands a choice now. The broad road is broad because it accommodates delay. It welcomes the man who intends to change, intends to pray, intends to repent—just not today. The narrow gate, by contrast, allows no postponement. It is not entered by accident or drift. It is entered by decision. Delay, therefore, is incompatible with discipleship. It is the broad road paved with good intentions.

One of the most sobering features of Jesus' teaching is that delay does not merely lead to judgment; it reveals judgment already at work. A soul that delays is a soul that has already become accustomed to living without God. Judgment is not the sudden imposition of divine anger but the unveiling of a life shaped by postponement. The man who delays prayer discovers at death that he has become a man who cannot pray. The woman who delays forgiveness discovers that she has formed herself into someone unable to receive mercy. The believer who delays conversion discovers that he has lost the very readiness that makes conversion possible. This is why Jesus' warnings are so severe. He is not threatening reluctant sinners; He is rescuing them from the consequences of their own delay.

This truth explodes in the parable of the rich fool. The man's barns are full. His plans are vast. His future feels secure. But his entire life rests on an assumption so deep he never bothers to articulate it: that he has time. He speaks in the language of delay: "I will say to my soul, Soul, you have ample goods laid up for many years; relax, eat, drink, be merry" (Lk 12:19). He believes the future belongs to him. God's response is the most devastating reversal in all the parables: "Fool! This night your soul is required of you." The judgment is not cruelty; it is reality. The man's sin is not wealth but delusion—the delusion that he controls the calendar of his soul. He planned for everything except death because he believed he had time to plan later.

Jesus tells this parable not to condemn ambition but to expose presumption. Presumption is faith's counterfeit. It assumes God will give what He never promised: more time. The rich fool imagined tomorrow. God gave him only today. The tragedy is that he never lived in the today God gave. He lived in a future that did not exist. His life was shaped by delay, and delay shaped him into a man incapable of readiness.

The fathers warn that presumption is more dangerous than despair because despair at least recognizes a problem. Presumption sees no need for urgency. It imagines that grace will always come when summoned, that repentance will be easier later, that holiness can be postponed without cost. Augustine describes presumption as "a thief of souls," not because it steals grace but because it wastes time. Basil calls presumption "the arrogance of tomorrow." Isaac the Syrian says presumption blinds a man to the fragility of the present moment. Each father is naming the same truth: the soul that presumes tomorrow forfeits today.

The spiritual psychology behind this is simple: delay feels safe because it avoids vulnerability. Obedience today requires trust. Repentance today requires humility. Forgiveness today requires surrender. Delay protects the ego by postponing all three. It allows the soul to remain unchanged while soothing itself with the promise of future change. It is the imitation of conversion rather than its reality. Jesus refuses to accept this imitation. He calls His disciples not to future obedience but to present obedience. Not to future repentance but to present repentance. Not to future vigilance but to present vigilance. The Christian life is a series of "now" moments, each one carrying the weight of eternity.

Delay becomes even more spiritually corrosive when it masquerades as humility. Many believers tell themselves they are waiting for the "right moment" to return to prayer, to seek reconciliation, to repair a relationship, to reorder their lives. They imagine that God will be more pleased with a later obedience performed with fuller sincerity. This illusion traps the soul precisely because it feels devout.

But God does not ask for a future version of the self. He asks for the heart as it is, now. To wait for ideal conditions is to deny grace its chosen hour. When Jesus calls fishermen, He does not wait for them to finish mending their nets. When He calls Matthew, He does not wait for him to balance his books. When He calls Zacchaeus, He does not wait for him to fix his finances. Their response—immediate, uncalculated—is the pattern for all discipleship. Grace speaks in the present because the present is the only place the heart can change.

This explains why Scripture continually warns against the hardness of heart that develops through delay. "Today, if you hear his voice, do not harden your hearts," the psalmist cries (Ps 95:7–8). The author of Hebrews repeats the warning twice, anchoring the urgency of salvation in the gift of "today." Hardness of heart is rarely instantaneous. It emerges subtly, almost imperceptibly, through countless occasions of postponed response. A man feels a nudge toward prayer and ignores it. A woman senses the need to repent and postpones it. A young believer feels inspired toward holiness but assumes he will have time later to pursue it. Each postponement forms a habit; each habit shapes a disposition; each disposition becomes a character. Delayed obedience slowly reshapes the soul into someone who *cannot* obey.

The fathers described this as the "creeping death of the inner life." Acedia, in its most advanced form, is not exhaustion but indifference. It is the soul that has quietly surrendered its vigilance. Evagrius calls it "the most oppressive of all the demons" because it attacks the will more than the intellect. Acedia does not argue; it dulls. It does not frighten; it numbs. It does not persuade the soul to reject God; it persuades the soul to wait. Its weapon is not temptation but postponement. Climacus observes that acedia "makes the hours seem long and the life of man seem endless." The illusion of endlessness is its strength. If life feels long, repentance feels less urgent. If death feels far away, holiness appears optional.

Jesus counters this illusion with uncompromising clarity. When He says, "You know not the hour," He is not speaking poetically but theologically. Human beings do not possess time; they receive it. Mortality is not a morbid fact but a covenantal truth: life is a gift with an end, and the Giver alone determines its span. Jesus speaks as one who loves His disciples too deeply to allow them to drift into the illusions that make love impossible. He does not frighten them with uncertainty; He frees them from presumption. To know neither the day nor the hour is to live with open hands. It is to receive each moment as a summons to fidelity. It is to measure life not by quantity of days but by quality of response.

Paul's insistence that "now is the day of salvation" takes on a sharper edge when read in this light. He does not say that now is the day of consideration or reflection or planning. He says salvation. Salvation is God's act, and God acts in the present. Paul stands in the long line of prophets and apostles who refuse to separate divine grace from the moment in which it is offered. The present moment is where heaven touches earth. It is where the soul encounters God. It is where decisions bend eternity. When Paul tells believers to awaken, he is not issuing a metaphor. He is calling them to live in the salvation that is available now and may not be offered in the same way tomorrow.

The psalmist's plea, "Teach us to number our days," expresses the wisdom Jesus embodies. Numbering one's days is not a mathematical exercise; it is a spiritual awakening. It teaches the soul to recognize the finite nature of earthly life and the infinite weight of eternal life. It reveals that time is not a possession but a stewardship. The person who numbers his days does not waste them. He does not delay the good he can do. He does not postpone reconciliation or forgiveness. He does not assume tomorrow will resemble today. Numbering one's days teaches a kind of holy realism: the recognition that every day carries the possibility of salvation or the loss of it.

This realism sharpens the Gospel's moral vision. The man who delays repentance is not simply procrastinating; he is resisting the God who calls him. The woman who delays forgiveness is not merely wounded; she is withholding mercy from the One who offered her mercy first. The believer who delays prayer is not simply distracted; he is postponing communion with the Living God. The consequences of delay are not psychological but theological. Delay tears at the fabric of covenant love. It trains the heart to live at a distance from God, and distance becomes alienation. What begins as a temporary pause becomes a permanent posture.

Delay also distorts a person's perception of God. The soul that postpones obedience begins to imagine God as someone who can be kept waiting. The heart that avoids repentance begins to think of God as someone who will always be available later. This is how presumption becomes a counterfeit form of trust. It claims to rest in God's mercy while refusing God's call. It imagines divine patience as divine indifference. It treats God's forbearance as endless elasticity. Scripture shatters this illusion. Divine patience is real, but it is not infinite. It exists to lead a person to repentance, not to excuse the postponement of repentance. Paul writes that God's kindness is meant to lead us to conversion, but warns that the heart storing up wrath is the heart that takes this kindness for granted. Delay turns mercy into fuel for judgment.

This distortion of God's character lies at the centre of Jesus' most severe warnings. The servant who says, "My master is delayed," is not only mistaken about time; he is mistaken about the master. He imagines him as inattentive, disengaged, and distant. This false image becomes the justification for his negligence. When the master returns suddenly, the servant's illusion is exposed, and the exposure is catastrophic because it reveals not a misunderstanding but a betrayal.

He lived as though the master's absence was permission to live without reference to him. Jesus speaks harshly here because the consequences are harsh: living without reference to God becomes dying without Him.

The parable of the ten virgins carries the same force. The foolish virgins do not doubt the bridegroom's arrival; they simply assume His timing will align with their readiness. They project their delay onto Him. When He arrives on His own terms, they are unprepared, and their exclusion is not arbitrary cruelty but covenant consequence. They wanted the feast, but they did not want the preparation the feast required. Their desire lacked urgency. Their hope lacked substance. Their hearts lacked readiness. Jesus' words—"Truly, I do not know you"—reveal a chilling truth: the relationship they presumed upon had never formed. Delay had hollowed it out.

Jesus amplifies this warning with the image of the narrow gate. The gate is narrow because discipleship is decisive. A person cannot pass through it carrying the weight of deferred obedience. Delay becomes baggage that will not fit through the entrance to life. Jesus says many will seek to enter and will not be able, not because they were unwelcome, but because they hesitated. They waited until the door was closing. They lived as though the invitation would remain open indefinitely. Jesus does not offer this as a theological abstraction. He is revealing the moral structure of the universe: love must be answered when offered. A heart that refuses to answer will slowly lose the ability to recognize the One who calls.

The fathers saw this clearly. Chrysostom writes that "no one is condemned for falling, but many are condemned for rising late." His point is not that sinners should despair but that sinners must rise quickly. Delay is more destructive than sin because sin can be repented of, but delay resists repentance itself. Basil says, "Repentance delayed is repentance denied." He is not being poetic; he is naming the spiritual physics of the soul. Every moment of delay reshapes the will, making repentance more difficult, not easier. Isaac the Syrian warns that "he who waits for a more convenient season is carried by the wind of his own negligence." Waiting becomes drifting, and drifting becomes separation.

Even the ascetical masters who emphasize gentleness speak with fierce clarity regarding delay. Dorotheos warns that the soul that postpones its conversion "plays with death," not because God is quick to condemn but because life is quick to end. Climacus observes that the devil rejoices more in delay than in open sin because delay keeps the soul asleep. Open sin at least can be confronted. Delay cannot be grasped. It slips through the fingers. It offers nothing to fight, nothing to confess, nothing to uproot. It is the silent desert of the unconverted heart.

This is why Jesus' words about vigilance carry such solemn joy. He is not merely describing the disposition of a good servant; He is revealing the nature of love. Lovers are attentive. They remain awake to the presence of the beloved. They do not postpone their affection. They do not schedule their devotion. They do not delay their response. Vigilance is the posture of a heart that desires God. Delay is the posture of a heart that desires itself. Jesus calls His disciples to watchfulness not because He wishes to burden them but because He wishes to free them from the illusion of control over time. When He says, "Stay awake," He is summoning the heart into the freedom of readiness. Love is ready. Indifference delays.

12

When Death Becomes Desire: From Holy Fear to the Longing for the Bridegroom

There is a wisdom that only mortality can teach. The monks understood this with a clarity the modern world has nearly forgotten. They fled into the desert not to escape life but to face it—its brevity, its fragility, its eternal stakes. The remembrance of death was not a shadow over their days; it was the lamp that illuminated them. Everything we have just traced in the deep monastic tradition—the battle with acedia, the discipline of nepsis, the exposure of delay—only makes sense when set against this single truth: a human being is moving toward an encounter with God. Not in theory. Not eventually. In reality. This encounter shapes the meaning of every hour we are given.

Acedia, in this light, is not merely fatigue or boredom. It is the refusal to live as one who will meet the Lord. It drains urgency from the soul by convincing it that tomorrow will resemble today, that the spiritual life can be postponed indefinitely, that holiness is an elective pursuit rather than the preparation for judgment. Acedia hides death from the mind, and by hiding death it hides God. It blinds a person to the truth that time is limited, that grace is offered in specific moments, that indifference toward those moments slowly unravels the capacity to respond at all. The Desert Fathers fought acedia because they knew it was a quiet revolt against the truth of mortality.

Nepsis—the guarding of the heart—is the opposite posture. It is the vigilance of someone who has remembered his end. A watchful Christian is not anxious; he is awake. He understands that thoughts matter because they shape desires, and desires matter because they shape choices, and choices matter because they follow him into eternity. The man who practices nepsis lives as though every moment carries weight, because it does. His life becomes ordered toward the One he will see face-to-face. His prayer sharpens. His repentance deepens. His love becomes deliberate. Vigilance is the virtue of someone who has allowed death to clarify life.

Delay, finally, is the tragedy of forgetting death altogether. It is the soul's quiet gamble that it will have more time—a gamble no one in history has ever won. Jesus exposes delay not because He wishes to frighten His disciples but because He wishes to free them from illusion. When He warns that the master returns suddenly, He is not describing an unpredictable deity but a predictable humanity: we do not control the hour of our death. The parables of the talents, the virgins, the unfaithful steward, and the rich fool are not scattered moral tales; they form a single revelation. Each shows what happens when a person forgets that life is limited, that grace is urgent, that time is sacred. Delay is the refusal to live as a mortal. It is the denial of memento mori.

Seen together, acedia, negligence, and postponement are not isolated vices. They are symptoms of a deeper amnesia. They reveal how easily the heart loses sight of its destiny. When a person forgets death, he forgets judgment. When he forgets judgment, he forgets love. When he forgets love, he forgets God. To remember death is not to become morbid; it is to recover the truth that every day is a preparation for meeting the One who gave it. The monks insisted on this not to cultivate fear but to cultivate clarity. Memento mori is simply honesty before God.

This is why the Christian tradition never separates mortality from hope. To remember death is to remember that life has a destination. It is to remember that our choices matter because they shape the soul that will one day stand before Christ. It is to remember that vigilance is not burdensome but liberating, because it clears away the illusions that numb the heart. It is to remember that grace is always offered today, not tomorrow. And it is to remember that the God who calls us to readiness is the same God who conquered death, not to terrify us but to lead us home.

Everything now moves toward that homecoming. The fight against acedia, the practice of watchfulness, the exposure of delay—all these disciplines clear the fog so that we can see what lies ahead. They form the soul to live not only with sobriety but with longing. For the Christian, death is not merely the end of earthly life; it is the threshold through which we meet the One who has loved us from before we were formed. Judgment is not the collapse of life but its unveiling. The warnings of Christ prepare us not for fear but for encounter. The Bridegroom is coming, and the heart that remembers its mortality is the heart that waits for Him with desire.

This is the turn the Gospel makes and the turn this book now makes with it. Mortality has shown us the seriousness of life. Vigilance has taught us to remain awake. The desert tradition has stripped away the illusions that keep us spiritually asleep. Now another truth comes into view—one that stands at the centre of Christian faith. The God we will meet at death is not a distant judge but the Bridegroom of the soul. His coming is sudden because love moves swiftly. His judgment is radiant because love reveals truth. His arrival is not meant to crush us but to complete us.

WHEN DEATH BECOMES DESIRE: FROM HOLY FEAR TO THE LONGING FOR...

The remembrance of death leads here, to this threshold of hope. It prepares the heart not simply to avoid peril but to welcome glory. It opens the eyes not only to human frailty but to divine fidelity. It awakens a longing that acedia cannot smother, that delay cannot steal, that death itself cannot end. The soul that lives in memento mori is the soul that begins to hear the ancient Christian cry with new clarity: *Maranatha—Come, Lord Jesus.*

IV

JUDGMENT, LOVE, AND THE BRIDEGROOM

13

What We Will See: The Face of Christ at Death

Death is a doorway, and judgment is what waits on the other side. Yet Scripture never speaks of judgment as a cold tribunal or a cosmic bureaucracy. Judgment is personal because it is Christological. "The Father judges no one," Jesus says, "but has given all judgment to the Son" (Jn 5:22). This means that the One who will look upon us at the moment of death is the same One who looked upon Peter after the denial, who looked upon the rich young man with love, who looked upon the widow offering her two coins. Judgment is not the moment Christ becomes a stranger. Judgment is the moment we see Him without veils, disguises, or illusions.

Everything the Christian life prepares us for converges here. We spend our days learning to desire the face we will one day behold. Death strips away the distractions that kept us from seeing clearly, and judgment reveals the truth that was always present but rarely recognized: the God we seek is the God who has always sought us. Augustine understood this with luminous simplicity. "You were within me," he writes, "and I was away." Judgment is the moment this distance ends. It is not primarily the exposure of sin but the revelation of God. Sin is exposed because God is revealed. Light does not accuse; it illuminates. When the soul stands before Christ, the truth of His love unmasks the false narratives we have told ourselves, not to crush us but to heal us.

Scripture speaks often of that unveiling. Paul says that the Lord "will bring to light what is hidden in darkness and will disclose the purposes of the heart" (1 Cor 4:5). Jesus promises that "nothing is covered that will not be revealed" (Lk 12:2). This is not divine surveillance; it is divine truthfulness. Judgment is the moment when God reveals who He is and who we are. The illusions that hid our motives, softened our faults, inflated our virtues, or excused our delays fall away. What remains is reality—God's and ours—meeting face to face.

This encounter is both radiant and terrifying, not because Christ is cruel, but because truth is weighty. John's vision of the risen Lord in Revelation captures this paradox. He sees "one like a Son of Man," clothed in glory, with eyes "like a flame of fire" and a voice "like the sound of many waters" (Rev 1:13–15). John, the beloved disciple, falls at His feet as though dead. The one who leaned on His breast at the Last Supper is overwhelmed in His presence. Yet Jesus touches him and says, "Fear not." This dual movement—overwhelming glory and tender reassurance—is the pattern of judgment. The face that reveals everything is the same face that saves.

Aquinas helps us understand why this encounter carries such weight. For him, the soul was made for one final end: the vision of God. Nothing else can satisfy it. Nothing else can complete it. "The beatific vision," he says, "is the final cause of the rational creature." It is what we were made for. Judgment is not the vision itself, but the threshold of it. The soul is shown the truth of its desires, its loves, its choices. It sees whether it has been shaped to receive the vision or has deformed itself away from it. Judgment reveals the degree to which we have become capable of beholding glory. The light of God is unchanging; what changes is the heart's capacity to endure it.

Isaac the Syrian offers a profound insight: "It is wrong to think that sinners in hell are deprived of the love of God." They are not deprived of His love; they are unable to bear it. Judgment, in this sense, is the unveiling of divine love experienced according to the state of the soul. For the saint, this encounter is beatitude. For the resistant, it is agony—not because Christ abandons them, but because they have spent their lives forming themselves into someone unable to receive what He offers. This is the meaning of Jesus' warnings: they are not threats but invitations to become capable of love.

The remembrance of death prepares us for this revelation. When we recall that we will see Christ, we strip away the pretences that prevent us from living honestly. Death becomes not the end of life but the end of illusion. This is why the Psalmist prays, "Your face, Lord, do I seek" (Ps 27:8). The desire to see God is not mere mysticism; it is the deepest orientation of the human heart. Every longing, every hunger for beauty, every ache for justice is, at its root, a desire to see the One who made us. Remembering death keeps this desire awake.

And it purifies our love. Augustine teaches that sin blinds the heart by dispersing it among many things. Judgment gathers the heart back into unity. In that single moment, all rival loves are weighed against the love of God. Not because God demands competition, but because divine love exposes what is false. The heart sees what it has clung to. It sees where its treasure lies. Jesus' words, "Where your treasure is, there will your heart be also" (Mt 6:21), are not metaphorical. They are prophetic. At judgment, the heart sees its treasure clearly—and cannot pretend.

The vision of Christ will therefore be healing for some and wounding for others, but the wound itself is love. The risen Lord still bears His wounds, not as scars of defeat but as signs of triumph. Thomas touches them and believes. Augustine says the wounds will remain eternally visible so that mercy will never be forgotten. Aquinas goes further: he says the wounds will shine in glory, "trophies of His victory." When the soul encounters Christ at death, these wounds will be the first things it sees. They will tell the truth. They will reveal whether we have allowed His sacrifice to shape our lives.

The tradition teaches that nothing hidden will survive the brightness of Christ's gaze. Not because Christ delights in exposure, but because love, by its nature, unveils. Augustine says in *City of God* that God's judgment "will not be a trial by which He learns, but by which He teaches." Judgment is not the moment God discovers who we are; it is the moment *we* discover who we are in His light. This is why the saints speak of judgment as illumination. What Christ reveals, He reveals with a purpose—to cleanse, to heal, to draw the soul toward its true end. Illusion cannot enter heaven. Self-deception cannot behold God. The soul must be real before the Real.

This is why the memory of death is not simply a stern reminder of mortality but a preparation for vision. The person who remembers death begins to practice transparency before God. He lives as though he will one day see the One whose eyes "are like a flame of fire" (Rev 1:14), not in terror but in expectation. He learns to welcome the truth rather than flee from it. He confesses his sins not as legal infractions but as obstacles to sight. He forgives others not merely as a moral obligation but because resentment blinds the heart. He repents not out of fear but out of longing: longing to see the Lord with a clean conscience, a purified love, and a heart unburdened by falsehood.

The moment of judgment is often imagined as a divine audit, yet Scripture's imagery is relational, almost intimate. The Psalms speak not of standing before a court but of standing before a face: "When shall I come and behold the face of God?" (Ps 42:2). Moses speaks with God "as a man speaks with his friend" (Ex 33:11). The prophets cry out that Israel's greatest hope is not deliverance from enemies but the shining of God's face upon them. All these longings converge in the Christian conviction that Christ is the visible face of the invisible God. "He who has seen me has seen the Father" (Jn 14:9). To see Christ at death is therefore to see the fulfilment of every biblical hope.

Yet this vision is not merely external. It is the encounter in which the soul is seen through and through. The light of Christ penetrates the recesses of the heart. It reveals not only acts but motives, not only choices but desires. Aquinas notes that in the presence of God, the soul becomes "manifest to itself." This is why the fathers insist that self-knowledge is impossible without God. We cannot see ourselves truthfully until we see ourselves in the One who is Truth. Judgment is the moment of perfect self-knowledge, and perfect self-knowledge is not misery but liberation. The lies we told ourselves die. The illusions we protected dissolve. The masks we wore fall to the ground. The soul stands naked and unashamed if it has lived in grace, or naked and trembling if it has lived in resistance to grace. But either way, the truth brings clarity.

The force of this encounter cannot be overstated. When the veil is lifted and the soul finds itself face to face with Christ, every earthly attachment is suddenly revealed for what it is. The loves that aligned with His love glow with the warmth of eternity. The loves that opposed His love collapse into dust. The heart sees, perhaps for the first time, the true measure of its life. Augustine says this moment will feel like a "flash of understanding," a comprehension of one's entire story in an instant. This is why Jesus' parables place such emphasis on readiness—not because He wishes to frighten His disciples, but because readiness allows love to recognize love.

In the presence of Christ, no excuses survive. No rationalizations, no delays, no half-hearted intentions retain their weight. The moment of judgment reveals whether we have allowed His grace to shape our hearts or whether we have shaped ourselves around our own desires.

It reveals whether we have sought His kingdom or our own comfort. It exposes the depth of our charity—not as a moral score but as the measure of our likeness to Him. Jesus says plainly that the standard of judgment is love: "As you did it to one of the least of my brethren, you did it to me" (Mt 25:40). This is not sentiment; it is ontology. Love is the only reality that survives the fire of judgment because love is the very life of God.

For those who have sought Christ, even in weakness, this encounter will be joy. It will be the homecoming for which the soul was made. For those who have resisted Him, this encounter will be sorrow—not because Christ condemns them, but because they cannot bear the brightness of the Love they never welcomed. Gregory the Great once wrote that "the face of the Judge is love." That line gathers the entire Christian understanding of judgment into seven words. The face that judges is the face that loves. The light that exposes is the light that heals. The truth that wounds is the truth that saves.

Yet this does not lessen the weight of the encounter. Love is demanding because reality is demanding. The moment of judgment is the moment every pretence collapses. It is the moment every desire is revealed. It is the moment the soul discovers what it truly worshipped, what it truly loved, what it truly served. And yet, for the Christian, this is the moment we were made for. We were formed from dust to behold glory. We were breathed into so that one day we might breathe the air of heaven. We were commanded to be vigilant not to avoid punishment but to be ready for love.

The soul that stands before Christ at death discovers that judgment is not a verdict spoken over life from the outside but the disclosure of life from within. Everything hidden becomes visible because everything is held within the sight of Christ. Nothing is lost to Him— not a single tear, not a single act of mercy, not a single moment of cowardice, not a single refusal of grace. His gaze gathers the whole of life, not piece by piece, but as a unified story that reveals what the person has become. The desert fathers often said, "A man becomes his choices," and in the light of Christ those choices are no longer scattered across years; they stand together as a single portrait of the heart.

This is why the saints urge us to remember death—not to cultivate fear but to cultivate truth. The one who practices memento mori lives each day as though he will one day see the face of Christ, because he will. This discipline forms a certain freedom: the freedom to live without illusion, the freedom to confess without hesitation, the freedom to detach from lesser loves in order to cling to the First Love. It shapes the soul into a vessel capable of receiving the light it will one day behold. Augustine writes in one of his sermons that the Christian must "prepare a place in the heart for the One who will come," and he adds that this preparation happens through humility, repentance, and love. Memento mori is simply the remembrance that this preparation has a deadline.

The power of the beatific encounter rests in the fact that the soul sees God and sees itself in God. Aquinas explains that in the beatific vision, "the intellect sees the divine essence, and in it all things," meaning that the soul comes to understand its own nature, its own journey, and its own grace in the very act of beholding God. This is why judgment is not a humiliation but a completion. It is the moment the creature stands before the Creator who formed it, redeemed it, sustained it, and called it. Judgment is not God catching us; judgment is God receiving us—receiving all that we have become through the mystery of freedom and grace.

Yet Scripture does not allow us to sentimentalize this moment. Jesus' own teaching presses upon the soul with moral seriousness. "Nothing is covered that will not be revealed, or hidden that will not be known" (Mt 10:26). "On that day," He says, "people will give account for every careless word they utter" (Mt 12:36). These aren't threats; they are descriptions of reality. In the presence of Perfect Truth, nothing false can endure. In the presence of Perfect Love, nothing unloving can remain concealed. The revelation is not cruelty—it is justice. More than that, it is clarity. The illusions that clouded our earthly life cannot survive the brightness of eternal life.

There is another dimension to this encounter that the tradition holds with great tenderness: the moment the soul sees Christ, it finally sees the One who has accompanied it in every moment of its earthly journey. The Judge is not a stranger. He is the Shepherd who sought the lost sheep, the Bridegroom who longed for the bride, the Physician who healed the wounds of sin, the Lamb who bore the weight of the world. Judgment is the unveiling of the Christ who has been quietly loving the soul from the beginning. Augustine says that in the beatific vision the soul will recognize that "He loved us before we loved Him," and it is this recognition that transforms judgment into joy for the righteous.

But joy is possible only for those whose hearts have been cleansed. "Blessed are the pure in heart, for they shall see God" (Mt 5:8). Purity here does not mean sinlessness; it means undivided love. It means a heart no longer fractured by competing loyalties. It means a soul that desires God more than anything else. The memory of death serves this purity by stripping life down to its essentials. It reminds us that the pleasures that once dazzled us will fade, the achievements that once consumed us will pass, and the opinions of others that once ruled us will fall silent. Only love will remain. Only the heart's orientation toward God will matter.

This is why vigilance is not a burden but a gift. The Christian remembers death so that life may be directed toward its true end. He practices humility so that he may rejoice in the truth. He practices repentance so that he may step into the light without fear. He practices charity so that he may recognize the Lord when He comes. When death arrives, the soul does not enter a courtroom; it enters a revelation. It steps into the light of the Face that has been calling it home across every season of life.

The saints insist that this encounter is the moment for which the soul was created. Gregory of Nyssa describes the beatific vision as "the soul stretching toward the Infinite," a stretching that will never cease because God is inexhaustible. Aquinas teaches that the soul will experience in that moment perfect rest and perfect desire—rest in having attained its end, desire in continually receiving more of the God who cannot be exhausted. The memory of death is the training for this moment, the schooling of the heart in longing for what will one day be revealed.

Yet none of this minimizes the drama of that first instant before Christ. The soul stands without disguise. All patterns of love and all refusals of love appear with sudden clarity. The call to conversion becomes unmistakable. The holiness of God becomes undeniable. But for the one who has lived with memento mori, this clarity is not crushing; it is consoling. The soul is ready—not because it has perfected itself, but because it has surrendered itself. It has learned to love the light before the light arrives.

The instant the soul sees Christ, the entire drama of salvation history focuses like a beam upon a single point: the relationship between the Creator and the creature. Everything God has ever done—calling Abraham, forming Israel, sending the prophets, becoming flesh, embracing the Cross, descending into death, rising in glory—was ordered toward this meeting. Judgment is not an interruption of that story; it is the consummation of it. The soul finally stands where it was always meant to stand: before the One who made it in love and redeemed it through His own blood.

This is why Scripture presents the encounter not only in juridical terms but in relational ones. Jesus speaks of servants meeting their master, bridesmaids meeting the Bridegroom, stewards meeting the returning owner, children meeting their Father. These images are not poetic decorations; they are lenses through which God reveals how He wishes to be seen. Judgment is severe because love is severe—severe in its clarity, severe in its honesty, severe in its refusal to let a lie remain a lie. Yet for that very reason it is beautiful. In the light of the Face of Christ, pretence collapses, masks disintegrate, shadows dissolve, and what is left is the person God intended us to be, either embraced or rejected through our own freedom.

The Fathers often describe this moment with reverent boldness. Augustine says that when the soul sees God, it will see itself "as God sees it," and that sight will either wound with remorse or flood with joy. Gregory the Great explains that the righteous "tremble with delight" because the God they feared in awe reveals Himself as the God they loved in faith. For the wicked, the same light becomes unbearable—not because God changes, but because the heart has trained itself to flee the light. Divine judgment is not arbitrary; it is the soul's encounter with unchanging holiness.

This is why the remembrance of death is not a morbid practice but a merciful one. It keeps us from forming a false self built upon vanities and distractions. It guards us from arranging life around a comfort that will not accompany us beyond the grave. It purifies the heart of divided loyalties. It awakens desire for the One who will be our judge precisely because He is our beloved. In this sense, memento mori is not merely preparation for death; it is preparation for love. It teaches us to live in truth now so that the truth will not overwhelm us later.

Aquinas offers a profound insight into the moment the soul sees God. He teaches that the beatific vision perfects every power of the human person. The intellect is elevated, the will is purified, the memory is healed. Everything that was wounded by sin finds its remedy not in self-effort but in the sheer radiance of God's presence. This is why the saints speak of judgment and heaven in a single breath. The fire of judgment and the fire of love are not two fires but one. The difference lies in the soul's readiness to receive it. For the saint, the fire consumes only what is false. For the hardened heart, the fire reveals what it refused to surrender.

The moment of death, then, is not simply the cessation of earthly life; it is the unveiling of life's deepest meaning. The soul does not wander into a void. It steps across a threshold into the presence of the One who has woven every moment of its existence with purpose. The God who saw every generosity, every hidden act of charity, every tear shed in prayer, every resistance to temptation, every whispered plea for mercy—is the God who stands before the soul at death. Nothing righteous is forgotten. Nothing loving is wasted. Nothing offered to Him in faith escapes His notice.

This is why the early Christians longed for the coming of Christ. Their cry "Maranatha" was not fear of judgment but desire for communion. They understood that seeing Christ meant seeing the fulfillment of every hope, every sacrifice, every struggle for holiness. They saw death not as the loss of life but as its completion. The one who remembers death rightly learns to see it this way: not as a thief but as an usher, guiding the soul into the presence of the Bridegroom. Judgment reveals the truth of love, and love gives judgment its meaning.

But this encounter also reveals the tragedy of a life lived without vigilance. Jesus' warnings about the unprepared servant, the closed door, the foolish virgins, and the man without a wedding garment all converge here. These teachings are not simply moral lessons; they are revelations of what happens when a heart refuses to love. Indifference is exposed. Negligence is laid bare. Complacency becomes visible as the refusal of grace it always was. The soul that arrives at death without having sought God receives the natural consequence of its own freedom: the sorrow of having rejected the very One who is now standing before it.

Memento mori is meant to keep that tragedy from becoming our story. It teaches the soul to live in such a way that the meeting with Christ becomes a moment of recognition, not surprise; a moment of fulfillment, not regret. It turns the eyes toward eternity, not to escape earthly duties but to fulfill them with love. It strengthens the will to choose what matters. It anchors the heart in the hope that the God who has accompanied us in shadows will meet us in light.

For the Christian, the remembrance of death is ultimately the remembrance of destiny. We were made to see God. We were made to be transformed by His beauty. We were made to become what we behold. The moment of judgment is the moment this vocation stands fully revealed. Everything in the Christian life prepares for it. Everything in Scripture points toward it. Everything in grace anticipates it. And everything in memento mori orders the soul toward that face-to-face encounter.

All of this reveals why the saints speak of death with both sobriety and expectation. They know that the moment a person sees Christ will be the most honest moment of their existence. Every earthly love, every wound carried, every longing awakened, every sacrifice offered, every sin repented of or clung to—everything is drawn into a single exchange of gazes between the creature and the Creator. Catherine of Siena wrote that "the soul, in seeing God, sees itself in Him," and in that mirror of divine charity the truth becomes irresistible. The soul beholds what it was made for. It beholds what it has become. It beholds what grace has worked and what freedom has resisted. And in that vision the whole mystery of life becomes clear.

This meeting with Christ is not the beginning of His relationship with the soul; it is the unveiling of it. The God who judges us is the same God who pursued us from the moment of our conception. He is the One who called us out of nothingness by love, guided us through years we scarcely understood, offered mercy in moments we squandered, and remained faithful when we were faithless. He is the Shepherd who searched for us, the Father who waited for us, the Physician who offered healing, the Bridegroom who longed for union. Judgment discloses this fidelity with unfiltered clarity. The soul sees, perhaps for the first time, how often God tried to save it, how many graces were poured into its life, how many invitations were extended, how many doors were opened. Nothing of God's mercy is hidden; nothing of His patience concealed.

This is what makes the remembrance of death a school of hope as much as of wisdom. To remember death is to remember that life is not drifting toward chaos but toward consummation. It is to remember that God has not left His world or His children to fate. It is to remember that the end toward which we move is not annihilation but encounter. The eyes that will look upon us have already wept for us in Gethsemane, already bled for us on Calvary, already healed us in the sacraments, already spoken our name in prayer to the Father. The Face we will see is the human face of divine love.

And yet this same remembrance guards the soul from presumption. The gaze of Christ is gentle, but it is also holy. His mercy is wide, but it is not indulgence. His desire for communion is fierce, but it is never coercive. The truth He reveals in judgment includes everything the soul refused to surrender, every lie it chose to inhabit, every call it chose to ignore. The moment of death is the moment when freedom reaches its final clarity. The heart either opens to the love it now beholds or recoils from it. Heaven and hell are not arbitrary assignments; they are the perfected expression of the heart's trajectory. Memento mori helps the soul choose that trajectory wisely.

When Augustine says that God will "crown His own gifts," he captures the paradox of the encounter. The virtues rewarded in judgment are virtues God Himself inspired. The holiness praised is holiness God Himself worked. The perseverance upheld is perseverance sustained by grace. Judgment becomes the celebration of divine generosity, not human achievement. The soul receives the crown of life from the One who forged it. This is why the saints speak of judgment with overflowing gratitude. They see that God has arranged everything so that mercy might triumph.

Aquinas deepens this vision by explaining that the blessed, in seeing God, enter into perfect rest because they finally possess what their hearts have always sought. The divine essence becomes the soul's joy, its stability, its satisfaction. Every longing is completed, every desire fulfilled, every sorrow answered. Judgment, for the righteous, is not the prelude to happiness—it is the threshold of it. It is the moment when the human person enters into the glory for which it was created before the foundation of the world.

The remembrance of death transforms daily life precisely because it illumines this horizon. It teaches a person to live each moment with the clarity of one who knows where he is going. It turns the ordinary into preparation, the mundane into offering, the difficult into purification. It frees the soul from the tyranny of trivial desires. It awakens the conscience. It purifies the love of God. It summons the will into readiness. The one who remembers death lives with a steadiness born of truth. He does not cling to the passing world, because his eyes are fixed on the Face that will never pass away.

This is the wisdom the Church wishes to give her children. Not fear of death, but preparation for glory. Not dread of judgment, but longing for communion. Not anxiety about the future, but confidence in the God who holds the future. Memento mori becomes, in this light, the most hopeful discipline of the Christian life. It summons the soul to vigilance so that nothing in this world distracts from the world to come. It invites the heart to shed illusions now so that the vision of God may be joy, not shock. It trains the eyes to recognise the Bridegroom when He comes.

In the end, the remembrance of death is the remembrance of Christ. It keeps before the believer the truth that the story of salvation is heading toward a face-to-face encounter, the moment when love speaks with finality and the soul responds without reservation. Every prayer, every sacrament, every act of charity, every moment of repentance prepares for this hour. And every whisper of memento mori strengthens the soul to meet it with hope.

There is a reason Christian art, liturgy, and Scripture all circle back to the theme of the Bridegroom. It is the image that gathers every thread of divine revelation into a single tapestry. God did not merely rescue Israel; He espoused her. Christ did not merely redeem the Church; He betrothed Himself to her. The Cross was not merely an atonement; it was a marriage proposal stretched across wood. Judgment, seen in this light, is the moment the Bridegroom lifts the veil. It is the hour when faith becomes sight, when promise becomes possession, when covenant becomes consummation.

The remembrance of death teaches the soul to wait for this unveiling with longing rather than fear. It teaches us that life is not a random sequence of events but a courtship—God pursuing the human heart across the years, through sin and repentance, through suffering and consolation, through darkness and light, until the moment He draws near to take us home. The Fathers never tire of this image. Ephrem speaks of Christ adorning the soul as a bride prepared for the feast. Origen describes death for the righteous as the Bridegroom entering the bridal chamber. Even Augustine, so often cast as severe, says that the heart at death "runs toward the One it loves," because love has prepared it for this very hour.

This is the truth memento mori protects. When a person remembers death, he remembers that life has a destination. He remembers that his choices are not isolated but covenantal. He remembers that his soul is being shaped for a meeting that will define eternity. He remembers that the God who will judge him is the same God who has loved him since before he was formed in the womb. This remembrance pierces the fog of acedia, the paralysis of delay, the illusion of self-sufficiency. It awakens the soul to reality: the Bridegroom is coming.

And when the soul finally stands before Him, all the fragments of life are gathered into unity. Every unanswered question, every hidden suffering, every sacrifice made in secret, every longing that seemed unfulfilled—everything becomes luminous in His light. The soul sees, perhaps for the first time, how God has been weaving its story into the story of His Son. It sees how divine providence was at work in moments that once felt empty. It sees how God's mercy was shaping it even when it resisted. Judgment becomes revelation, and revelation becomes rest.

Yet the same encounter reveals the tragedy of a heart that has loved too little. Jesus warns of this not to condemn but to awaken. The parables of vigilance, the images of doors closing, the admonitions against lukewarmness—they are not threats; they are pleas. Christ does not shout because He is angry. He shouts because He loves. The urgency in His voice is the urgency of a Bridegroom who does not want the bride to miss the feast. The severity of His warnings is the severity of love confronting the danger of indifference.

For this reason, the remembrance of death is not merely a practice among monks or mystics. It is a grace meant for every Christian. It teaches us to number our days so that we may gain a heart of wisdom. It teaches us to keep our lamps filled with oil so that we may welcome the Bridegroom when He comes. It teaches us to hold lightly to the things that pass away and firmly to the One who does not. It teaches us to live every day as an act of preparation, not in fear but in fidelity.

The one who remembers death rightly becomes free—not obsessed with dying, but liberated for living. He becomes the kind of person who forgives quickly, repents promptly, loves generously, prays earnestly, and watches with expectation. He becomes a disciple who no longer drifts through life but walks toward eternity with clarity. He becomes the kind of soul who will recognise Christ when he sees Him, because he has been looking toward Him all along.

Christians throughout the ages have prayed for a "holy death," not because they feared God's wrath, but because they feared losing sight of His love. Memento mori guards against that loss. It keeps the eyes fixed on the Bridegroom, the heart anchored in hope, and the life attuned to eternity. It allows a person to approach judgment with confidence—not the confidence of presumption, but the confidence of one who has learned to trust the One who will judge.

And when the final hour comes, the soul that has lived in this remembrance will discover something marvellous: death is not the moment God stops loving us; it is the moment He loves us into fulfillment. The Face that appears is the Face that sought us, forgave us, strengthened us, and waited for us. The light that surrounds us is the light that guided us in shadows. The voice that speaks our name is the voice that spoke the world into being.

The remembrance of death, embraced through all the pages that came before, prepares us to hear that voice with joy.

14

Death as the Arrival of the Bridegroom

When Jesus speaks of the end—whether the end of the age or the end of an individual life—He does not place His disciples inside a courtroom or a throne room, though those images are certainly present in Scripture. More often, He places them inside a wedding. The surprising, even disarming claim of the Gospel is that death is not merely the moment of judgment; it is the moment the Bridegroom arrives. Everything Christ teaches about vigilance—every warning, every parable, every call to readiness—is framed by this deeper reality: God approaches His people as a lover approaching His beloved. Judgment is real, but it is wedding judgment. It is the Lover stepping into full view. It is the arrival of the One who seeks union with the soul that bears His image. The early Christians grasped this immediately. Their language, liturgy, and longing all reveal that they understood death not primarily as departure but as arrival—not as the closing of a door but as the opening of one.

This is why the New Testament so often speaks of Christ as Bridegroom. John the Baptist, when his own disciples worried that Jesus was attracting more followers, answered with a clarity that pierces every age: "He who has the bride is the bridegroom; the friend of the bridegroom rejoices greatly at the bridegroom's voice" (Jn 3:29). John casts himself not as rival but as witness, rejoicing simply because the Bridegroom has come. Jesus Himself deepens this imagery when questioned about fasting. "Can the wedding guests mourn as long as the bridegroom is with them?" (Mt 9:15). He is not offering metaphor; He is revealing identity. The Bridegroom has entered the world, and His presence begins the great preparation for the feast that will crown creation.

This wedding vision does not begin in the New Testament. It is the flowering of a covenant planted long before. The prophets repeatedly speak of God as husband and Israel as bride. Hosea declares, "I will betroth you to me forever" (Hos 2:19). Isaiah promises, "As the bridegroom rejoices over the bride, so shall your God rejoice over you" (Isa 62:5). These are not soft images. They reveal the deepest inner logic of salvation history: God's desire is union. His covenant is marital in nature. His commandments are the shape of fidelity. His mercy is the restoration of intimacy. When Jesus arrives and speaks of the kingdom in bridal terms, He is not inventing a symbol; He is fulfilling one.

This is why the parable of the ten virgins (Mt 25:1–13) stands at the centre of Christian eschatology. It is not simply a story about being ready; it is a story about desire. The wise virgins carry oil not because they fear punishment but because they long to meet the Bridegroom with lamps burning. Their readiness comes from love. The foolish virgins are not condemned for wickedness but for indifference. They want the feast but not the preparation. They want joy without vigilance. They want communion without desire. Jesus makes the contrast unmistakable: the Bridegroom comes suddenly, unexpectedly, beautifully—and only those whose love has remained awake enter into the feast. The Fathers saw in this parable the soul's final hour. Origen says that the closed door represents the separation between those whose hearts burned for Christ and those whose hearts remained cold. Gregory of Nyssa teaches that the oil symbolizes the inner likeness to God that forms through charity, and that only such likeness can recognize the Bridegroom when He comes.

The early Church lived inside this imagery. They ended their liturgies, their letters, and their prayers with the cry: "Maranatha! Come, Lord!" (1 Cor 16:22). They were not begging God to rescue them from the world; they were yearning for the Bridegroom who had promised to return. Revelation closes with the same longing: "The Spirit and the Bride say, 'Come'" (Rev 22:17). The Spirit—that is, God's own life—teaches the Bride—the Church—to desire the Bridegroom's arrival. Union is written into the fabric of creation and into the heart of every believer who listens to grace. Augustine says that all of Christian life is "a holy longing," and that the final encounter with Christ is the fulfillment of that longing. Bernard of Clairvaux writes that the soul awakens when it recognizes the voice of the Bridegroom, for "love is the language of this meeting." Ephrem the Syrian describes the departing soul as adorned for the feast, rising to meet Christ with joy: "The Bridegroom comes; blessed is the soul made ready for Him."

Yet the most astonishing dimension of Jesus' teaching is not the bridal imagery itself but the way He binds it to suddenness. The Bridegroom comes at midnight. The master returns when the servants do not expect Him. The Son of Man arrives "like a thief in the night" (Mt 24:43). These images are not meant to produce anxiety. They express the nature of love. Lovers come swiftly. Lovers do not wait until it is convenient. They arrive in the fullness of their desire. When Jesus insists that His coming will be sudden, He is not cultivating fear but revealing fervour. His swiftness is mercy. It prevents calculation, manipulation, or the illusion that discipleship can be negotiated. It ensures that the meeting between God and the soul takes place in truth.

The early saints understood this. Ignatius of Antioch, on his way to martyrdom, called death "the birth pangs" of his soul because he would at last "reach God." Origen describes the hour of death as "the Bridegroom leading the bride into the chamber of light." Ambrose, writing of his brother Satyrus, says that death is "the moment the Bridegroom kisses the soul." These images may sound too tender for modern ears, but they express the Church's deepest conviction: death is not abandonment. It is arrival. It is the Bridegroom keeping His promise.

The Christian prepared for death is not the Christian who trembles, but the Christian who yearns. Readiness is not fear sharpened to a point; it is desire strengthened through fidelity. The wise virgins represent not anxiety but longing. The faithful steward is not terrified of the master's return; he is motivated by love. The vigilant disciple is not obsessed with signs; he is attentive to the voice he knows by heart. Jesus teaches that where a person's treasure is, there the heart will be (Mt 6:21). The one who treasures Christ will desire His arrival. Judgment becomes joy when desire is rightly ordered.

This helps explain why the Church has always turned to the Song of Songs when speaking of the soul's final encounter with God. The text is no mere poetic relic; it is a prophetic unveiling of the mystery fulfilled in Christ. Origen, in his homilies on the Song, teaches that the Bridegroom's sudden appearance—leaping over mountains, knocking at the door, calling in the night—symbolizes Christ's coming both at death and at the end of the age. The Bride, half-asleep, hears His knock and hesitates. When she finally rises to answer, she discovers that He has withdrawn. Origen sees in this moment the whole tragedy of delayed desire. Christ comes swiftly because He loves swiftly; the Bride lingers because she loves with hesitation. Yet the Bridegroom's departure inflames her longing, and she begins to seek Him with renewed fervour. The Church preserved this reading because it illumines the paradox embedded in all of Jesus' parables: suddenness is mercy because suddenness purifies love.

Gregory of Nyssa develops this further. He writes that the soul at death is "awakened by the Bridegroom's kiss," a kiss that is not sensual but spiritual—the infusion of divine life into the purified heart. The kiss reveals truth, burns away illusion, and draws the soul into union. It is this revelation that transforms judgment from dread into consummation. The same divine light that exposes the soul's falsehoods also heals them. The Bridegroom comes not to shame but to sanctify, not to condemn desire but to fulfill it. This is why Gregory calls death "the beginning of true life," because it is the moment when the soul's deepest longing meets its true Beloved.

The early Christians lived this hope with disarming simplicity. They greeted one another with "Maranatha"—not as ornament but as orientation. To say "Come, Lord" was to affirm everything Christianity proclaims: that God has come, that God is coming, and that God will come again in glory. This anticipation was woven into their liturgy. The Eucharist itself concludes with an eschatological pledge: "Until He comes." Every Mass is a rehearsal for the wedding feast of the Lamb (Rev 19:9). The altar is the table at which the Bride tastes the presence of the Bridegroom. The chalice is the cup of the covenant. The Communion procession is the movement of the heart toward union. The early Church understood that sacramental life is bridal in its very structure. The Bridegroom nourishes the Bride with His own life so that she may be readied for the final wedding.

This is why martyrdom held a place of such reverence in the early Church. Martyrs did not seek death; they sought Christ. Their courage sprang not from disdain for the world but from desire for the Bridegroom. Ignatius of Antioch begged his fellow Christians not to prevent his martyrdom, saying, "My love is crucified, and there is no fire in me for anything else." To modern ears this sounds extreme, but to the early Church it was simply the logic of love. They believed Christ was truly waiting for them beyond the veil. They believed the Bridegroom would receive them with joy. Their longing was not deathward but Godward. Their hope was not escape but embrace.

This same hope permeates Paul's words to the Philippians: "My desire is to depart and be with Christ, for that is far better" (Phil 1:23). Paul is not romanticizing death; he is articulating desire. His longing is relational. The Bridegroom who appeared to him on the Damascus road now draws him toward union. That desire intensifies, not diminishes, as Paul grows in holiness. This is why he describes the Christian life as a race—not toward annihilation, but toward the prize, which is Christ Himself (Phil 3:14). The finish line of the Christian race is the Bridegroom's embrace.

Yet love demands readiness. The bridal imagery in Scripture drives this point again and again. The Bride must keep her lamp lit. The servants must be awake. The steward must remain faithful. These demands are not burdens; they are invitations to desire. Jesus does not ask for vigilance because He delights in severity but because He delights in love. He asks for readiness so that the soul will experience His arrival not as intrusion but as fulfillment. The difference between joy and terror at the moment of death is not found in external circumstances but in the state of the heart. Augustine captures this beautifully when he writes, "Love Him now, and you will not fear to see Him." The one who loves Christ in life will recognize Him in death. The one who desires Christ now will desire Him more when He comes.

This is why the Church insists that holiness is fundamentally an orientation of love. The commandments, the sacraments, the virtues, the works of mercy—all of these shape the heart to desire God. They prepare the soul for the Bridegroom's arrival. They train desire so that it does not attach to passing things. They purify the eyes so that the soul may behold God without shrinking back. Preparation is not punishment; it is purification. The Bride must be adorned for her Husband (Rev 21:2). This is the inner logic of Christian discipleship: every sacrifice, every act of charity, every moment of repentance makes the soul more transparent to love.

What begins to emerge through all of this is the truth that preparedness is not driven by fear of judgment but by longing for union. Jesus is not trying to terrify His disciples into obedience; He is trying to awaken their desire. Fear may jolt the sluggish heart, but only love sustains the vigilant one. The wise virgins stay awake because they want to see the Bridegroom. Their oil is the oil of desire—fuelled by devotion, replenished through fidelity, guarded through prayer. The foolish virgins fail not because they are ignorant but because they are indifferent. Their lamps do not go out from lack of intelligence but from lack of love. They wanted the celebration without the commitment, the joy without the journey, the feast without the Bridegroom. In this sense, Jesus' parable is not only eschatological but diagnostic. It reveals the secret orientation of every heart.

This is the same truth embedded in the parable of the wedding garment (Mt 22:1–14). The man who enters the feast without proper attire is not rejected because he violated a rule; he is rejected because he did not desire the Bridegroom enough to prepare for Him. The garment symbolizes the transformed heart—what Augustine calls "the clothing of charity" and Gregory the Great calls "the habit of holiness." The refusal to wear it is the refusal of love. This is why Augustine says that the terrifying phrase "Bind him hand and foot" is spoken not over the ignorant, but over the indifferent. The one cast out is the one who wished to enter the kingdom without being conformed to the King.

Bridal theology pulls all these teachings into a coherent whole. The relationship between God and the soul is not legal but nuptial. It is not merely commanded; it is wooed, won, and consummated. When Paul says that marriage is a "great mystery" and that it refers to "Christ and the Church" (Eph 5:32), he is unveiling the deepest structure of reality. The Bridegroom does not seek servants but lovers; He does not desire fear but fidelity; He does not demand submission but communion. Holiness, in this light, becomes something very different from rigid obligation. It becomes readiness for the feast.

This helps explain why suddenness is part of the Gospel's grammar. Jesus repeatedly insists that the day and hour of His coming are unknown. Modern readers often interpret this as a threat, but the spiritual masters saw it differently. Suddenness protects love from calculation. It guards the sincerity of devotion. It ensures that the heart remains oriented toward the Bridegroom Himself rather than toward the timing of His arrival. Origen says that the Bridegroom comes "when the soul least expects Him, so that it may learn to expect Him always." Maximus the Confessor adds that the soul which trains itself in continual remembrance of God will find His arrival not frightening but familiar. Each moment lived in grace becomes a rehearsal for the final meeting.

The Song of Songs gives poetic flesh to this truth. "I slept, but my heart was awake; the sound of my beloved knocking" (Song 5:2). The Bridegroom arrives unexpectedly, calling in the night. The Bride hesitates, rises late, and discovers He has passed by—yet His absence kindles fresh yearning. The Church preserved this scene because it reveals the drama of love's timing. Christ knocks at the door of the soul again and again; delay dulls the heart, but desire awakens it. The sudden arrival of the Bridegroom is not meant to shame the Bride but to awaken her to the greatness of the One who seeks her.

This desire is what the early Christian cry "Maranatha" carried. It was not a sigh of fear but a song of expectation. The Bride longed for the Bridegroom. The martyrs felt this so deeply that they walked into death singing hymns, not because they despised life but because they loved Christ more. Polycarp, facing execution, prayed, "I bless You that You have deemed me worthy this day and hour." He believed the Bridegroom was near. This is the logic of the saints: the one who loves Christ in life longs to meet Him in death. The one who is purified by grace now will be perfected by glory then.

Everything in the Christian life is shaped by this orientation. The commandments are not arbitrary restrictions; they are forms of fidelity. Prayer is not self-improvement; it is spousal conversation. The sacraments are not rituals; they are the kisses of the Bridegroom, given to strengthen and sanctify His Bride. Baptism is the washing that prepares her. Confirmation is the sealing of her love. The Eucharist is the foretaste of the wedding banquet. Confession is the restoration of intimacy after infidelity. Every sacrament is ordered toward the marriage feast of the Lamb.

To live memento mori in this context is to live with the Bridegroom in view. Death becomes not the feared moment of divine exposure but the awaited moment of divine embrace. The remembrance of death teaches the soul to say "Come, Lord" with increasing sincerity. It detaches us from the passing world so that we may be attached to the eternal one. It frees us from fear by anchoring us in desire. It teaches us to read the signs of our life not as random events but as invitations from the One who is preparing us for Himself.

All of this reveals something that runs deeper than emotion: preparedness is the shape that desire takes in time. The soul prepares because it loves. The Bride adorns herself because she wants to be beautiful for the Bride groom who delights in her. This is why Scripture describes holiness in bridal terms. Paul tells the Corinthians, "I betrothed you to one husband, to present you as a pure bride to Christ" (2 Cor 11:2). The language is not metaphorical window dressing; it is theological architecture. To be a Christian is to be engaged to Christ. To live as a Christian is to live in preparation for union. To die as a Christian is to enter the bridal chamber.

This truth helps us understand the severity in Jesus' warnings. The closed door, the foolish virgins, the unfaithful servant, the man without a wedding garment—these images are not threats; they are revelations of love's demands. Jesus speaks sharply because love is sharp when it confronts indifference. Lukewarmness wounds the heart of God. Indifference to grace is infidelity of the soul. When Jesus says, "I will spit you out" (Rev 3:16), He is not revealing cruelty; He is revealing the incompatibility between divine fire and human half-heartedness. The Bridegroom does not desire a bride who tolerates Him. He desires a bride who loves Him.

Desire, therefore, is the key to understanding readiness. The saints teach this repeatedly. Augustine writes, "The entire life of a good Christian is a holy longing." He explains that God delays the fullness of His presence not to frustrate the soul but to enlarge its capacity for joy. "He stretches our desire," Augustine says, "and in stretching it, He enlarges our soul that it may contain more." The longing that defines Christian life is not emptiness but expansion. God teaches us to desire what only He can satisfy. The Bridegroom withholds the wedding feast not to taunt the Bride but to transform her into someone who can receive it.

Aquinas deepens this by explaining that beatitude—the vision of God—is the perfection of desire. Human longing finds its fulfillment not in some impersonal glory but in a Person who knows the soul by name. Aquinas says that the beatific vision perfects both intellect and will: the mind is flooded with truth, and the will is flooded with love. Nothing remains unfulfilled. The final union is not the erasure of desire but its completion. Grace does not destroy longing; it crowns it. The arrival of the Bridegroom is the moment when the heart ceases to hunger because it finally possesses the One for whom it was made.

This is why the remembrance of death must never be reduced to fear. Fear may awaken, but only love sustains. Fear may shake the soul, but only love keeps the lamp burning during the long night. Memento mori, properly understood, is not the grim stare into the grave but the hopeful gaze into the wedding feast. It is the Bride watching for the Bridegroom. It is the soul rehearsing the moment it will hear His voice. It is the Christian living every ordinary day in the light of an extraordinary promise: "I go to prepare a place for you... I will come again and take you to Myself" (Jn 14:2–3).

The suddenness of His coming becomes sweet rather than frightening when viewed through this lens. Lovers do not want a scheduled arrival; they want a surprise filled with eagerness. The unknown hour protects the intimacy of the encounter. It ensures that the heart is shaped by fidelity rather than calculation. Suddenness preserves sincerity. Chrysostom makes this point when he says that the uncertainty of the hour "keeps the soul in a state of loving attention." He does not interpret Christ's teaching as a threat but as a means of cultivating desire. When the hour is unknown, every hour becomes an opportunity to love.

This is why the saints look at death differently from the world. For those far from God, death is the end of everything they have loved. For those near to God, death is the beginning of everything they have longed for. The difference lies not in circumstance but in desire. The Bride who has fallen in love with the Bridegroom anticipates His coming even in darkness. She listens for His footsteps. She waits for His voice. She prepares her heart. She purifies her love. She adorns her soul with virtue. She remains faithful not out of grim duty but out of joyful expectation.

The early Christians bore witness to this with remarkable clarity. Many inscriptions in the Roman catacombs speak not of loss but of hope. They use wedding language. They speak of "entering the peace," of "being called home," of "meeting the Lord." Death was not an interruption but a homecoming. Tertullian even says that the Christian soul "goes to Christ as the bride goes to the bridegroom." This was not sentimental rhetoric; it was the worldview of those who believed that mortality had been transfigured by resurrection. Christ had entered death and turned it into a doorway. The one who remembers death rightly lives as someone awaiting the knock on that door.

This is the horizon that memento mori restores. When death is remembered as the Bridegroom's arrival, life is immediately reoriented. Time ceases to be something we endure or squander; it becomes the arena where fidelity is forged. Moments once dismissed as trivial become opportunities for love. Sacrifices once avoided become offerings made in secret. Temptations once indulged become occasions for choosing the One who is coming. The remembrance of death trains the soul to value each day not because it is precarious but because it is precious. Each hour is another step toward the bridal chamber.

This is why Christ insists that His disciples learn to watch. Watchfulness is not paranoia; it is love's attentiveness. The watchful heart is the heart that has discovered what matters. It does not drift. It does not yawn its way through life. It does not postpone conversion. It does not grow numb to grace. It lives awake. It lives desiring. It lives leaning toward the horizon. In the ancient Church, the practice of keeping vigil—especially the Easter Vigil—was a direct embodiment of this longing. The Bride watched for the Bridegroom in the night. The Church stood in darkness with lamps lit, waiting for the cry, "The Lord is risen!" Every vigil taught the soul to interpret its life in eschatological terms—to prepare as one who knows the Bridegroom's arrival will be sudden and glorious.

This desire for the Bridegroom also sheds light on why holiness often feels costly. Love always costs something. The Bride who prepares for the wedding does so with joy, but also with discipline. She adorns herself, purifies her heart, removes what does not belong, chooses what magnifies her beauty. Holiness is this bridal work in the soul. When the Christian prays, fasts, forgives, repents, resists sin, or embraces charity, he is adorning the soul with the garments of love. This is why Revelation speaks of the wedding garment as "the righteous deeds of the saints" (Rev 19:8). These deeds are not accomplishments to boast of; they are the embroidery of love upon the fabric of the soul. They prepare us to meet Him.

The Fathers emphasize this. Ephrem says that each virtuous act "weaves a thread of light" into the garment the soul will wear before the Bridegroom. Basil teaches that holiness consists in "a readiness to meet Christ without shame," which means allowing grace to purify desire so that we long for Him above all things. Maximus writes that the soul's journey is the gradual transformation of eros—natural human longing—into agapē, divinely infused love. When eros is purified, he says, "the soul runs swiftly to the Bridegroom," no longer stumbling under the weight of divided affections. This is why asceticism, properly understood, is not punishment but preparation—training the heart to desire rightly.

Viewed in this light, the Christian who lives in haste toward sin is the one who forgets the Bridegroom. The one who delays repentance is the one who has allowed desire to grow faint. The one who forgets death is the one who forgets the wedding. Memento mori is not intended to frighten but to focus, not to depress but to direct. It is a discipline that burns away illusions. It reminds the soul that it is being prepared for Someone. It reminds the soul that nothing in this world can satisfy what it was made to contain. It reminds the soul that the Bridegroom is not far off but drawing near.

DEATH AS THE ARRIVAL OF THE BRIDEGROOM

This nearness is the secret pulse of all Christian spirituality. Christ is not a distant figure waiting at the end of history; He is the One who comes now—sacramentally, spiritually, silently—and who will come again in glory. Each moment of grace is a knock at the door. Each movement of conscience is a whisper of His approach. Each longing for holiness is the stirring of His presence. Bernard of Clairvaux describes this beautifully when he says that Christ comes to the soul "in many visits," preparing it for the final coming when He will take it wholly to Himself. These visitations are gentle rehearsals for the soul's death—moments when the Bridegroom draws near to deepen desire, awaken love, and heal what is wounded.

But the fullness of His arrival—whether at the end of the world or at the end of a single human life—will surpass every foretaste. Paul tells the Thessalonians that when Christ comes, the faithful will be "caught up… to meet the Lord in the air" (1 Thess 4:17). The Greek word he uses for "meet" (apantēsis) refers to the custom of citizens going out to greet a king or bridegroom and escorting him the rest of the way. The point is not escape from earth but welcome of the One who comes to glorify it. Death, in this view, becomes the soul's apantēsis—its joyful rush to meet the Bridegroom who comes to fulfill His covenant.

This is why suddenness cannot frighten the soul that loves Christ. Suddenness becomes sweetness. It becomes the thrill of the beloved appearing at last. It becomes the final breath before the embrace. For the saint, the unknown hour is not a threat but a promise. It means the Bridegroom may come when the heart is most ready to love Him. It means He may arrive in a moment soaked with fidelity. It means the entire mystery of salvation—the calling, the cleansing, the forgiving, the sanctifying—may reach its fulfillment in a single luminous encounter.

In the end, the arrival of the Bridegroom is the moment for which the entire Christian life has been preparing us, even when we did not know it. Every confession cleansed a stain from the garment we would one day wear before Him. Every act of charity embroidered another thread of light upon it. Every temptation resisted strengthened the heart to love Him more. Every prayer, whispered in weakness or offered in strength, trained the ears to recognize His voice. Nothing given to God in this life—no sacrifice, no hidden act of fidelity, no humble obedience—is wasted. All of it becomes part of the soul's beauty when the Bridegroom arrives.

And when He comes, there will be no confusion about what is happening. The soul will know Him. Even the one who has never seen Him with bodily eyes will recognize Him instantly, for grace has been engraving His likeness upon the heart throughout a lifetime. Augustine says that the soul will "run toward the One it loves," not because of compulsion, but because love is the most natural motion of a heart awakened by grace. This running is the fulfillment of every longing, every ache, every restless desire that haunted the human spirit. Our entire earthly pilgrimage has been a school of desire, teaching us to hunger for the One who alone can satisfy.

Yet as soon as the Bridegroom appears, something else becomes clear: the soul must be able to endure the light of His love. The saints insist that the brightness of His presence is joy to the pure but agony to the impure—not because Christ changes, but because the soul must be prepared to receive Him. This is why vigilance matters. This is why desire must be purified. This is why holiness is not optional ornamentation but the very capacity to see and embrace God. The Bride must be adorned. The heart must be readied. Love must be strong enough to endure glory.

This is where the truth of divine mercy becomes astonishing. God does not simply wait for us at the end; He prepares us for the end. He shapes us through Scripture, Eucharist, repentance, suffering, friendships, vocations, and hidden graces we barely perceive. He loves us into readiness. He purifies desire, prunes attachments, heals wounds, and enlarges the soul's ability to love. Bernard of Clairvaux says that God "wounds in order to heal" and "embraces in order to perfect." Even our trials become part of the bridal preparation. They remove what cannot enter the feast so that the soul may enter unhindered.

Still, when the Bridegroom arrives, most souls will not be fully prepared for the intensity of His love. Scripture and tradition do not hide this. The vision of God is overwhelming. The light of Christ reveals everything, and whatever in the soul has not yet been healed will recoil. But Christ does not abandon the beloved in this moment. The Bridegroom completes the preparation that life began. The final cleansing, the last healing, the purification of love that could not be finished on earth—all of this takes place in His presence. Purgatory is not the rejection of the Bride. It is the final act of divine tenderness making her ready for union.

This is why the remembrance of death is inseparable from hope. Death is not the moment God begins to love us; it is the moment His love reaches fullness. It is the moment the Bridegroom steps forward, the veil is lifted, and the covenant is consummated. It is the moment desire ceases to ache and begins to possess. It is the moment faith gives way to sight, promise to fulfillment, longing to embrace. The Christian who lives in memento mori walks toward this hour not with dread, but with devotion. He does not fear the arrival of the Bridegroom because he has learned to love Him already.

Everything in the Gospel, everything in the sacraments, everything in the life of prayer prepares the soul for this meeting. The remembrance of death teaches us to live each day as an act of preparation—not anxious, but attentive; not fearful, but faithful; not indifferent, but in love. The Bridegroom will come. He has promised to come. And when He does, the soul that has longed for Him will discover that its entire existence has been ordered toward this single, radiant encounter.

The Bridegroom arrives. The Bride rises. The wedding feast begins.

15

Purgatory: The Last Mercy Before the Wedding Feast

Death is not the end of God's work in the soul. Scripture describes judgment with images of revelation and fire, but neither of these is merely punitive. Each reflects the love of a God who refuses to abandon His creatures to the unfinished state in which He finds them. From the opening pages of the Bible to the final visions of the Apocalypse, the God of Israel reveals Himself as the One who purifies His people with the fire of His holiness, not to destroy but to render them capable of communion. This is why the Fathers spoke of death not simply as a boundary but as a threshold where the human person meets a love too immense to leave anything unhealed. Purgatory emerges within this vision—not as a medieval invention or a morbid speculation, but as the final movement of divine mercy preparing the soul for the wedding feast of the Lamb.

The Christian imagination has sometimes reduced purgatory to a holding cell—an unfortunate delay on the way to heaven. Yet the tradition presents it with far greater depth. The Letter to the Hebrews describes God as "a consuming fire" (Heb 12:29), a phrase echoing Deuteronomy's declaration that "the Lord your God is a consuming fire, a jealous God" (Deut 4:24). The fire here is not arbitrary wrath. It is the radiance of divine holiness itself, the burning of love that tolerates no rivals and purifies every distortion that prevents communion. Augustine understood this fire not as something external to God, but as the very presence of God received by a soul that is not yet fully healed. "If they have built upon Christ gold, silver, precious stones, they will receive a reward; but if wood, hay, stubble, they shall be saved, yet as through fire" (cf. *Enchiridion* 69). He interprets Paul's teaching in 1 Corinthians 3:10–15 as a revelation of this mystery: the soul is saved, but the encounter with divine truth burns away all that is false, all that is misaligned with love.

The apostle does not speak here of punishment in the retributive sense. He speaks of *loss*—the painful unveiling of what could have been a greater likeness to Christ. This is why the Church calls purgatory a purification, not a penalty. The soul desires God fully at the moment of death, because grace has already awakened this desire. Yet the soul also sees, often for the first time with perfect clarity, how deeply it needs healing. The encounter with the Holy One discloses what still remains untransformed, not to shame the soul but to free it from every shadow.

Athanasius hints at this dynamic when he writes that Christ "became man that we might become God" (*De Incarnatione* 54). If theosis—the transformation of the human person by divine life—is the goal of salvation, then purgatory is simply the completion of this process for those who die in grace but not yet perfected in love. The Eastern Fathers often speak of this in terms of light rather than fire. Gregory of Nyssa, in his *Life of Moses*, describes the soul's ascent into God as a movement into ever-deepening light that exposes and dissolves all impurities. For him, the soul meets God's glory as both sweetness and purification. "The divine is by nature pure," he says, "and admits no communion with what is impure." The removal of impurity is therefore not a punishment but a condition for joy.

In the West, this understanding parallels Aquinas' teaching that purgatorial cleansing arises from the soul's own burning desire for God. "The souls in purgatory suffer from the delay of the vision of God," he explains, "and this delay is itself the greatest pain" (*ST* Suppl. q. 71, a. 2). It is not God inflicting torment; it is the soul awakening fully to its destiny and feeling the ache of separation from the One it loves above all things. This longing is purifying because love itself consumes what does not belong to love. For Aquinas, the fire of purgatory is metaphorical in its material description but literal in its effect: it is the intensity of divine charity acting upon a soul now perfectly open to truth.

Such a vision aligns deeply with the biblical portrayal of God's dealings with His people. When the prophet Malachi announces the coming of the Lord, he asks, "Who can endure the day of his coming? For he is like a refiner's fire and like fuller's soap" (Mal 3:2). The imagery is unmistakable: God purifies as a goldsmith purifies precious metal—by applying heat that separates the pure from the impure. The goal is not destruction but restoration, the recovery of what the metal was always meant to be. Isaiah declares something similar when he speaks of God refining His people "in the furnace of affliction" (Isa 48:10). Neither prophet imagines a God who delights in suffering; both reveal a God who uses fire only for the sake of beauty.

This is why purgatory belongs naturally within the message of memento mori. To remember one's death is not merely to brace oneself for judgment; it is to prepare consciously for healing. The remembrance of death awakens the heart to the unfinished work within us, the patterns of sin that remain stubborn, the affections that resist surrender, the attachments that obscure love. When Christians meditate on the last things, they do not do so to paralyse themselves with fear. They do so to place themselves beneath the radiance of God's truth now, so that the purifying work that awaits them may begin already in this life.

The Psalms capture this longing with surprising tenderness. "Search me, O God, and know my heart; try me and know my thoughts" (Ps 139:23). The psalmist invites divine scrutiny not as a terror but as a mercy. He desires the fire because the fire reveals and sets free. In another place he prays, "You have tested us, O God; you have tried us as silver is tried" (Ps 66:10). These are not the prayers of a man afraid of God. They are the prayers of a man who knows that God's testing is God's love in action. Jerome once remarked that the Christian "fears nothing but sin" because sin alone disfigures the soul's capacity for God. Purgatory, then, is simply the final liberation from sin's residue.

Yet there is another dimension to this mystery: purgatory is not simply the fire of truth; it is the fire of love. Catherine of Genoa, whose *Treatise on Purgatory* remains one of the most luminous accounts in Christian history, insists that the souls undergoing purification experience "a joy so extreme that no tongue can describe it," even as they endure a pain "like that of hell, except that guilt is absent." The paradox arises because love itself is both delight and purification. "The souls in purgatory," she writes, "love God so greatly and are drawn to Him with such force that they are in a kind of violent joy." For Catherine, purgatory is not God's anger but God's embrace—a consuming closeness that removes every obstacle to perfect union.

This is why the Church speaks of purgatory as a "final purification" (*CCC* 1031). It completes the sanctification begun in baptism, nourished in the Eucharist, deepened through confession, shaped by charity, and refined by suffering. In this sense, purgatory is not a divine exception but a divine consistency. God finishes what He starts. The One who began a good work in us will bring it to completion (Phil 1:6), and that completion includes the removal of all that clings to sin.

Nothing unclean shall enter the heavenly Jerusalem (Rev 21:27), not because God is severe, but because heaven is communion with the All-Holy One.

Purgatory thus reveals something essential about God's fidelity. He refuses to let His children settle for mediocrity in love. He refuses to allow the distortions of sin to remain forever embedded in the soul. He is a Father who insists on finishing the work of our transformation. Memento mori, when embraced faithfully, trains the heart to welcome this final mercy. It frees us from clinging to the illusions that will one day be burned away anyway. It teaches us to cooperate now with the purifying grace that will perfect us then.

The Fathers often insisted that the soul's purification after death is not fundamentally different from the purification God begins in this life. What changes is the soul's clarity. In this world, our minds and hearts are clouded by distraction, self-deception, and the inertia of habit. Sin rarely appears to us in its true form; we justify, rationalize, minimize, and hide. At death, these veils fall. Augustine teaches that in the next life "every man's conscience shall be clearly revealed to himself" (*City of God* 20.14). He means that the soul finally sees what God has always seen. This revelation is graced, not grim. The soul is not condemned for beholding the truth; it is liberated by it.

Gregory the Great describes this moment with pastoral realism. In his *Dialogues* (Book 4), he speaks of souls who "do not enter the heavenly kingdom unless they are first cleansed by the purifying fire." For Gregory, this is not a speculative idea but a pastoral necessity. He knows that even the faithful depart this life with a mixture of virtue and frailty. He recognizes that charity may be alive but imperfect, that humility may be present but undeveloped, that forgiveness may have been chosen but not yet made complete. Gregory's insight illuminates the logic of purgatory: the God who calls us to perfect love does not abandon us when we fall short; He completes what we could not finish.

This is why the early Christians prayed for the dead. Far from imagining purgatory as a place of divine abandonment, the ancient Church understood it as a stage of God's ongoing care. Inscriptions in the catacombs bear witness to this conviction. Families offered Eucharistic memorials for their loved ones, confident that their prayers assisted the deceased in the final stages of purification. The Second Book of Maccabees, written long before Christ's coming yet embraced by the Church as inspired Scripture, records how Judas Maccabeus took up a collection "to provide for a sin offering" for the dead, "because he took thought of the resurrection" and believed it was "a holy and pious thought to pray for the dead" (2 Macc 12:43–46). This is not a peripheral detail in Israel's faith; it is a window into the communal heart of salvation. God perfects us, yet He calls His people to participate in one another's sanctification.

Aquinas expands this logic by insisting that charity binds the living and the dead in a mystical communion. "The suffrages of the living are available to the dead," he writes, "because all the faithful are one body" (*ST* Suppl. q. 71, a. 1). In other words, the Body of Christ does not dissolve at death. Love endures. Intercession continues. The prayers, sacrifices, and Masses offered by the faithful on earth become channels through which God accelerates the purification of those who have gone before us. The purifying fire is God's work, but the Body participates in that work through the communion of saints. Purgatory is therefore not merely a doctrine about individuals; it is a doctrine about the Church.

This ecclesial dimension carries with it a profound consolation: no one who dies in friendship with God journeys toward the wedding feast alone. Even in purification, they are surrounded by the love of the Body, upheld by the prayers of the saints, strengthened by the Eucharistic offerings of the Church on earth. Catherine of Genoa marvels at this in her treatise: "The souls in purgatory are so united with the will of God that they accept all that He wills, and they are more consoled by our prayers than by any other earthly good." Their consolation arises not because they suffer in loneliness, but because they suffer in love. They know they are being prepared for a joy beyond imagination, and they know that the Church is helping to carry them toward it.

Yet the purification itself is real. Scripture does not veil this truth. Paul declares that "each man's work will become manifest, for the Day will disclose it, because it will be revealed with fire" (1 Cor 3:13). He adds that some will "suffer loss," though they themselves "will be saved, but only as through fire" (v. 15). The apostle distinguishes between the person and the work. The believer is saved because Christ is the foundation. The believer's works are tested because love demands integrity. This distinction is crucial. It shows that purgatory is not a second chance for the damned; it is the refinement of the saved. The one who has built with straw needs purification; the one who has built with gold receives reward. The fire reveals the difference.

The Fathers extend Paul's image with vivid consequences. Origen, though speculative in many places, nevertheless captures a truth the Church would later clarify: "God is a consuming fire, and the fire that purifies is the same fire that punishes; it is only the disposition of the soul that determines how the fire is received" (*Homilies on Jeremiah* 20.3). Origen's language must be read carefully, yet it contains an essential insight: the divine presence is experienced according to the soul's condition. For the wicked, the encounter is agony because they have rejected love. For the righteous, the encounter is purification because they desire love but are not yet perfected in it. The same fire burns differently depending on what it touches.

This theological insight reveals why memento mori is indispensable. If God will purify every soul that dies in grace, then the remembrance of death invites us to cooperate with that purification now. The monks understood this with striking clarity. The remembrance of death was not merely a spur toward repentance but a training in desire. It taught them to love the light that would one day expose their hearts completely. It taught them to welcome now the cleansing that would free them then. Basil the Great insisted that "the remembrance of death is the daily death of the passions" (*Homily on Psalm 33*). In other words, what purgatory completes, memento mori begins. The one prepares the soul to receive the other.

The relationship between purgatory and memento mori becomes even clearer when we contemplate Christ's own death. In the Paschal Mystery, death becomes the place where divine love transfigures everything it touches. Christ enters death not as a captive but as a conqueror, descending into its depth in order to flood it with light. Hebrews declares that He shared our flesh and blood so that "through death he might destroy him who has the power of death" and "deliver all those who through fear of death were subject to lifelong bondage" (Heb 2:14–15). If death has been conquered, then purgatory cannot be a lesser death. It must be the triumph of the risen Christ applied to the soul in its final stages of healing. It is the victory of Easter completing its work in us.

This is why, in the tradition, purgatory is always oriented toward joy. It is a place—better, a state—of upward movement. The soul advances toward God with unhindered longing because every fibre of its being desires Him. The purification is painful only because the soul wishes to be fully God's but still carries the remnants of self-love, pride, and attachment. Gregory of Nyssa describes this beautifully when he speaks of the soul "stretching forward" into God, leaving behind whatever impedes its ascent. "The soul becomes itself by approaching Him who is," he writes (*Homilies on the Song of Songs*). This approach is purgation and illumination at once.

The holiness that awaits us is not merely moral improvement; it is communion with a God whose beauty our language cannot describe. The mystics strain for metaphors—the fire, the furnace, the light, the kiss of the Bridegroom—because no single image captures the reality. What all these metaphors share is motion: God draws the soul upward, inward, onward. Purgatory is the final pull of this divine magnetism, the irresistible attraction of perfect love. It is mercy insisting on completion.

The soul that enters this final purification is therefore not a soul in terror but a soul in truth. It has crossed the threshold of death with faith intact and love alive, even if that love is still imperfect. It sees now, with unclouded clarity, the God for whom it was made. That vision does not wait for the end of purgation; rather, as Aquinas argues, the blessed dead "see God in a certain manner" even while they are not yet admitted to the fullness of the beatific vision (*ST* Suppl. q. 70, a. 3). They see Him enough to desire Him without reserve. They know Him enough to surrender to His purifying work. They love Him enough to welcome the burning that brings them home.

This is why the saints speak of purgatory with such surprising joy. Catherine of Genoa's testimony remains unparalleled in spiritual literature. She insists that if there were a more painful purgation available, the souls would choose it rather than enter heaven with the slightest stain remaining. "They cannot turn toward themselves," she writes, "because they are entirely occupied solely by the operation of God's love" (*Treatise on Purgatory*). Their suffering is not despair but desire. It is the ache of a soul being stretched to contain the immensity of divine love. It is the painful joy of a heart learning how to breathe the air of heaven.

In this way, purgatory reveals the paradox at the centre of Christian hope. God demands perfection, not because He is severe, but because He is generous. He will not allow us to dwell eternally in anything less than perfect love. Augustine makes this point with luminous simplicity: "He who made you without you will not justify you without you" (*Sermon 169*). The soul must cooperate, even after death, with the grace that shapes it into Christ's likeness. Purgatory is that cooperation brought to completion. It is love consenting fully to be loved.

Yet this raises a striking implication: if purgatory is the final stage of sanctification, then the remembrance of death is its beginning. Memento mori is not morbid introspection. It is a rehearsal for the clarity that awaits us. It trains us to see our sins as God sees them, to desire healing rather than delay, to welcome the refining fire now rather than be surprised by it later. It awakens in us a holy impatience to be made whole.

The desert monks grasped this instinctively. When Abba Isaac declared that "the remembrance of death is the foundation of all virtues," he was not courting despair but inviting realism. The monk who remembers his death prays more honestly. He forgives more readily. He strips away the excess that clutters the heart. He offers his sins to God with fewer excuses and more humility. In short, he cooperates with the purification that purgatory will one day complete. He welcomes the divine fire in its gentlest form—the fire of repentance, of tears, of conversion—rather than wait for the more intense healing that may be required after death.

This continuity between earthly repentance and final purification has profound consequences. It means that purgatory is not an interruption in the spiritual life but its culmination. It is not a detour but a destination along the way to perfect love. The soul that enters purgatory is a soul that has chosen God, that has left sin behind in principle if not yet in totality, that has died in grace but has not yet grown into the full stature of Christ. Purgatory finalizes the choice already made. It completes the journey begun at baptism.

It consummates the longing awakened by grace and strengthened through trial.

Here we see the deep coherence of the economy of salvation. God's justice and His mercy are not opposed. His mercy is not indulgence; His justice is not cruelty. Both are expressions of His unwavering commitment to transform us into the image of His Son. If judgment reveals truth, purgatory heals the wounds that truth illuminates. If Christ conquers death, purgatory frees us from everything within us that still belongs to death. If heaven is communion with the living God, purgatory removes the obstacles that prevent perfect communion. In every respect, purgatory is mercy in motion.

This understanding dissolves the caricature of purgatory as a cosmic waiting room or as a punitive torture chamber. The Church has never taught such images, though they have lingered in popular imagination. The true doctrine is far more beautiful and far more demanding. It insists that heaven is a realm of perfect love and that perfect love cannot coexist with the residue of selfishness, pride, bitterness, or disordered attachment. It insists that God loves us too much to leave us half-healed. It insists that the soul must be radiant to behold the radiance of God.

Aquinas articulates this with unparalleled clarity when he writes that "nothing unclean can enter the kingdom of God" (*ST* Suppl. q. 86, a. 3). He does not mean that God rejects the imperfect; he means that God refuses to stop loving us halfway. He will finish what He started. He will burn away every trace of sin, not because He delights in our pain but because He delights in our holiness. Purgatory is the last act of divine fidelity.

The medieval theologians expressed this through the imagery of gold being purified. Gold is precious precisely because it can withstand fire; indeed, it becomes more beautiful because of the fire. So too the soul in purgatory. The fire does not destroy; it reveals. It does not consume; it refines. It does not punish; it perfects. This is why the saints were unafraid of purgatory. They viewed it not as a threat but as a promise. It was the guarantee that God would finish what He had begun.

In this light, memento mori becomes not merely a spiritual discipline but a participation in God's own work. When we remember our death, we anticipate the cleansing that awaits us. We learn to surrender the sins that cling so closely. We practice humility, detachment, forgiveness, patience. We allow the Spirit to purify us through trials, disappointments, and struggles. We carry our crosses not as burdens but as instruments of healing. We embrace suffering not as defeat but as purification. This is purgatory begun on earth.

What happens at death is, therefore, not foreign to what happens in life. It is the same God, the same love, the same fire, the same call to holiness. The difference is that in death the work becomes swift, clear, and irresistible. We no longer resist grace. We no longer cling to illusions. We no longer negotiate with our sins. We are seized by love and drawn toward its fullness.

The Church's teaching on purgatory, rightly understood, restores depth to the Christian vision of death. It reminds us that death is not merely the end of earthly life; it is the threshold into divine life. It is the moment when God's eternal purpose becomes visible, when His love becomes our environment, when His holiness becomes the measure of our being. Yet if that holiness is the measure, then love must transform us completely. Purgatory is the assurance that such transformation will not remain unfinished. It is the promise that God will make us saints. Not admirers of holiness. Not spectators. Saints.

This is why the saints themselves welcomed the thought of purgatory. They did not imagine it as a prison but as a forge. They wanted nothing more than to be made like Christ, and they knew that this likeness could be painful. Teresa of Ávila once admitted that she would gladly suffer "a thousand deaths" if that suffering would increase her love for God by the smallest degree. This is the heart that purgatory perfects—a heart so inflamed with love that the very fire of God is joy.

Dante, though a poet rather than a theologian, captures this with unforgettable precision in the *Purgatorio*. As the souls ascend the mountain of purification, he observes that their suffering is marked by hope, not despair. Their pain is oriented upward. Their tears are luminous. Their longing is stronger than their agony. The poet is not inventing doctrine; he is dramatizing what the Church teaches: purgatory is ordered toward heaven, and every movement within it is a movement of love.

This perspective dismantles the modern aversion to any talk of purgation. Our culture recoils from the idea of discomfort. We equate love with ease. We imagine that God's mercy must be gentle in the sense of being painless. Yet Scripture does not share this assumption. "The Lord disciplines him whom he loves," says Hebrews, "and chastises every son whom he receives" (Heb 12:6). Discipline is not cruelty. Chastisement is not rejection. Both are expressions of a Father's devotion to His children. God's goal is not our comfort but our transformation. His mercy refuses to settle for anything less than our holiness.

If this is true in life, it must be true in death. The God who purifies us through trials, who prunes us so that we bear more fruit, who refines us like gold in the furnace, will not cease this work at the moment we die. Death does not cancel sanctification; it consummates it. The purification that begins in baptism, that deepens through confession, that is nourished in the Eucharist, that is strengthened through suffering—this purification reaches its fullness in purgatory. It is the final ascent of the soul into the likeness of Christ.

Seen in this light, memento mori becomes not merely practical wisdom but theological realism. To remember our death is to remember our destiny. It is to keep before our eyes the truth that we were made for God and that nothing less will satisfy us. It is to recognize that every sin is a distortion of the self, a chain around the soul, a refusal of love. It is to live with the knowledge that the God who calls us to holiness will not stop calling until holiness is complete. The remembrance of death is thus the remembrance of sanctification. It is the anticipation of purification. It is purgatory begun in the present moment.

This insight is crucial because it preserves the continuity between mortal life and eternal life. The spiritual habits we cultivate now shape the way we enter death. The virtues we practice now dispose our souls to receive God's cleansing fire with joy rather than fear. The repentance we undertake now lessens the purification needed later. The detachment we embrace now frees us from the painful release of attachments after death. The love we choose now becomes the measure of the love we can receive when we behold God face to face.

The saints understood this intimately. They did not approach death as an abrupt rupture but as the culmination of a journey. They viewed life as a training in desire, a preparation for the vision of God. They believed that holiness is not an instant transformation but a gradual surrender. "The soul is shaped by what it loves," wrote Augustine (*Confessions* 13.9), and purgatory is simply the final shaping of the soul that loves God imperfectly but sincerely. Life teaches us how to love rightly; death completes what life begins.

This perspective casts a new light on the urgency of conversion. If purgatory is the final mercy, then every moment of life is an opportunity to begin that mercy here and now. Every confession is a foretaste of purgation. Every act of forgiveness is a release from bondage. Every sacrifice is a loosening of the grip of self. Every trial accepted in faith is a burning away of pride. Every moment of prayer is a descent of divine fire into the heart. In this sense, purgatory is not a remote doctrine but a present reality. It is the shape of the Christian life.

And because it is the shape of the Christian life, it is also the shape of Christian hope. We do not hope in a God who overlooks our sins; we hope in a God who heals them. We do not hope in a God who tolerates our mediocrity; we hope in a God who transforms it. We do not hope in a God who merely admits us into heaven; we hope in a God who makes us capable of delighting in heaven. Purgatory is the assurance that this hope will be fulfilled.

Thus, memento mori is not simply the remembrance of our death; it is the remembrance of our destiny. It is the remembrance that we are being prepared for glory. It is the remembrance that holiness is not an optional decoration but the very condition of beatitude. It is the remembrance that the God who created us in His image will not rest until His likeness is restored in us completely.

When we remember our death, therefore, we remember our purification. When we remember our purification, we remember the One who purifies. And when we remember the One who purifies, we remember that every moment of life is an invitation to let His fire burn a little brighter within us.

The final mercy of purgatory also reveals something essential about the nature of divine judgment. Judgment, in Scripture, is never portrayed as God standing at a distance tallying faults. Judgment is the moment when the truth of God meets the truth of the human person. It is the unveiling of relationship. It is encounter. To be judged by God is to be seen by Love. That vision is what purifies. That encounter is what transforms.

This is why the Fathers insist that divine judgment is not a contradiction to divine love but its expression. Isaac the Syrian makes this point with disarming simplicity: "We know nothing of God's justice; only His mercy" (*Ascetical Homilies*, Homily 51). Isaac does not deny judgment; he reframes it. He sees that God judges by loving, and that God loves by revealing. This revelation is the fire. This love is the purification. What we call purgatory is simply love insisting on being itself.

The love that purifies is the same love that forgives. It is the love that sent Christ to the cross. It is the love that breathed the Spirit into the Church. It is the love that descended into death to break its chains. It is the love that raised Christ from the grave. When this love confronts a soul still tainted by pride, or wounded by sin, or entangled in disordered desires, it cannot help but burn. Yet the burning is not the destruction of the soul but the destruction of everything within the soul that is not love.

This is why purgatory is the last mercy before the wedding feast. The bridal imagery that runs through Scripture—from Hosea to the Song of Songs, from John the Baptist's proclamation of Christ as Bridegroom to Paul's teaching in Ephesians 5, from the parable of the Ten Virgins to the vision of the New Jerusalem—finds its consummation here. The Bride must be made ready. The Groom desires nothing less than a spotless bride, radiant with holiness, adorned with charity, free from every stain of sin. Revelation declares this explicitly: the Bride "was granted to be clothed with fine linen, bright and pure," and "the fine linen is the righteous deeds of the saints" (Rev 19:8). Yet those deeds are not ours alone; they are God's work in us. Purgatory perfects what grace has begun, clothing the soul in the very beauty it longs to offer the Bridegroom.

This bridal preparation is not a peripheral theme; it is the heart of salvation. Christ came to unite humanity to Himself in a covenant of love. The cross is the moment when the Bridegroom gives Himself completely. The resurrection is the moment when He triumphs for His Bride. The sacraments are the channels through which

He continues to sanctify her. Purgatory is the final stage of that sanctification, the last cleansing before the eternal union of heaven. Aquinas captures this when he writes that the soul's purification is ordered toward "the full participation in the divine good" (*ST* Suppl. q. 71, a. 1). Participation means communion. Communion means union. Union means the wedding feast of the Lamb.

The realization that purgatory prepares us for union with God helps correct a subtle but widespread misconception: the idea that purgatory is primarily about punishment. It is not. Punishment is a deficient word for what purgatory accomplishes. Even when the imagery of fire is used, it is never the fire of wrath but the fire of holiness. It is the fire Isaiah experienced when the seraph touched his lips with a burning coal (Isaiah 6:6–7), not to punish but to purify, not to condemn but to commission. The coal is taken from the altar of sacrifice—the place where God meets His people in mercy. In that temple vision we see the whole logic of purgatory: a God who purifies so that we may stand before Him without shame and serve Him in everlasting joy.

If purgatory is the coal from the altar, then memento mori is the vision of the temple. It is the conscious act of placing ourselves before God even now, of seeing our sins as they truly are, of acknowledging that we are not yet ready for the fullness of His glory. This is not despair; it is hope in practice. It is the hope that longs for holiness, the hope that seeks purification, the hope that says with the psalmist, "Create in me a clean heart, O God, and renew a right spirit within me" (Ps 51:10). When we remember our death, we remember that this plea will be answered fully and finally.

In this sense, purgatory is not an interruption in our relationship with God but its fulfillment. It is the final act of God's tenderness toward the soul. It is the moment when He removes the last obstacles to intimacy. It is the moment when He prepares us for the direct vision of His face. Just as a bride adorns herself before meeting her groom, the soul in purgatory is adorned by God Himself. "He loved the Church and gave Himself up for her," writes Paul, "that He might sanctify her, having cleansed her by the washing of water with the word… so that she might be holy and without blemish" (Eph 5:25–27). Purgatory is the consummation of this cleansing, the final washing, the last touch of love before the wedding.

This is where the doctrine becomes not only consoling but thrilling. Purgatory means that our destiny is nothing less than **face-to-face communion with God**. It means that our wounds will not follow us into eternity. It means that the habits of sin that plagued us in this life will be burned away forever. It means that every tear of repentance shed in this life prepares the soul to receive the fire of purification with joy. It means that holiness is not beyond us but promised to us. It means that the God who began a good work in us will bring it to completion (Phil 1:6).

Thus, the remembrance of death is ultimately the remembrance of glory. It is the anticipation of the transformation that awaits us. It is the quiet certainty that sin will not have the last word. It is the conviction that God will finish what He started, no matter how incomplete our efforts may seem. It is the trust that the fire that awaits us is the fire of love.

The deepest mystery of purgatory, then, is not its fire but its nearness to heaven. The soul undergoing purification is already held within the gravity of glory. It is already oriented toward God with a longing unencumbered by earthly distraction. It is already surrendered to love more completely than it ever was in life. The soul is not wandering in uncertainty; it is being drawn, irresistibly, into the heart of the Trinity. This is why the Church Fathers speak of purgatory not as a descent but as an ascent. Gregory of Nyssa calls it the soul's "upward movement," a gradual illumination as the divine beauty becomes clearer and clearer. The fire does not push downward; it pulls upward. It is not the fire of exclusion, but the fire of embrace.

Seen from this angle, purgatory reveals its harmony with the Paschal Mystery. Christ descended into death so that even the realm of the dead might be filled with His presence. He sanctified the grave from within. He turned death itself into a passageway of grace. If death has become a doorway to life, then the purification that follows death must be understood as Christ's own work. He is the one who purifies, the one who heals, the one who restores. "He who began a good work in you will bring it to completion" (Phil 1:6). Purgatory is the final stroke of that divine artistry. The divine Physician continues His healing. The divine Bridegroom continues His preparation of the Bride. The divine Potter continues shaping the clay until it reflects His design without distortion.

This Christological orientation prevents us from treating purgatory as a mechanical process. It is not a cosmic machine; it is a personal encounter. It is the soul face-to-face with the One who loved it into existence. The healing is personal. The purification is personal. The fire is personal. It is the fire of the Sacred Heart. It is the love that pours from Christ's wounded side. It is the love that suffered agony in Gethsemane, that endured the cross, that descended into death so that we might rise. When this love touches the soul, it awakens desire, dissolves pride, consumes impurity, and frees the will. This is purgatory. It is Christ fulfilling His work of redemption in the individual soul.

Understanding this changes the way we live. Memento mori becomes not just an awareness of death but an awareness of what awaits beyond death: the God who refuses to leave us unfinished. The remembrance of death becomes the remembrance of love's final victory. It reminds us that holiness is not merely a moral ideal but a supernatural destiny. It reminds us that purification is not a threat but a promise. It reminds us that our death will be the moment God draws nearer than ever before, not to condemn but to complete.

Yet this truth also carries a challenge. If purgatory is the final purification, then every day of life should be a cooperation with that purification. The sacraments cease to be mere rituals and become instruments of transformation. Confession becomes a foretaste of fire. The Eucharist becomes a pledge of glory. Fasting becomes the loosening of attachments that would otherwise burn away painfully later. Acts of charity become the polishing of the soul. Forgiveness becomes the release of chains. Patience becomes endurance through which love matures. The trials God allows become the slow purgation of pride. Every hardship becomes an invitation to let the divine fire work now rather than later.

This is the wisdom of the saints. They lived with the end in view. They offered their sufferings as purification. They welcomed humiliations as medicine. They embraced prayer as exposure to divine light. They practiced self-examination not as a form of anxiety but as an act of hope. They remembered their death because they remembered their destiny. They lived in the shadow of eternity, and that shadow was not darkness but radiance.

The remembrance of death thus becomes the remembrance of the beatific vision. It keeps before us the truth that we will one day see God "face to face" (1 Cor 13:12). It keeps before us the truth that nothing impure can endure that vision. It keeps before us the truth that our entire life is a preparation for that gaze. The monks understood this better than anyone. Their constant meditation on death was a constant meditation on glory. "When the mind is vigilant," wrote Hesychios in the *Philokalia*, "it is ready for the vision of God." Vigilance was preparation for the light. Purification was preparation for union. Death was preparation for joy.

This understanding carries an extraordinary consolation: nothing good will be lost, and nothing sinful will remain. God wastes nothing in the soul that loves Him. Every act of love is preserved. Every sacrifice is remembered. Every struggle endured in faith becomes material for glory. Even our failures become occasions of mercy that deepen humility and expand the heart's capacity for God. Purgatory ensures that every fragment of grace, however small, is brought to completion.

And here the remembrance of death becomes a source not of fear but of gratitude. Death is no longer a threat; it is a threshold. It is the moment when the soul falls into the hands of the God who has pursued it since birth. It is the moment when the divine Potter takes the vessel He has shaped through the years and perfects it with the final touch. It is the moment when the soul sees at last that every tear, every burden, every cross, every disappointment was part of the refining, part of the preparation, part of the ascent. Death reveals that love was the author of every chapter.

This is why memento mori belongs not to despair but to hope. It is the hope that the fire awaiting us is the fire of a love that will not let us remain fragile, wounded, or half-formed. It is the hope that the God who fashioned us from dust will not rest until we shine like crystal in the New Jerusalem. It is the hope that death is not the end of sanctity but its climax. It is the hope that we will enter the wedding feast not as strangers but as a Bride made beautiful by grace.

The more deeply we contemplate this mystery, the more clearly we see that purgatory is not an isolated doctrine but the luminous thread that ties together the whole Christian vision of judgment, mercy, sanctity, and destiny. It reveals that God is unsatisfied with partial healing. It reveals that love aims at completion. It reveals that the beatific vision requires a heart that has been freed of every residue of sin. It reveals that sanctification is not optional ornamentation but the very structure of eternal joy. And it reveals that nothing in the Christian life is wasted—not a single trial, not a single prayer, not a single moment of repentance.

This is why the Church, for all her realism about sin, is infinitely hopeful about the sinner. She knows that God's grace is relentless. She knows that Christ's victory over death extends into the depths of the soul. She knows that purification is not punishment but promise. She knows that the divine love that descended into the tomb will descend into every corner of the human heart. She knows that the Spirit, who hovered over the waters at creation, still hovers over the chaos of our imperfections, ready to bring forth new beauty. She knows that the Bridegroom who gave Himself on the cross will not cease to beautify His Bride until she radiates with His own splendour.

In this sense, the doctrine of purgatory stands as a rebuke to despair. It declares that we are not defined by our failures. It declares that sanctity is not reserved for the few. It declares that God's purposes cannot be thwarted by our weakness. It declares that even the wounds we carry into death can become windows of grace through which divine light enters more deeply. It declares that holiness is not a distant dream but an imminent destiny. The God who called us from dust will not abandon us until we shine with His glory.

But purgatory is also a rebuke to presumption. It reminds us that sin matters. It reminds us that attachments matter. It reminds us that grace must be received, not merely acknowledged. It reminds us that the Christian life is a path of real transformation, not an abstract declaration of righteousness. It reminds us that cheap grace is not grace at all. It reminds us that our choices echo in eternity. It reminds us that the soul must be purified because love demands integrity. Purgatory is the revelation that God refuses to settle for half-love, half-repentance, half-discipleship. He wants us entirely.

Here memento mori becomes the hinge between life and eternity.

When we remember our death, we remember that this purification is inevitable. We remember that the God who will one day complete our sanctity is already at work in us now. We remember that every decision either cooperates with His fire or resists it. We remember that every day is an invitation to welcome the purification that awaits us. We remember that holiness is not a burden but a promise. We remember that the Bridegroom is preparing us for a union that exceeds all earthly joy.

The remembrance of death thus becomes a school of hope. It teaches us to live with the end in view, not as people terrified of judgment but as people longing for the embrace of the One who loves us. It teaches us to see suffering as purification, not punishment. It teaches us to see repentance as freedom, not shame. It teaches us to see trials as preparation, not obstacles. It teaches us to see the fire of God as illumination, not destruction. When we remember our death, we remember that the love that purifies us now will perfect us then.

And when the final moment comes—when the soul takes its last breath and steps into the radiance of God's presence—the remembrance of death becomes the experience of glory. The veil is lifted. The heart is cleansed. The fire is love. The wounds are healed. The soul rises. And the Bridegroom, who has pursued us through every chapter of our lives, welcomes us into the wedding feast of the Lamb.

Purgatory, then, is the last mercy before that feast. It is the assurance that we will not meet the Bridegroom unprepared. It is the guarantee that our love will be made whole. It is the promise that our destiny is nothing less than union with God. And it is the invitation, even now, to cooperate with the fire that will one day make us radiant.

For the God who formed us from dust will not rest until we shine with glory. His mercy is the fire. His justice is the fire. His love is the fire. And purgatory is the final proof that His love always, always has the last word.

16

The Nearness of the Bridegroom: Letting the End Shape the Everyday

The mysteries we have considered—judgment as revelation, death as the arrival of the Bridegroom, and purgatory as the final mercy of love—have shown that the Christian vision of death is neither bleak nor abstract. It is relational. It is covenantal. It is the culmination of a love story that began when God breathed life into dust and called us His own. Death is not the moment when God turns His face from us; it is the moment when His face becomes unavoidable. It is the hour when love breaks through every veil, when truth and mercy meet, when the Bridegroom comes in glory and the soul can hide nothing from the One who fashioned it. Everything in the Christian life is a preparation for that encounter. Everything in salvation history points toward it. And everything that Christ teaches about vigilance, holiness, and readiness finds its fulfillment there.

This is why memento mori is not a morbid fixation but a luminous key. To remember one's death is to remember one's destiny. It is to live with the Bridegroom's arrival in view. It is to understand that judgment is not primarily about accusation but about revelation: the unveiling of who we are and who God is. It is to see that death is not the extinguishing of desire but its perfection. It is to recognize that purgatory is not God's anger but God's determination that nothing unlovely will remain in the soul that He intends to embrace forever. When the Christian remembers death rightly, he remembers love rightly. Death becomes the doorway where the promises of God reach their completion.

Yet this places an extraordinary truth before us: everything that awaits us beyond death has already begun within us. The revelation of judgment begins when we allow God's word to search our hearts. The arrival of the Bridegroom begins when we open the door of the soul to His presence. The purification of purgatory begins when we yield to the Spirit's refining fire in repentance, humility, and surrender. What God completes in the next world, He begins in this one. What He purifies then, He invites us to purify now. What He will reveal in glory, He begins to reveal in prayer. Memento mori is therefore not merely a meditation on the end; it is a summons to live the beginning differently.

This is where the remembrance of death takes on its deepest meaning. It teaches us to see the whole Christian life as preparation for union with God. It exposes the illusions we cling to, the attachments we defend, the sins we excuse, the pride we protect. It reveals how easily we forget the love that will one day judge us and the judgment that will one day purify us. It compels us to ask not merely, "What will happen when I die?" but, "How should I live if the Bridegroom could arrive at any moment?" When the Christian remembers his death, he remembers that the time for transformation is now. Not later. Not someday. Now.

The saints understood this. They lived with the end in view, not as those terrified of punishment but as those longing for the fullness of love. They practiced vigilance not because they feared God's anger but because they desired His face. They embraced purification not as suffering to be avoided but as the final polish of love. They prayed, fasted, forgave, served, repented, and watched—not because they were anxious, but because they were awake. In them, memento mori was not merely a phrase; it was a posture of the soul. They remembered their death so that they might remember their bridegroom. They remembered the fleeting nature of this life so that nothing would prevent them from reaching the life that never ends.

Yet remembering is not enough. If the mysteries of judgment, arrival, and purification have shown us what awaits beyond the veil, they now call us to shape our days accordingly. If the Bridegroom will come suddenly, then the heart must learn to desire Him daily. If the soul will be purified by divine fire, then the will must learn to surrender now. If death will be the moment when God reveals the truth of our lives, then we must practice living in truth while time remains. Memento mori must move from meditation to practice, from awareness to habit, from insight to imitation of Christ. It must become a way of life.

This is the purpose of all that follows. The mysteries we have contemplated are not meant to remain lofty or distant. They must enter the ordinary rhythm of Christian living, shaping prayer, ordering desire, refining habits, and consecrating the hours. If we are to be ready for the Bridegroom's arrival in death, we must learn to live ready for His coming in every moment. If we are to welcome His purifying love then, we must cooperate with it now. If we are to behold His face in glory, we must begin seeking His face in the routines, disciplines, and sacrifices of this life.

The remembrance of death leads naturally, even necessarily, into a life of deliberate practices. Daily disciplines become acts of preparation. Simplicity becomes a training in detachment. Silence becomes a rehearsal for judgment. Prayer becomes an opening of the heart to the fire that will one day cleanse it completely. Mercy toward others becomes practice for the mercy God will show us. Sacrifice loosens the grip of earthly comforts. Repentance purifies the affections. Forgiveness frees the will. Every spiritual practice becomes a way of stepping toward the wedding feast, a way of cooperating with the grace that will one day perfect us.

Thus the path forward opens with clarity: if the mysteries beyond death are real—and they are—then the practices of the Christian life must be shaped by them. To remember death is to choose life. To contemplate judgment is to seek holiness. To anticipate purgatory is to welcome purification now. To expect the Bridegroom is to live awake, alert, and available to grace. It is time to adopt the habits of a people preparing for glory. Everything that awaits us beyond death calls us to a life that is ready.

And readiness begins now.

V

A LIFE THAT IS READY

17

Daily Practices of Memento Mori

The Christian who remembers death does not withdraw from life; he enters it more deeply. There is a clarity that comes only when the heart keeps the end in view, a clarity that pierces through distraction and noise, and exposes the weight and wonder of every moment. From the earliest days of the Church, this remembrance was not an idea to be admired but a discipline to be lived. The psalmist's plea—"Teach us to number our days that we may gain a heart of wisdom"—was not poetry for the liturgy alone; it was instruction for how to shape a day, a habit, a life. Wisdom is not simply knowledge but vision, the ability to see life in the light of eternity, to perceive the divine story unfolding beneath the ordinary movements of time. Memento mori is the practice by which that vision becomes steady.

 The spiritual masters understood that the way we begin the day shapes the entire interior landscape of the soul. Morning is not merely the start of hours but the renewal of creation within the heart. Each sunrise recapitulates Genesis: darkness gives way to light; God speaks again; life is offered anew. To wake is to be given another invitation into the covenant. It is a small resurrection, a reminder that God has carried us through the night and restored breath to our lungs. The first thoughts of the day, then, bear extraordinary theological weight. If the soul begins the morning adrift, carried along by impulse or anxiety, the rest of the day follows in its wake. But if the soul begins by remembering its mortality—by acknowledging that this day is a gift, that this breath is unearned, that this moment might be the last—then everything takes on the gravity of grace.

The Desert Fathers began each morning as though it were their first and lived it as though it were their last. Abba Poemen taught that a monk should rise with the thought that he will not see evening; Abba Evagrius that the remembrance of death purifies the intentions at dawn. They were not courting dread but cultivating vigilance, teaching the soul to see life as fragile and therefore precious. The Christian who begins his day under the gaze of eternity finds that his desires are reordered almost effortlessly. Gratitude springs up before complaint. Patience appears where irritation usually thrives. The small sacrifices that fill the day—listening when one would rather speak, serving when one would rather rest—become offerings rather than burdens. When the heart whispers, "This day may be my last," it discovers how to love while there is still time.

This is why the Church's morning prayers often place judgment and mercy side by side. The Byzantine tradition begins the day by asking God to "grant me to pass this day without sin," while the Roman liturgy offers the Invitatory Psalm, reminding the soul: "Today, if you hear His voice, harden not your hearts." Morning is not simply a moment of beginning but a moment of decision—a summons to choose God again. Memento mori sharpens that summons. It reminds us that we will one day give an account for how we loved, and that today is part of that account. Every morning becomes a small rehearsal for the final awakening, the dawn that will not end, when the soul rises to see God face to face.

The remembrance of death in the morning cultivates not fear but wonder. It opens the heart to the mystery that life is a gift sustained by God moment by moment. Augustine observed that God is closer to us than we are to ourselves, yet we move through life as though our existence were self-sustaining. By remembering death at dawn, the Christian remembers dependence. He recognizes that life flows from God's generosity, not from his own strength. He begins the day in humility, a humility that becomes fertile soil for charity, patience, and joy. The soul that remembers death becomes less entitled and more grateful. It becomes less hurried and more attentive. It becomes less self-centred and more open to grace.

Yet the remembrance of death is not a fleeting morning exercise. It must shape the entire arc of the day, especially the evening. If morning is a small resurrection, evening is a small judgment. The tradition of the examen—present in the monastic East, the patristic West, and perfected in Ignatius—arose from the belief that the Christian must not allow a day to end without truth. The day must be handed back to God as an offering, examined in the light of His word, purified by contrition, and entrusted to His mercy. The examen is not an inventory of failures but a dialogue of love. It is standing before God and allowing His light to reveal not only what we have done but who we are becoming.

Augustine practiced this long before the word "examen" existed. In the *Confessions*, he recounts how each evening he weighed his desires, tested his thoughts, and sought to understand how God had been drawing him closer throughout the day. For him, examining the heart was an act of hope. It signalled a trust that God was forming him even through his weaknesses. Cassian, in his *Conferences*, insists that monks must "call the soul to account each night," not to condemn but to convert. The daily reckoning is a rehearsal for the final reckoning—a way of training the heart to face the truth of its own story with humility and confidence in God's mercy.

When the Christian examines his day with the remembrance of death, he sees time differently. He recognizes that each action is a seed planted in eternity, that each word leaves a mark on the soul, that each moment carries within it the possibility of grace or refusal. He begins to grieve the wasted hours not with despair but with resolve. He begins to cherish the moments of fidelity not with pride but with gratitude. He learns to see sin not as a slip to be excused but as an obstacle to union with God. And he learns to receive mercy not as cheap comfort but as the refining fire that will one day purify him completely.

As the day draws to its close, the remembrance of death takes shape most beautifully in the Church's night prayer. Compline is the liturgy that teaches the Christian how to die well. It is the prayer of surrender, of handing the soul back to God, of trusting Him in the darkness. From the earliest centuries, Christians concluded the day by placing themselves under God's protection: "Into your hands, O Lord, I commend my spirit." These words, first spoken by the psalmist, were placed on the lips of Christ as He died; they become the final prayer of the believer each night. Compline is the Church's quiet catechesis on mortality. It teaches us that the soul must return to God with trust, not fear; with repentance, not regret; with longing, not anxiety.

The Eastern Churches express this even more vividly. Each night they ask God for "a Christian ending to our life: painless, unashamed, peaceful." This prayer is stunning in its simplicity. It does not ask for exemption from death but for preparation for it. It acknowledges that the end of life should mirror the posture of the soul: humble, reconciled, at peace. Every night becomes a rehearsal for that final surrender. Every act of entrusting one's spirit to God becomes a step toward the moment when that entrustment will be complete and irreversible. To sleep is to practice dying; to rise is to practice resurrection. The rhythm of the Christian day thus becomes a sacrament of eternity.

The power of the Church's night prayer lies not only in the surrender it teaches but in the honesty it demands. The soul cannot commend itself to God without first acknowledging the truth of its day. Compline traditionally includes a brief examination of conscience, a simple but profound act of truthfulness. The Christian stands before God, not offering explanations or excuses but presenting the heart as it is. Sin is named; grace is recognized; the day is surrendered. This nightly act shapes the soul toward humility, which Aquinas calls the foundation of all virtue. It is humility that allows the soul to die well, because humility opens the heart entirely to God. Through nightly repentance, the Christian slowly becomes the person who can say with peace, "Lord, into Your hands."

This daily rhythm—morning remembrance, evening examen, night surrender—forms a spiritual architecture. It shapes the soul to live in the present moment with vigilance and love. It trains the heart not to postpone conversion. It teaches the Christian to see each day as a gift and each night as a threshold. Memento mori becomes woven into the very structure of time. The day is framed by resurrection and judgment, by gift and surrender, by promise and truth.

Yet the Church has never been content with interior practices alone. Christians throughout history have surrounded themselves with reminders of mortality—icons, crucifixes, prayer ropes, monastic cells marked by simplicity. These physical signs serve as anchors for the mind and heart. The body is part of the spiritual life, and what the eyes see often shapes what the soul remembers. The early monks kept skulls not out of morbidity but out of sobriety. They believed that to look upon the relic of a life once lived was to encounter a silent homily. That skull had once laughed, wept, hoped, sinned, prayed. It had known joys and sorrows, labours and temptations. And now it spoke only one truth: "You will follow me."

The monk who prayed beside a skull was not flirting with despair but embracing the truth that wakes the heart. Death was not his enemy in that moment; forgetfulness was. The skull became a teacher, a witness to the frailty of man and the mercy of God. Basil the Great wrote that the remembrance of death "sobers the soul" and guards it against pride. It is difficult to boast when one prays before the bones of someone once equally full of plans and illusions. It is difficult to cling to anger when reminded how brief life truly is. It is difficult to waste time when confronted with the truth that time is finite. The skull served as a sacrament of honesty.

Most Christians will not pray beside skulls, but all Christians can cultivate visible reminders of mortality that draw the heart toward wisdom. A crucifix is the most perfect of these reminders, not only because Christ died but because He died for us. The crucifix reveals both the reality of death and the glory that transforms it. It shows the cost of sin and the triumph of love. To begin the day under the crucified Christ is to remember that life is serious, that holiness matters, that love requires sacrifice. To end the day beneath His gaze is to remember that mercy is real, that forgiveness is possible, and that death is not a wall but a door.

Icons serve a similar purpose in the Eastern tradition. An icon of Christ Pantocrator reminds the believer that each moment unfolds under His sovereignty and judgment. An icon of the Bridegroom—Christ in the purple robe of His Passion—teaches the soul that the One who will judge us is the One who already gave Himself for us. Icons shape the imagination. They inscribe truth on the senses. They remind the soul that prayer is not merely an interior whisper but an encounter with the living God. In the presence of sacred images, the remembrance of death becomes the remembrance of divine love.

The saints often kept a particular prayer or phrase close at hand to anchor their remembrance of death. "O Lord, grant me a holy end," prayed Augustine. "Lord Jesus Christ, Son of God, have mercy on me," prayed the hesychasts, letting the Name itself shape every breath. The early Christians greeted one another with "Maranatha"—"Come, Lord"—a simple expression that placed life under the shadow of Christ's return. These prayers are not magical formulas; they are small hinges on which the heart turns back to God throughout the day. They keep the soul awake. They fight against the creeping illusion that time belongs to us.

Yet the most powerful visible reminder of mortality is simplicity of life. Simplicity is memento mori made visible. It is the quiet refusal to anchor the heart in possessions that cannot follow us into eternity. The Church Fathers warned frequently that excess creates forgetfulness. Clutter dulls the soul, multiplying distractions and dispersing desire. A life swollen with things becomes a life too heavy to rise toward God. But simplicity—spacious, humble, intentional—makes room for grace. It reminds the soul that it is a pilgrim, not a settler. It frees the heart from the tyranny of accumulation. It teaches the believer to live as one who knows the journey is short.

This is why monastic cells are bare, why hermits live with so little, why saints often embraced voluntary poverty. They understood that possessions are not neutral; they shape the imagination. An overstuffed life makes neglect easy. It encourages delay. It whispers that there is always more time, always another season, always another chance to begin again. But a simple life—lean, uncluttered, disciplined—keeps the soul alert. It teaches the body to align with the truths the mind professes. It becomes a quiet form of vigilance.

Yet simplicity is only one part of the Christian's rule of life. A rule is the trellis on which discipleship grows. It is not a set of restrictions but a structure that guards love. Families have rules; friendships have rhythms; covenants have obligations. Without structure, even the most sincere intentions wither. The monastic traditions of East and West understood this well. Benedict's Rule, the Desert Fathers' sayings, the Philokalia's instructions—all assume that holiness is impossible without deliberate patterns of life. Memento mori must therefore be built into the rule, not left to inspiration. It must be scheduled, practiced, revisited, renewed.

Christians who wish to remember death in a life-giving way will find it helpful to establish daily moments dedicated to this wisdom. Morning, noon, evening, and night can each carry a brief act of remembrance: a psalm, a prayer, a moment of silence, the sign of the cross, a short reading from Scripture. The goal is not to overwhelm the day with rituals but to let truth punctuate it. Each reminder becomes a small turning of the heart, keeping the soul from drifting into forgetfulness.

There is a distinct emphasis in the Eastern Christian tradition that deepens this practice even further: the repeated invocation of "the hour of our death" in prayer. This phrase appears constantly—in the hymns of Great Lent, in the prayers of Compline, in the supplications to the Mother of God. It teaches the soul to view every moment through the lens of the final moment. It is not morbid repetition; it is spiritual realism. The hour of our death reveals the truth of our life, the orientation of our love, the depth of our surrender. By remembering it daily, the Christian prepares to meet it with peace rather than panic.

This Eastern emphasis on the hour of death is not a narrow devotional habit but a theological vision. It flows from the conviction that the whole Christian life is ordered toward union with Christ, and that death, for the believer, is the final liturgy of that union. Every hour prepares for that hour. Every prayer anticipates that meeting. Every act of repentance is a rehearsal for the moment when the soul will stand before the Bridegroom. This vision saturates the prayers of the East, where the Christian continually asks for "a Christian end to our life, painless, unashamed, and peaceful, and a good defence before the dread judgment seat of Christ." The prayer is not asking for ease but for readiness. It is asking for the grace of truth, courage, and peace.

This readiness is cultivated not by extraordinary feats but by the accumulated weight of ordinary fidelity. Small acts of remembrance, repeated over years, engrave truth into the soul. The early monks believed that consistency mattered more than intensity. A short, honest prayer said every day is more transformative than a long, emotional prayer offered sporadically. A brief moment of silence kept faithfully is more fruitful than a dramatic resolution abandoned after a week. This patient fidelity is what shapes the soul for eternity. It is the slow awakening of the heart that gradually aligns desire with truth.

One of the most overlooked daily practices of memento mori is gratitude. Gratitude is a remembrance of gifts, and every gift implies a giver. To live gratefully is to recognize that nothing is owed and everything is received. Gratitude is the opposite of presumption, which is one of the roots of spiritual sloth. The presumptuous heart believes there will always be more time, more chances, more mercy, more opportunities. Gratitude shatters that illusion. It teaches the soul to see each moment as unrepeatable, each person as irreplaceable, each breath as undeserved. A grateful heart cannot drift into forgetfulness because it is constantly awakened by the surprise of grace.

Gratitude also disarms fear. The soul that gives thanks daily is not easily frightened by the thought of death, because gratitude trains the heart in the logic of gift. Life has been a gift; death will be a gift; eternal life is the fulfillment of all gifts. Gratitude prepares the soul to see death not as theft but as consummation. It roots the Christian in trust, the virtue that Aquinas identifies as the proper response to divine providence. To trust God daily is already to practice the surrender that death will one day require.

Alongside gratitude, the discipline of silence is indispensable. Silence is the environment in which the remembrance of death becomes fruitful. The modern world is allergic to silence. Noise fills every space, not simply to entertain but to distract. Noise prevents the soul from thinking about what matters. It keeps the mind occupied so that the heart never confronts its fears, its sins, its longings, its mortality. Yet the saints insist that silence is where God speaks. Elijah encountered the Lord not in the wind or fire but in the "still small voice." Silence is where the soul hears the truth about itself. Silence is where the remembrance of death becomes the remembrance of God.

To practice silence daily is to reclaim the interior life. It creates space for reflection, repentance, and prayer. It allows the heart to listen. It reveals desires that must be purified and wounds that must be healed. Silence exposes the illusions that comfort can hide. It is in silence that the Christian feels the weight of time, the brevity of life, the seriousness of love. Silence turns the mind toward eternity. The remembrance of death without silence becomes anxiety; the remembrance of death within silence becomes wisdom.

Yet silence alone is not enough. The Church insists on the necessity of the sacraments. The sacramental life is the deepest daily practice of memento mori, because the sacraments place the Christian inside the mystery of Christ's death and resurrection. Every Mass is a remembrance of death—the death of the Lord, given so that we might live. Every Eucharist is a foretaste of the final banquet. Every Confession is a preparation for judgment. Every anointing is a strengthening for the final battle. The sacramental life teaches the soul to die daily and rise daily, to live under the sign of the Cross and the promise of resurrection.

A Christian who remembers death without the sacraments may drift toward fear. A Christian who receives the sacraments without remembering death may drift toward complacency. But the union of both—frequent Confession, reverent Communion, faithful participation in the liturgy—forms a soul that is sober and joyful, humble and confident, awake and at peace. The sacraments root memento mori in grace rather than effort, in divine action rather than human striving.

Among the sacraments, the Eucharist holds the central place because it unites the believer to the death and life of Christ. The Eucharist is the victory over death made present. It is the pledge of eternal life. It is the food of pilgrims who know the road is short. The early Christians received the Eucharist as viaticum—not only at the hour of death but as preparation for it. Every Communion was a rehearsal for the final meeting. Every Amen was a yes to God's will, a yes to His call, a yes to the journey home. The Eucharist makes the Christian a person who can die well, because the Eucharist teaches the soul how to live well.

The daily remembrance of death also requires a certain discipline of speech. Words shape the heart. Idle talk disperses the mind, while truthful and restrained speech gathers it. The Desert Fathers were relentless about this. Abba Poemen said, "A man may seem silent, but if his heart condemns others he is speaking." True silence is purity of heart. True watchfulness includes watchfulness over the tongue. To speak less is to listen more—to God, to conscience, to reality. To refrain from gossip and idle chatter is to cultivate the interior attention needed for memento mori.

These practices—gratitude, silence, simplicity, sacramental life, disciplined speech—form the scaffolding of a Christian life that is awake. But the centre of all these practices is love. Memento mori is not driven by fear; it is driven by love. The remembrance of death teaches the soul to cherish what matters, to love with urgency, to forgive quickly, to repent sincerely. Death reveals the truth of love. The one who remembers death becomes attentive to relationships, patient in suffering, generous in service. Memento mori is not a withdrawal from life; it is a deeper immersion into it.

This is why the saints were never gloomy people. They remembered death constantly, yet they lived with radiant joy. Francis of Assisi embraced Lady Death as a sister. Thérèse of Lisieux spoke of death as the moment she would "fall asleep in love." The remembrance of death purified their vision. It stripped away the trivial. It magnified the eternal. It taught them to live in the presence of God, not tomorrow but today.

The saints reveal that when memento mori is woven into daily life, it produces not heaviness but freedom. The heart that remembers death is liberated from the tyranny of comparison, ambition, and anxiety. It no longer needs to prove itself or defend itself, because it knows the truth: only one thing is necessary. This is why the remembrance of death is never solitary. It draws the soul into charity. A person who knows he will die soon learns to see others through the lens of eternity. Impatience softens. Grudges lose their force. Forgiveness becomes easier. Love becomes simpler. When the brevity of life becomes clear, love becomes urgent.

Yet it is not merely human relationships that memento mori clarifies. It also restores prayer to its proper place. Many Christians struggle to pray because they imagine prayer as one activity among many, something to fit into the day if there is time. But the remembrance of death reverses this logic. It teaches the soul that prayer is the heart's preparation for eternity. Prayer is not a task; it is the training of desire. It is where the soul learns to recognise the voice of the Shepherd it will one day meet. It is where the mind is shaped to love what God loves. When prayer is seen in this light, even the simplest acts—making the sign of the Cross, whispering the Jesus Prayer, lifting up a moment of intercession—become seeds of eternal life.

The tradition of the Church is rich with simple, daily prayers that align the heart with this vision. One of the oldest is the Kyrie eleison. To say "Lord, have mercy" is to place oneself truthfully before God: needy, grateful, hopeful. It is a prayer shaped by humility, and humility is the virtue most opposed to acedia. Acedia whispers, "Why bother? Nothing will change." The Kyrie responds, "Everything changes when I turn to God." The humble prayer becomes an act of resistance against the spiritual paralysis that keeps the soul asleep.

Among the most powerful daily practices is the Jesus Prayer: "Lord Jesus Christ, Son of God, have mercy on me, a sinner." This prayer is the heartbeat of Eastern Christianity, a constant remembrance of God, an anchor for the wandering mind. The hesychasts—those who pursued interior stillness—believed that repeating this prayer slowly, attentively, and consistently could purify the heart. They taught that the name of Jesus carries divine power, shaping the soul that invokes it. The Jesus Prayer is, in its own way, a form of memento mori, because it keeps the soul mindful of its dependence upon God and its need for mercy at every moment of life, especially at the final moment.

This daily rhythm of prayer inevitably deepens the virtue of humility. Humility is crucial for memento mori because it is the virtue that tells the truth about the self. The humble person knows he is a creature. He knows he is dust. He knows he depends upon God for every breath. Humility is not self-loathing; it is self-knowledge. It is the recognition that the soul is made for God and cannot find rest apart from Him. The remembrance of death is incomplete without humility, because only humility allows the soul to surrender with peace.

To cultivate humility daily is to practice remembering one's limits, one's sins, one's need for grace. The tradition offers many small ways to do this: asking forgiveness promptly, thanking others sincerely, serving without seeking attention, accepting correction patiently, offering inconveniences to God. These practices of hidden obedience soften the heart and prepare it for the final surrender. At death, the soul will give itself entirely to God. Daily humility is the rehearsal for that gift.

Another element of daily memento mori is the discipline of ordering one's desires. The Fathers teach that desire is not eliminated by holiness; it is purified. The heart always wants something. The question is whether it wants what leads to life or what leads to death. The remembrance of death clarifies desire. It asks the soul, "What will matter when everything else falls away?" This question becomes the measure of choices. It becomes the standard by which the Christian discerns how to use time, money, energy, and attention.

This is why the saints warn against the scattering of desire, the fragmentation produced by too many attachments. St. Maximos the Confessor teaches that the passions arise when desire is misaligned, when the heart clings to what is passing instead of to what is eternal. The remembrance of death realigns desire. It reminds the soul that the world is good but temporary; that pleasure is a gift but not a god; that success is useful but not ultimate. Desire must be ordered toward the kingdom. This ordering is a daily task. It is the soul's slow training in wisdom.

The practice of remembering death also impacts how the Christian approaches work. Scripture teaches that work is a participation in God's creative activity, not a means of self-exaltation. When a person remembers death, work is transformed. It becomes a gift rather than a burden, an offering rather than an identity. The Christian who remembers death becomes diligent but not anxious, industrious but not frantic. He labours with the awareness that his time is short and his work is offered to God. This produces excellence rooted in humility. It cures perfectionism and vanity. It frees the soul from the pride that imagines achievements can grant immortality.

This remembrance extends even into rest. Rest is not idleness; it is the restoration of the soul. The one who remembers death understands the need for sabbath. The sabbath is a weekly memento mori because it interrupts work, reminds the believer that the world does not depend upon him, and turns the heart toward eternal worship. Rest is not a luxury but a commandment. It teaches the soul that its destiny is not endless labour but eternal communion. Rest is the weekly anticipation of the final rest in God.

All of these practices—prayer, humility, gratitude, silence, sacramental life, ordered desire, holy work, sabbath rest—form a single pattern. They are threads of one garment: the garment of readiness. The Christian who weaves this garment daily becomes a person who can meet death with peace. Not because he is perfect, but because he is prepared. Not because he is fearless, but because he trusts the One who conquers fear. Not because he has mastered life, but because he has surrendered it.

At the heart of these practices is love. The remembrance of death is ultimately a remembrance of love. God has given us life as a gift. He has numbered our days. He has prepared a home for us. He has promised that He will meet us at the hour of death. To remember death daily is to remember His love. It is to live with the awareness that every moment is held by God, every breath sustained by Him, every step guided toward Him. The Christian who remembers death becomes a person who sees life as a pilgrimage of love. The road is short, the journey is sacred, and the destination is joy.

The remembrance of death also reshapes how Christians understand time itself. Modern life treats time as a possession, something to manage or maximise. Yet Scripture teaches that time is not owned but given. It flows from the generosity of God. The remembrance of death frees the soul from the illusion of control. It awakens reverence toward time, because each hour becomes a gift placed in our hands with a purpose. Every day is a space where grace is offered and received. This is why the Apostle Paul urges, "Look carefully then how you walk... making the most of the time, because the days are evil." When the Christian remembers death, the temptation to waste time begins to lose its grip. The soul grows attentive, not frantic but intentional, willing to give full presence to the task and the person before it.

This attentiveness naturally cultivates simplicity. The one who remembers death sees through the clutter of unnecessary obligations, possessions, and distractions. He begins to choose what matters. Simplicity is not minimalism; it is clarity. It is the virtue that frees the heart from being weighed down by the trivial. The remembrance of death is its great teacher because it forces the soul to distinguish between the essential and the ephemeral. The saints lived simply not because they despised the world but because they understood its transience. They held earthly goods lightly because they were reaching for a kingdom that cannot pass away.

Simplicity is strengthened by the daily discipline of letting go. This may be as small as releasing an unkind thought or as large as surrendering an ambition. Every act of relinquishment loosens the fingers of the heart from what it clings to apart from God. It creates inner space. It widens the capacity for grace. A Christian who learns to let go a little each day is preparing for the final letting go. This is why the remembrance of death does not weaken joy; it enlarges it. When the soul is freed from needless anxieties and burdens, it becomes capable of delight. It becomes alive to God's gifts, awake to beauty, alert to mercy.

The remembrance of death is also a powerful antidote to fear itself. Many fears arise from attachment—fear of loss, fear of failure, fear of illness, fear of insignificance. When the soul remembers that everything except God is passing, fear begins to loosen. Death, which once seemed terrifying, becomes the moment of truth when all illusions fall away and love alone remains. The saints were bold not because they possessed natural courage but because they practiced remembering what lasts. Their fearlessness was the fruit of clarity. They lived with their eyes fixed on the eternal.

This clarity also shapes how Christians handle suffering. The remembrance of death teaches that suffering is not the final word. It situates suffering within the horizon of eternity. The sufferings of this present time are real, weighty, and often shattering, yet they are not permanent. The remembrance of death helps the soul see suffering as a participation in the Cross and as a preparation for glory. It allows the Christian to endure with hope, because he knows that every sorrow—if united to Christ—becomes seed for resurrection. The remembrance of death does not trivialise pain; it transfigures it.

This transfiguration is particularly clear in the Christian practice of offering up suffering. To offer one's pain to God is to unite it to the suffering of Christ, allowing grace to flow through it. This is a daily practice, sometimes repeated dozens of times in an hour. It forms the soul in patience, fortifies the will, and deepens compassion. A person who remembers death becomes surprisingly gentle with the wounds of others, because he knows how fragile life is. The remembrance of death tenderises the heart. It breaks the hardness that often forms through self-protection. It opens the soul to mercy.

Forgiveness becomes easier, too. When the soul remembers death, grudges lose their weight. Resentments feel absurd. Anger appears wasteful. The Christian who remembers death learns to ask, "Will this matter when I stand before Christ?" Most of the time the answer is no. Forgiveness becomes not merely an obligation but an act of freedom. It liberates the heart from the prison of bitterness and restores the peace that vigilance requires.

And with forgiveness comes compassion. Compassion grows naturally from the remembrance of death because it reveals the shared condition of humanity. We are all dust. We are all fragile. We are all walking toward the same horizon. The remembrance of death dissolves pride, because pride depends on illusions of superiority and control. When the soul faces the truth of its mortality, those illusions crumble. Compassion replaces judgment. Understanding replaces cynicism. The Christian becomes capable of seeing others through the eyes of Christ, who looked upon the crowds "because they were harassed and helpless, like sheep without a shepherd."

The remembrance of death also positions the Christian within the communion of saints. Memento mori makes the believer aware that he is part of a much larger story—one that includes the faithful who have gone before and the faithful who will come after. This awareness transforms daily life. It infuses the smallest acts with meaning. A hidden sacrifice, a whispered prayer, a quiet act of charity—each one ripples through the Body of Christ. The remembrance of death is therefore not merely personal; it is ecclesial. It unites the soul to the great cloud of witnesses who have run the race before us.

This ecclesial awareness strengthens hope. The one who remembers death remembers heaven. He remembers that he is not meant for this world but for the kingdom to come. Hope becomes the atmosphere of daily life. It is not an escape from the present but the illumination of it. Hope enables the Christian to persevere in love, because hope is anchored in the promise that love will triumph. The remembrance of death is the training of hope, because it keeps the Christian looking toward the fulfillment of all desire: the face of God.

Finally, memento mori restores joy. This may seem paradoxical, yet it is the testimony of every saint. The remembrance of death removes the burden of pretending that this life is ultimate. It frees the soul from the pressure to manufacture meaning. It releases the heart from the dread of loss. Joy arises when the soul rests in God, trusting that He holds every moment. Joy is the fruit of realism, not denial. The Christian who remembers death lives lightly, gratefully, expectantly. He is not crushed by fear because he knows he is loved by the One who conquered death.

These daily practices—humility, prayer, gratitude, silence, sacramental life, simplicity, ordering of desire, holy work, rest, compassion, forgiveness, ecclesial awareness, hope, and joy—form a life that is truly awake. They convert doctrine into discipline, belief into habit, mortality into mission. They turn the remembrance of death from an idea into an environment, a way of seeing that transforms every moment into preparation for eternity.

A life shaped by the remembrance of death also discovers the profound importance of constancy. Modern spirituality often prizes emotional intensity—grand resolutions, dramatic conversions, sudden insights. Yet the Church, from her earliest centuries, has insisted that holiness is built on persevering fidelity. Constancy is the ability to do the right thing again and again, especially when it feels small, unseen, or unremarkable. It is the quiet strength that refuses to let the soul drift. The remembrance of death fuels this constancy because it anchors the believer in the truth that every day, even the most ordinary, carries eternal weight.

Constancy resists the subtle temptation to measure progress by feelings. Feelings rise and fall; constancy endures. A Christian who practices daily remembrance becomes less concerned with emotional experience and more concerned with faithful response. Over time, this steadiness becomes the character of the soul. It forms the kind of resilience that can face trial without collapsing, temptation without despair, dryness without quitting. The saints excelled not because they felt strong but because they remained faithful in weakness.

Memento mori strengthens this fidelity by reminding the soul of the goal: the face of Christ.

This constancy is sustained by another daily discipline: repentance. Repentance is not merely a reaction to sin; it is a posture of the heart. It is the willingness to turn again and again toward God. The remembrance of death makes repentance urgent but not despairing. It reveals the seriousness of sin, since sin shapes the soul we will bring before God, yet it also reveals the depths of mercy. Repentance becomes a source of hope because it places the sinner in the hands of the One who heals. A Christian who repents daily keeps the heart soft and pliable. The remembrance of death protects against both presumption ("I have more time") and despair ("It is too late for me"). It instils the truth that today is the day of salvation.

From repentance flows reconciliation. The remembrance of death teaches that broken relationships cannot be taken lightly. Time is short. Wounds left unattended fester. Words left unsaid become regrets. The Christian who remembers death seeks peace quickly. He refuses to let anger linger or coldness harden. This does not mean excusing evil or denying justice. It means refusing to let the sun set on bitterness. A reconciled heart is a ready heart. At the hour of death, nothing will matter more than love given and love received.

This truth naturally extends into how Christians treat their bodies. The remembrance of death reminds the believer that the body is both fragile and sacred. It is the vessel that carries the soul toward eternity, yet it is also the instrument through which holiness is lived. Daily care for the body—through rest, moderation, and discipline—is not vanity but stewardship. It honours the Creator who formed the body from dust and breathed life into it. Even ascetic practices, when done rightly, are rooted in this reverence. They teach the body obedience so that the soul may be free. The remembrance of death protects asceticism from becoming self-punishing. It places bodily discipline within the context of love and preparation.

The remembrance of death also teaches discernment. Discernment is not simply choosing between good and evil but recognising what leads the soul toward God and what leads it away. Daily memento mori sharpens the conscience because it asks, "Will this draw me closer to Christ or distract me from Him?" This question simplifies choices. It exposes hidden motivations. It reveals the subtle ways in which the enemy sows delay, complacency, and distraction. A Christian who remembers death becomes more alert, more honest, and more courageous in decision-making.

This courage extends into the realm of mission. When the soul remembers that life is short, evangelisation becomes urgent. Not frantic, but earnest. Every person we meet is walking toward eternity. Every conversation carries possibility. The remembrance of death dissolves the fear of awkwardness or rejection. It makes the Christian bold in charity. The early Church grew because ordinary believers lived with the vivid awareness that souls were at stake. They spoke of Christ with joy and seriousness. They invited others into a kingdom they knew was near. A life shaped by memento mori becomes naturally missionary because it sees time through the eyes of eternity.

The remembrance of death also purifies how Christians engage with the world's pleasures. Pleasure is not evil; it is a gift. But pleasure becomes destructive when it becomes ultimate. The soul that remembers death learns to enjoy earthly goods without clinging to them. Food becomes thanksgiving, not excess. Beauty becomes praise, not possession. Friendship becomes communion, not control. Entertainment becomes recreation, not escape. The remembrance of death reorients delight toward its proper end: God. It frees the soul from the restlessness that seeks satisfaction in passing things.

Similarly, memento mori reshapes how the Christian approaches ambition. Ambition itself is not sinful. It becomes dangerous when it disregards the eternal. The remembrance of death teaches the soul to ask, "What am I striving for, and why?" It exposes ambitions that are rooted in ego rather than service. It illuminates paths that honour God and discard those that obscure Him. A Christian who remembers death may still pursue excellence, leadership, or achievement, but with purified intention. The goal is no longer self-glory but stewardship of God-given gifts. This kind of ambition becomes virtue—magnanimity—when it seeks great things for the sake of love.

Even leisure is transformed. True leisure is not idleness but rest in what is good, true, and beautiful. It restores the soul and reminds it of its final rest in God. Leisure shaped by memento mori avoids the counterfeit versions of rest—mindless scrolling, shallow entertainment, self-indulgent escape. It chooses activities that nourish the heart and open it to grace: reading, conversation, nature, music, silence. Leisure becomes a rehearsal for heaven.

Within this rhythm of work, rest, prayer, and repentance, the Christian also cultivates the daily act of surrender. Surrender is the core of readiness. It is the willingness to place one's life entirely in God's hands, trusting His wisdom more than our own plans. Each day offers countless opportunities to practice this surrender: accepting a disappointment, yielding control, embracing an unforeseen sacrifice, entrusting a fear to God. The remembrance of death makes surrender not frightening but reasonable. If the final moment of life will be an act of surrender, then the wise Christian practices now.

And finally, the remembrance of death produces a posture of anticipation. The Christian does not merely prepare for death; he longs for the Bridegroom. The remembrance of death awakens desire for God. It transforms the soul from a reluctant servant into a waiting bride. It teaches the heart to whisper daily, "Come, Lord Jesus." This longing is not escapism but fulfillment. It is the desire planted by the

Spirit, the desire that will be satisfied when faith becomes sight.

These daily practices—constancy, repentance, reconciliation, bodily stewardship, discernment, mission, purified pleasure, holy ambition, true leisure, surrender, anticipation—shape a life that is not merely ready for death but ready for Christ. They draw the Christian into a pattern of living in which every moment becomes preparation for eternity. Through them, memento mori becomes not a grim reminder but a joyful orientation toward the kingdom that is coming.

A life steeped in the remembrance of death also cultivates a deeper reverence for the ordinary. Modern spirituality is often tempted to chase the extraordinary—ecstatic experiences, dramatic signs, emotional highs. Yet Scripture and tradition reveal that sanctity takes root in the soil of daily life: the mundane tasks, the unnoticed sacrifices, the small obedience's. When the Christian remembers that each day may be his last, he learns to perceive the ordinary through the lens of eternity. Simple actions—washing dishes, answering an email, listening attentively to a friend—become offerings. The remembrance of death dignifies the small, because it reveals that nothing small is insignificant when done in love.

This reverence for the ordinary is intimately connected to patience. Patience is the quiet strength that endures the slow pace of growth, the unanswered questions, the delays that grace requires. Memento mori strengthens patience because it reminds the soul that God works on an eternal timeline. Impatience is born from the illusion that the present moment must satisfy every desire. The remembrance of death breaks that illusion. It teaches the Christian to trust that God is shaping him for eternity, often through processes that seem painfully slow. Patience becomes easier when the heart knows that its true fulfillment lies beyond this world.

Patience also protects the soul from despair. Despair often arises when the Christian forgets the end of the story. The remembrance of death keeps that end before the eyes. It whispers that suffering will pass, sin will be healed, and death will be defeated. This perspective allows the Christian to persevere through dry seasons of prayer, prolonged temptations, and difficult relationships. The remembrance of death does not minimize these struggles—it situates them within a larger hope. The soul that remembers death becomes difficult to discourage.

Alongside patience stands perseverance. Perseverance is the virtue that refuses to quit even when every feeling says to stop. It is the refusal to abandon prayer, charity, or faithfulness despite dryness or exhaustion. The remembrance of death fuels perseverance because it reminds the Christian that the battle is temporary and the reward eternal. The saints persevered not because they were naturally strong but because they recognised the brevity of life. They knew that trials, temptations, and labours would one day end. Perseverance becomes a form of hope in action, a daily yes to God even in darkness.

This daily yes is strengthened by community. The remembrance of death creates a longing not only for God but for the communion of saints, both living and departed. It teaches the Christian to value the people God has placed in his life. Community becomes a means of preparation, a support in vigilance, a source of encouragement. The early Church lived with a vivid awareness of death, and it bound them together in profound unity. They prayed for one another, forgave one another, carried one another's burdens. They knew that they would stand before God together, as one body. The remembrance of death makes Christian community not optional but essential.

Within community, spiritual friendship plays a unique role. A spiritual friend is someone who sees your soul and desires your salvation. Such a friend reminds you of your end with love and truth. The remembrance of death makes these friendships deeper, more honest, more grace-filled. It teaches believers to speak words that matter: encouragement, correction, intercession, gratitude. A spiritual friend becomes, in a sense, a witness to your life—a person who helps you live ready for the judgment and the feast to come.

This communal dimension extends to the way Christians pray for the dead. The remembrance of death connects the living and the departed in a bond of charity that transcends time. Praying for the dead is a daily act of love, a way of participating in God's mercy toward those who have gone before us. It is a reminder that the Church is not limited to those who walk the earth. It also purifies the heart from the illusion that love ends at death. The saints teach that our prayers assist those undergoing purification. In praying for them, the soul becomes more aware of its own need for mercy and more eager to prepare for its own encounter with God.

The remembrance of death also ennobles fasting. Fasting reminds the body of its limits and the soul of its dependence. It sharpens attention, strengthens resolve, and makes room for prayer. When joined to memento mori, fasting becomes a daily participation in the dying and rising of Christ. It trains the soul to relinquish comfort for the sake of love. It purifies desire. It prepares the heart to meet God with hunger for righteousness rather than attachment to pleasure. Fasting, when done with humility, aligns the soul with the Cross, where death becomes the gateway to life.

Almsgiving, too, becomes transformed. The remembrance of death turns generosity into an investment in eternity. Jesus teaches that what we give to the poor becomes treasure in heaven. A Christian who remembers death becomes free from the fear of loss, because he knows he cannot take earthly wealth beyond the grave. Generosity becomes joyful rather than burdensome. It becomes a declaration of trust: that God will provide, that love is eternal, that the kingdom is worth more than possessions. Almsgiving is one of the most concrete ways to live ready for judgment, because Jesus identifies Himself with the needy and promises reward to those who serve them.

Another essential daily practice is the discipline of intentional presence. Modern life scatters the mind. Distraction fragments attention. The remembrance of death gathers the soul. It teaches the Christian to be present—to people, to tasks, to God. Intentional presence is a spiritual discipline because it resists the temptations of acedia, which thrives on distraction and fragmentation. When the Christian chooses to be fully present—to listen deeply, to pray attentively, to work carefully—he honours the God who is ever-present. Presence becomes a form of vigilance, a way of refusing to sleepwalk through life.

Intentional presence also enriches prayer. When the mind is present, prayer becomes encounter rather than recitation. Even brief prayers, when prayed with full attention, unite the soul more deeply to God. The remembrance of death prompts this attentiveness. It whispers, "This may be the last prayer you ever pray." Not to frighten, but to awaken. Not to burden, but to elevate. When the Christian prays with this awareness, prayer becomes more earnest, more sincere, more loving.

Finally, all these daily practices converge in a single invitation: to live each day as if it were one's last. This does not produce recklessness or despair. It produces clarity, sobriety, and peace. To live each day as if it were the last is to live each day with open hands, a clean conscience, and a heart that is reconciled to God and neighbour. It is to live with intention rather than drift, with gratitude rather than entitlement, with love rather than indifference.

A life that practices memento mori daily becomes a life that is fully alive. It sees the world truthfully, loves people deeply, and seeks God wholeheartedly. It becomes a life that anticipates the final moment with hope, because that moment will unveil the One the heart has learned to love in every small act of daily faithfulness. Through these practices, the Christian becomes not merely prepared for death but prepared for union, prepared for joy, prepared for the Bridegroom who comes.

All these threads—prayer, silence, gratitude, repentance, constancy, community, sacramental life, simplicity, holy desire, purified ambition, fasting, almsgiving, reconciliation, and intentional presence—form a single tapestry. It is the tapestry of a Christian who lives awake. Not frantic, not fearful, not morbid—awake. Awake to the shortness of life, awake to the love of God, awake to the kingdom that draws near. The remembrance of death, practiced daily, becomes a spiritual atmosphere in which the soul breathes more freely. It clears the fog that often settles over the Christian life, cutting through triviality and revealing the eternal beneath the ordinary.

To remember death daily is to refuse the illusion of endless tomorrows. It is to choose today. The Christian who lives this way stops postponing conversion, stops delaying forgiveness, stops drifting through sacraments, stops sleepwalking through relationships. He becomes a person who answers grace without hesitation. He becomes a person who knows that life is not a rehearsal but a pilgrimage, and that every step of that pilgrimage is precious. This is why memento mori is not a morbid fixation but a liberation. It frees the soul from the tyranny of the unimportant.

And this liberation does not lead to detachment from life but to deeper engagement with it. When the Christian remembers death, he loves more fiercely, because he knows that love alone endures. He forgives more quickly, because he knows that grudges will look absurd in the light of eternity. He prays more sincerely, because he knows that prayer is a foretaste of the communion that will one day be eternal. He seeks virtue with greater seriousness, because he knows that the soul he shapes today is the soul he will offer to God.

The remembrance of death infuses daily life with meaning. When the Christian wakes, he sees the morning as a gift. When he works, he sees labour as participation in God's creation. When he suffers, he sees sorrow as the Cross that prepares him for resurrection. When he rests, he sees sabbath as a rehearsal for heaven. When he prays, he sees eternity breaking into time. The remembrance of death turns life into a sacrament of readiness.

This readiness is not rooted in fear but in longing. The more the Christian remembers death, the more he learns to desire God. The heart begins to sense that this life is not the final chapter but the threshold of something infinitely greater. The remembrance of death does not dull desire; it intensifies it. It forms within the soul a quiet ache for the Bridegroom—a longing that transforms vigilance from duty into delight. The Christian becomes like the wise virgins who kept their lamps trimmed, not because they feared the night, but because they desired the One who would come in it.

At its core, memento mori is the daily embrace of truth: the truth about life's brevity, the truth about the soul's dignity, the truth about God's faithfulness. When the Christian remembers death daily, he begins to see everything else in the proper light. Trials become temporary. Temptations become battles with eternal consequences. People become unrepeatable gifts. Time becomes sacred. And Christ becomes the horizon toward which every moment moves.

This is the fruit of memento mori. By remembering death, the Christian remembers what matters. By seeing the end, he understands the journey. By living each day as preparation for the final day, he discovers the secret of the saints: that those who are most ready to die are the ones who are most alive.

In these daily practices, the remembrance of death becomes the remembrance of love. It shapes a soul that does not fear the final hour but welcomes it as the moment when faith becomes sight. It trains the heart to hear, even now, the distant echo of the Bridegroom's voice. And it forms within the Christian a life that is ready—ready not merely to end, but to be completed in the One who conquers death.

18

Detachment: Freedom from the Tyranny of Comfort

From the beginning, the people of God have struggled with the same quiet danger: the temptation to make life comfortable enough that the soul forgets why it was created. The ancient idols have changed their names, but not their nature. The heart that once bowed before Baal now bows before convenience. The spirit that once feared famine now fears discomfort. The world promises relief, ease, distraction, and control, and even the faithful often mistake these promises for peace. Yet the Scriptures speak with unsettling clarity: the human being cannot be free while enslaved to comfort. What we cling to becomes our master. What we refuse to surrender shapes the borders of our love.

Jesus does not hide this truth; He reveals it with a severity born of love. "If any man would come after Me, let him deny himself, take up his cross daily, and follow Me" (Lk 9:23). These words stand at the centre of discipleship. They do not describe a heroic spirituality reserved for the advanced. They describe the daily posture of every Christian who has understood the cost of love. Self-denial is not repression; it is the refusal to let self-rule eclipse God-rule. It is the decision to dethrone comfort so that Christ may reign. The cross is not a symbol of sadness but of freedom—the place where the false self dies so that the true self may live.

This same urgency pulses through Jesus' discourse on the cost of discipleship. "Whoever does not renounce all that he has cannot be My disciple" (Lk 14:33). The command strikes modern ears as excessive. Yet Christ is not demanding contempt for creation; He is demanding sovereignty over the heart. The "renunciation" He speaks of is not hatred for the good things of earth; it is the reordering of love according to the Kingdom. He is naming a spiritual truth that has always governed human existence: the heart cannot be divided and remain whole. The disciple must choose his treasure, because the treasure he chooses will become his master. "For where your treasure is, there will your heart be also" (Mt 6:21).

This reordering is not merely a discipline—it is salvation's logic. Scripture shows again and again how divided affections disintegrate the soul. Lot's wife turned back because her heart was still in Sodom. Demas abandoned Paul "because he loved this present world" (2 Tim 4:10). The seed in Jesus' parable that fell among thorns grew for a time but never bore fruit, "for the cares of the world and the delight in riches and the desire for other things enter in and choke the word" (Mk 4:19). The language is unyielding: these attachments choke, suffocate, and consume the potential of grace. They do not merely distract the soul; they deform it.

The Fathers understood this with piercing insight. Origen spoke of the Christian life as the "exodus of the heart," the slow departure from Egypt's bondage toward the freedom of God. To cling to the world, he said, is to "tie one's soul to the carts of Pharaoh," dragged where one does not wish to go. St. Basil taught that attachment to wealth or honour is not simply imprudent; it is a form of imprisonment. "The more a man possesses," he wrote, "the more he is possessed." St.

Gregory of Nyssa observed that the soul must be "lightened" if it is to ascend toward God, because "no one runs swiftly while carrying a weight." Their collective witness points to one truth: love becomes expansive when freed; constricted when bound.

This is why the monastic tradition speaks so starkly of death—not merely the death of the body, but the death of the self-will. The monk's renunciation is not an escape from the world; it is the restoration of desire. Detachment is the soil in which love becomes possible. In the desert sayings, Abba Alonius declares, "If a man does not say in his heart, 'I alone and God are in the world,' he will not find peace." This is not individualism but interior freedom—the ability to live without being ruled by the environment, by possessions, or by the opinions of others.

The monastic understanding of the "double death" belongs here as well. The Christian dies twice: once to the world, and once in the world. The first death is voluntary. It is the death of ego, pride, self-protection, and the endless search for comfort. The second is inevitable, the natural end of mortal life. The Fathers insist that the first prepares for the second. "Die before you die," they say, "so that when you die, you will not die." This paradox echoes the words of Christ: "He who loses his life for My sake will find it" (Mt 10:39). Death to the world is the discovery of the Kingdom. Detachment is the birth of freedom.

The Scriptures reinforce this movement. Jesus declares, "No one who puts his hand to the plow and looks back is fit for the Kingdom of God" (Lk 9:62). The backward glance is not nostalgia; it is captivity. It is the refusal to fully enter the future God offers. It is longing for Egypt while walking toward the Promised Land. St. Paul deepens the same truth when he writes, "We brought nothing into the world, and we cannot take anything out of the world" (1 Tim 6:7). The apostle is not speaking cynically; he is reminding the Church that life is pilgrimage. Only what is given to God endures.

This pilgrimage of detachment is not bleak. It is luminous. It restores the heart to its true size. The soul that clings to lesser goods becomes small; the soul that surrenders them becomes spacious. Augustine wrote that humanity is shaped by love's direction: "Two loves built two cities." The love of self to the contempt of God builds the earthly city. The love of God to the contempt of self builds the heavenly one. Detachment is the turning of love toward its true home. It is the refusal to let temporary desires eclipse eternal joy.

The remembrance of death sharpens this truth. Memento mori does not despise the world; it reveals its fragility. It teaches the soul to hold lightly what it cannot keep. It frees the heart to cherish what it can never lose. When the Christian remembers death, he discovers the value of every moment and the boundaries of every earthly good. The illusion of permanence dissolves. Gratitude deepens. Priorities reorder. Love clarifies. The soul becomes awake.

The modern world, perhaps more than any age before it, finds detachment unintelligible. We live within an unspoken creed that equates fullness of life with fullness of possession, that identifies happiness with ease, that interprets inconvenience as injustice. Entire economies turn on the cultivation of desire, and entire vocabularies have developed to justify indulgence. The human will, once trained by Scripture to rise toward God, is now trained by culture to curve inward, seeking constantly to be served, soothed, and spared. This is the tyranny of comfort. It dulls the edge of longing. It blinds the inner eye. It lulls the soul into a quiet belief that the present arrangement of conveniences is all that life requires.

Yet beneath the surface of this cultivated ease lies a more ancient truth: the heart grows restless when it is fed with what cannot satisfy. Augustine's famous confession—"Our hearts are restless until they rest in You"—is not an abstract proverb. It is an anthropology. The human being was not made to be comfortable; the human being was made to love. Comfort, when enthroned, begins to suffocate that capacity. It shrinks desire rather than fulfilling it. It creates small joys at the cost of great ones. It pacifies the soul into a manageable shallowness. And Christ refuses to leave His disciples in such captivity.

This is why the Gospels are filled with Jesus' hard sayings. He speaks not to punish but to purify. He lays bare the attachments that keep the heart confined and calls the disciple into a greater spaciousness of love. His command, "Deny yourself" (Lk 9:23), is not the suppression of joy but the restoration of it. It is the refusal to let the small self eclipse the true self—the self created for communion, for holiness, for the love of the Father. Jesus names the posture that makes this possible: "Whoever does not bear his own cross and come after Me cannot be My disciple" (Lk 14:27). In these words, the Lord is not glorifying suffering for its own sake; He is describing the death of the false self, the surrender of the ego's demands, the dismantling of pride's fortress.

The cross, then, is not primarily an exterior burden. It is the interior freedom that comes from letting go of what binds. It is the acceptance of God's way over one's own way. It is the daily death that allows the daily resurrection. The early Christians understood this with clarity. Hermas, in *The Shepherd*, speaks of the Christian as one who must "put away double-mindedness and the desires of this world" if he wishes to stand firm. The Epistle to Diognetus describes believers as those who "dwell in the world but are not of the world," living a paradoxical freedom because their hearts are anchored elsewhere.

The parable of the sower amplifies this truth with sobering precision. Jesus identifies a particular danger: "the cares of the world, and the delight in riches, and the desire for other things" (Mk 4:19). These are not the gross sins that the believer easily recognizes and rejects.

They are the subtle entanglements that weave themselves into daily life almost unnoticed. They do not attack the word; they choke it. They do not deny the Gospel; they smother it. They do not destroy the seed; they starve it of space. Christ reveals that the soil of the heart becomes fertile only when it is spacious enough for the Word to take root. Detachment is the cultivation of that spaciousness.

There is a deep wisdom in the Fathers here. Gregory the Great observed that "earthly desires are like smoke: they rise for a moment and then dissipate, leaving the eyes stung and blinded." Chrysostom warned that "even small attachments, if left unchecked, can weigh down the wings of prayer." Maximos the Confessor offered a penetrating diagnosis: the passions are not destroyed by force but by the reordering of love. "The one who loves God," he wrote, "loves nothing merely for its own sake." This is the essence of detachment: the refusal to love anything apart from God, so that everything can be loved rightly within God.

Memento mori intensifies this process. The remembrance of death pierces illusions of permanence. It dissolves the lie that comfort can protect us, prolong us, or define us. It reminds the soul that every earthly good, no matter how noble, will one day be surrendered. The Christian who remembers death is not a pessimist; he is a realist. He sees the world as gift, not possession. He receives without clinging. He enjoys without worshipping. He releases without despairing. The remembrance of death draws the horizon of eternity close enough to touch, and in that light, the things that once ruled the heart lose their throne.

Detachment, then, is not a flight from creation but a flight toward its meaning. The heart that releases its claim on lesser goods becomes capable of receiving greater ones. Poverty of spirit is not the refusal of joy but its preparation. Jesus blesses the poor in spirit not because they lack but because they are free. Their hands are open. Their hearts are uncluttered. Their desires are not diluted by competing loves. They are capable of seeing God because nothing obstructs the view.

The tradition often speaks of earthly life as pilgrimage. This is not metaphor; it is identity. The pilgrim does not build his home along the road. He travels light because weight slows love's journey. He carries only what he must, and even these belongings are held loosely. St. Peter calls the faithful "aliens and exiles" (1 Pet 2:11), not as a rebuke but as a reminder of dignity. Our citizenship is in heaven. Our hearts are made for a homeland we have not yet seen. Detachment is the refusal to mistake the road for the destination.

This interior freedom transforms how the disciple engages the world. Simplicity becomes not a form of austerity but a dynamic form of clarity. Poverty of spirit becomes not a spiritual minimalism but a maximal openness to God. The soul begins to understand what St. Isaac the Syrian meant when he wrote, "The one who has found the Kingdom within needs nothing from without." The less the heart depends on the fragile promises of the world, the more it discovers the indestructible promises of God.

Detachment is best understood not as subtraction but as expansion. When Christ calls the disciple to denial of self, He is not diminishing the self but liberating it. The self that clings fiercely to possessions, positions, and preferences is a cramped self, one whose horizons have closed in upon its own small orbit. But the self surrendered to God becomes wide, spacious, and capacious—capable of receiving a life infinitely larger than the one it tried to secure. This is why the saints could give everything away and yet never become diminished. Their poverty was abundance. Their surrender was victory. Their losses were gains, because their hearts had room for God.

The monastic fathers understood this with remarkable precision. Their teachings on the "double death" reveal a spiritual anthropology of extraordinary depth. Death to the world—voluntary, interior, decisive—is the first death. It is the renunciation of the illusions that bind. It is the death of self-will, the death of the passions' tyranny, the death of the ego's endless hunger for recognition. This death is not repressive; it is creative. It clears the interior ground so that divine love can take root. Then comes the second death: the natural end of earthly life. For the one who has already died voluntarily, this death becomes a passage rather than a terror. The first death prepares for the second; the first death transforms the second. As the desert fathers say, "If you die before you die, you will not die when you die."

These ancient voices were not romanticizing asceticism. They were describing a law written into the human condition: the soul that refuses to let go will eventually be torn away. The soul that learns to release finds peace. Detachment trains the heart for the moment when every earthly attachment must be surrendered. It frees the Christian to greet death—not as an intruder, but as the final stripping away of what was never permanent. This does not trivialize grief or minimize suffering. It simply places them within the horizon of truth.

St. John Climacus saw this clearly. In his *Ladder of Divine Ascent* he writes, "A detached man is not one who has no possessions, but one who is not possessed by them." Detachment is an interior condition, not an exterior arrangement. A wealthy man who holds loosely what he has may be more detached than a poor man consumed by envy or fear. Poverty of spirit is measured not by the inventory of one's life but by the orientation of one's heart. Climacus likens attachment to a thread: even if it is thin, it binds. Even a light cord prevents flight. The smallest love, if wrongly ordered, becomes the chain that restrains the soul.

This teaching is echoed by Cassian, who warns that the most dangerous forms of attachment are not gross or obvious. They are subtle. They hide within habits, comforts, unspoken expectations, and unexamined desires. He writes that the devil prefers to tempt monks not with great luxuries but with small delights—"for a small delight, when clung to, becomes a great snare." Detachment begins not with dramatic renunciations but with the quiet honesty that names what holds the heart. It is the prayerful recognition of what we cannot let go.

In this sense, detachment and memento mori belong together. The remembrance of death shines a gentle but relentless light on the heart's concealed attachments. It reveals what we fear losing. It uncovers the illusions we have built to feel secure. It shows us the small idols we have tucked into our pockets, hidden under the folds of daily life. Death has a way of exposing truth. The Christian who remembers death regularly becomes wise because he lives with the clarity that nothing in this world can be kept. The Christian who forgets death becomes vulnerable to illusion because he tries to build permanence out of what is passing away.

Jesus names this logic repeatedly. "Do not store up for yourselves treasures on earth," He says, "where moth and rust destroy and thieves break in and steal" (Mt 6:19). The fragility of earthly treasure is not a threat; it is a revelation. What rust can touch is not worth clinging to. What thieves can steal is not worthy of fear. Christ invites the disciple to place his heart where no thief can enter, no rust can corrode, no death can reach. "Store up for yourselves treasures in heaven… for where your treasure is, there your heart will be also" (Mt 6:20–21). Detachment becomes, therefore, the practical expression of heavenly investment. It is the reallocation of desire toward eternity.

The call to relinquish what binds is not abstract. Jesus makes it painfully concrete when He says, "No one who puts his hand to the plow and looks back is fit for the Kingdom of God" (Lk 9:62). The backward glance is the gesture of nostalgia, the unwillingness to release the familiar, the reluctance to trust God's future. It is the longing for Egypt even as one walks toward freedom. Lot's wife embodies this truth—turned into a pillar of salt not out of cruelty, but as a witness to divided desire. She left the city with her feet but not with her heart. Jesus warns that divided hearts cannot enter the Kingdom because they cannot bear its fire. The gaze fixed backward reveals a heart that is not ready for God.

The early Church fathers return again and again to this image of the backward glance. Cyril of Alexandria interprets it as the soul's refusal to let go of worldly patterns. Augustine uses it to illustrate the inner battle between two loves. Maximos sees in it the divided self caught between pleasure and virtue. The common theme is unmistakable: attachment is a direction of the heart, not merely a possession of the hands. What the heart clings to determines what the heart becomes.

Here, simplicity emerges not as an aesthetic preference but as a spiritual strategy. A simple life is a life unburdened. It is a life whose freedom is safeguarded by restraint. Simplicity is the virtue that takes the excess weight off the soul so that love can move swiftly. It frees the mind from clutter, the desires from excess, the will from paralysis. It clarifies what matters. It makes the heart agile. It teaches the Christian how to live lightly in a world heavy with distractions.

The tyrannies of the modern age—consumerism, entertainment, noise, digital saturation—are not new in essence, only in form. They operate on an ancient principle: distract the heart long enough, and it will forget to desire God. Detachment is the antidote. It is the reminder that nothing the world promises can be kept, and everything God promises will be fulfilled. It is the interior stance that says, quietly and firmly, "My life is not here to be comfortable; it is here to become holy."

The saints, who lived this truth rather than merely speaking of it, reveal how detachment becomes the architecture of Christian freedom. Consider Francis of Assisi, who renounced wealth not out of disdain for beauty but out of love for the One who is Beauty itself. When he cast off his rich garments, he was not becoming less himself; he was becoming more himself. He discovered that the heart is not enlarged by acquisition but by surrender. His poverty was not a rejection of creation; it was a refusal to let the gifts of God eclipse the Giver. In the same way, Thérèse of Lisieux embraced "spiritual childhood," a posture of radical trust that required letting go of every illusion of self-sufficiency. She wrote, "The only thing I desire now is to love until I die of love." Such love is possible only for the heart unbound.

But if the saints reveal the heights of detachment, the monks reveal its training ground. The monastic life is structured around intentional limits—silence, simplicity, obedience, poverty, stability—not to punish the soul but to purify it. Abba Moses taught that detachment frees a monk to see reality clearly: "Sit in your cell, and your cell will teach you everything." The "cell" is not merely a physical space; it is a spiritual posture. It is the place where distraction withers because there is nothing left to distract. It is the furnace where unnecessary desires are burned away. It is the school where the soul learns to desire God without rival.

St. Benedict, perhaps the most influential architect of Western monasticism, wove detachment directly into his Rule. The monk is not permitted to hoard, to cling, or to claim. He is to receive what is given and release what is taken. His stability in place—the vow to remain rooted—fosters stability of heart. He is not permitted to flee discomfort, because discomfort reveals what the heart still fears. Detachment is the training of desire, the formation of a heart trained to respond to God swiftly and joyfully. The more lightly the monk lives, the more readily he can say, "My heart is ready, O God, my heart is ready" (Ps 57:7).

And here memento mori becomes the gentle mentor of the Christian soul. The remembrance of death awakens urgency without anxiety, sobriety without despair. When death is forgotten, the soul drifts. It delays. It bargains. It imagines it has endless tomorrows. But when death is remembered—quietly, steadily, truthfully—the heart becomes sharp. It learns to measure moments not by their comfort but by their eternal weight. Detachment begins to feel natural rather than forced. Simplicity becomes appealing rather than burdensome. The illusions of permanence dissolve, and the soul begins to breathe freely again.

The remembrance of death is also the great equalizer of attachments. It teaches the Christian that nothing he fears losing will survive his death anyway. It exposes the folly of hoarding, the absurdity of vanity, the fragility of worldly fame. Death whispers, "You will carry none of this with you." Yet this whisper is not meant to terrify; it is meant to reorder. It invites the believer to hold possessions as though lending them, to hold relationships with gratitude rather than grasping, to hold time as a gift rather than a guarantee. The Christian who remembers death often becomes paradoxically more generous, more joyful, more liberated, because his heart is no longer chained to what must one day be surrendered.

This interior freedom has profound implications for how the disciple engages suffering. When comfort is no longer enthroned, suffering loses much of its power. It still wounds, but it does not define. It still tests, but it does not enslave. Suffering becomes not the collapse of one's world but the moment when faith reveals its strength. Detachment prepares the soul to meet suffering with courage because the soul has already relinquished the illusion that life can be controlled. The Christian who has practiced letting go is not undone when the world takes something away.

Here, again, the monastic tradition provides clarity. St. Isaac the Syrian teaches that "the heart that has embraced simplicity is not troubled by the loss of anything." He does not deny grief; he denies bondage. For Isaac, simplicity is the crown of detachment—the interior state in which nothing but God can rule the heart. When earthly goods are removed, the heart remains whole because it was never dependent on them for its identity. This is not indifference but liberation. It is not coldness but strength.

St. Paisios of Mount Athos expressed the same truth in modern terms when he warned that "comfort is the tomb of the soul." He did not mean that comfort is evil; he meant that when comfort becomes the measure of life, life withers. Growth requires risk. Holiness requires sacrifice. Love requires vulnerability. Detachment protects the heart from the paralysis that comfort creates. It teaches the Christian to desire God more than ease, truth more than approval, holiness more than security.

Jesus exemplifies this in His own earthly life. He had nowhere to lay His head (Mt 8:20). He entered cities without possessions. He taught His disciples not to worry about what they would eat or wear because "your Heavenly Father knows that you need them all" (Mt 6:32). His detachment was not poverty for its own sake; it was perfect trust. It was freedom from the tyranny of fear. It was the life of a Son who knew He was secure in the Father's love. For Jesus, detachment was the natural posture of a heart anchored in eternity.

His teaching reflects this identity. When He says, "Sell your possessions and give to the poor" (Lk 12:33), He is not imposing a burden; He is inviting freedom. When He warns that the rich will enter the Kingdom only with difficulty, He is not condemning wealth; He is revealing the spiritual gravity that wealth exerts. When He declares that the one who seeks to save his life will lose it, but the one who loses his life for His sake will find it (Mt 16:25), He is unveiling the paradox at the heart of Christian existence. Life is found in surrender.

Freedom is found in letting go. Joy is found not in accumulation but in communion.

Detachment also restores the Christian's relationship with time. The attached soul lives in a constant tension between the past it refuses to release and the future it anxiously tries to control. It clings to what once offered security and grasps at what might offer more. Time becomes adversarial. The past feels heavy, the future feels threatening, and the present feels insufficient. Jesus repeatedly addresses this spiritual distortion. "Do not worry about tomorrow," He says, "for tomorrow will worry about its own things" (Mt 6:34). The invitation is not carelessness but trust. The one who seeks first the Kingdom can live in the present because he is not enslaved to outcomes. Detachment frees the heart to inhabit today.

This is the wisdom of the manna in the wilderness. Israel was given enough for the day, never for the week, so that they might learn to trust God rather than store anxiety. When they attempted to hoard, the manna rotted. When they relied on God, they were fed. The lesson was simple: security rooted in possession leads to decay, but security rooted in God leads to peace. Detachment is the spiritual manna of the Christian life. It teaches the soul to live without hoarding, without grasping, without trying to secure a future that belongs to God alone. "Give us this day our daily bread" becomes not only a petition but a posture.

The remembrance of death sharpens this disposition. When the Christian reflects on the brevity of life, he sees the futility of anxiety. Death exposes the illusion of control. It reveals that every earthly plan and every great accumulation will one day be surrendered. Yet far from inducing despair, memento mori can produce deep gratitude. Time becomes precious precisely because it is finite. Each day becomes a gift rather than an entitlement. The present moment becomes the place where eternity touches earth. The Christian who remembers death is freed to live fully—not in fear of losing time but in wonder at receiving it.

Detachment also reorders the imagination. The attached soul imagines happiness as comfort, pleasure, ease, or recognition. It imagines holiness as a path that should not cost too much. It imagines God as Someone who ought to bless its plans. The detached soul sees differently. It imagines happiness as communion with God. It imagines holiness as participation in the life of Christ. It imagines suffering as opportunity, sacrifice as love, and the future as a horizon of hope. Detachment is not the shrinking of life but the enlargement of imagination. It trains the heart to see as God sees, to love as God loves, to hope as God promises.

The saints testify to this transfigured imagination. Catherine of Siena wrote that "all the way to heaven is heaven, because Jesus said, I am the Way." Julian of Norwich, amid suffering and turmoil, could say, "All shall be well," not because her circumstances were easy but because her heart was anchored in God. Their lives demonstrate that detachment is not emotional suppression but spiritual clarity—the ability to view the world through the lens of eternity. When the heart is no longer dominated by attachment, it becomes capable of joy even in hardship and peace even in uncertainty.

This clarity reveals another truth: attachment is rarely about objects. It is about identity. People cling to possessions because they fear insignificance. They cling to comfort because they fear pain. They cling to approval because they fear rejection. They cling to control because they fear vulnerability. The object is not the idol; the insecurity is. Detachment therefore does not target things but the fears that animate them. It asks the Christian: *Where does your security come from? What defines your worth? Whose voice determines your identity?* Every attachment answers these questions falsely. Every act of detachment answers them truthfully.

Jesus addresses this identity-rooted attachment when He says, "One's life does not consist in the abundance of possessions" (Lk 12:15). Life consists in relation—to the Father who creates, to the Son who redeems, to the Spirit who sanctifies. Possessions cannot protect life; they cannot prolong it; they cannot deepen it. They can only distract from it. This is why Christ calls His disciples to become like children. Children trust. Children receive. Children release. Their identity is given, not achieved, and therefore their freedom is intact. Detachment restores this childlike trust—not naivety, but a mature simplicity that relies entirely on God.

In this light, poverty of spirit becomes not deprivation but abundance. It is the realization that everything good comes from God and everything necessary will be provided. It is the refusal to root identity in anything fragile or fading. Jesus blesses the poor in spirit because their hearts are unencumbered and therefore receptive. They are not weighed down by the turbulence of competing desires. They are not pulled apart by the demands of self-worship. Their poverty is wealth because it makes space for God.

When detachment matures into simplicity of life, it colours every detail of daily existence. Simplicity is not the rejection of beauty but the refusal to be drowned by excess. It is the gentle discipline of choosing less in order to love more. It is the quiet decision to live with open hands rather than clenched fists. The Christian who embraces simplicity discovers that joy becomes easier, gratitude becomes deeper, and prayer becomes more natural. The noise of unnecessary desires fades. The heart becomes a place where God can speak.

Here the remembrance of death performs its final work. It reminds the Christian that comfort cannot accompany him into eternity. It reveals that the things most fiercely hoarded here will be forgotten there. It shows that the life lived lightly is the life lived well. When the soul acknowledges its mortality, it stops demanding from the world what only God can give. It becomes less anxious, less frantic, less divided. It begins to live not for the sake of accumulating but for the sake of becoming. Detachment becomes the path by which the soul learns to desire heaven more than earth.

Detachment restores the meaning of sacrifice. In a culture that treats sacrifice as loss, Jesus reveals it as gain. "Whoever loses his life for My sake will find it" (Mt 16:25). The vocabulary is jarring only when measured by worldly standards. Measured by the Kingdom, the logic is luminous: sacrifice enlarges the heart because it frees it from the tyranny of self. Sacrifice teaches the Christian to value what endures. Sacrifice sharpens vision, deepens compassion, strengthens resolve. The attached heart resists sacrifice because it believes it will be diminished; the detached heart embraces sacrifice because it knows it will be transformed. This is why the saints do not fear giving away what the world treasures—they have discovered treasures the world cannot see.

The cross itself is the supreme revelation of this truth. Jesus renounces not only possessions but reputation, comfort, and even the natural right to life. His poverty on Calvary is not humiliation but triumph. He gives all because He desires all. His total detachment is the fullest expression of divine love. Yet what appears as abandonment is in fact consummation. St. Paul declares, "Though He was rich, for your sake He became poor, so that by His poverty you might become rich" (2 Cor 8:9). The poverty of Christ is the wealth of the Church. In His self-emptying, He reveals the pattern of redeemed humanity: life poured out becomes life restored. In His surrender, the mystery of detachment reaches its perfection.

The early martyrs lived this logic with breathtaking clarity. They faced death not because they despised life but because they loved eternal life more. When St. Ignatius of Antioch begged his fellow

Christians not to rescue him from martyrdom, he was not displaying morbid zeal; he was expressing the freedom of a heart no longer enslaved by fear. "Let me be food for the beasts," he wrote, "that I may become the pure bread of Christ." His detachment was not nihilism; it was nuptial. He longed for union with the One he loved. Martyrdom, in his mind, was not loss but consummation. The world can make no sense of such courage because the world cannot imagine a love stronger than comfort.

This same pattern appears in quieter, more hidden forms of detachment. Parents who sacrifice their ambitions for the good of their children. Spouses who surrender pride to preserve unity. Priests who renounce earthly security to shepherd souls. Monks who give up the noise of the world for a life of unbroken prayer. These sacrifices are not punishments; they are freedoms. They are the daily renunciations that make love possible. Detachment is not merely an idea; it is a habit of self-giving lived in kitchens, workplaces, monasteries, and parishes. Every act of surrender is a small victory over the tyranny of comfort. Every sacrifice is a confession of the heart's true treasure.

St. Gregory Nazianzen once wrote, "What is not assumed cannot be healed; what is not surrendered cannot be saved." He spoke of Christ's incarnation, but the principle applies to the Christian life as well. What we refuse to surrender cannot be transformed. What we cling to becomes the measure of our bondage. Detachment is the offering of the whole self to God so that the whole self can be made whole. This is not a transaction; it is a transformation. The heart learns to say, "Take what must be taken, give what must be given—only let me be Yours."

The remembrance of death strengthens this disposition brilliantly. When the Christian considers that everything he clings to will one day be taken from his hands, he begins to practice letting go early.

He anticipates the final surrender by voluntary surrenders now. This is what the monks meant by dying twice. The first death prepares the second. The first death sanctifies the second. The Christian who practices detachment daily discovers that, little by little, the fear of losing anything diminishes. The terror of death loses its teeth. The soul meets mortality with a strange calm because it has already surrendered what death will one day claim.

Here the pilgrimage imagery becomes indispensable. Earthly life is a journey, not a destination. The pilgrim travels light because unnecessary weight slows the pace. The pilgrim keeps moving because the homeland is ahead, not behind. The pilgrim expects difficulty, not because he despises comfort, but because he trusts the path. Scripture saturates this insight. "We seek the city that is to come" (Heb 13:14). "Our citizenship is in heaven" (Phil 3:20). "We walk by faith, not by sight" (2 Cor 5:7). Detachment is the pilgrim's virtue—the refusal to pitch one's tent where God has not asked one to remain. The one who clings to this world becomes stuck; the one who lets go becomes free.

The fathers often warned that nothing hinders prayer more than attachment. Evagrius says, "A wandering heart begets wandering thoughts." What causes the heart to wander? Desire without order. Fear without trust. Possession without surrender. The one who clings to comfort finds prayer difficult because he is pulled in too many directions. His loves are divided; his heart is crowded. But for the one who has embraced detachment, prayer becomes natural. His heart has space. His desires are simplified. His attention is clear. He becomes like Mary of Bethany, who sits at the feet of Jesus because she has chosen "the one thing necessary" (Lk 10:42). The attached heart is restless; the detached heart is at rest.

This rest is not passivity; it is readiness. The Christian who has embraced detachment becomes alert, watchful, spiritually agile. He does not cling to earthly securities because he is anchored in divine security. He does not fear loss because his treasure cannot be lost. He does not hesitate to obey because no earthly attachment contends for his loyalty. Detachment forms a heart that can say "yes" to God before knowing what the cost will be. It forms a soul that can receive the unexpected without panic, the difficult without despair, the joyful without idolatry. Detachment strengthens the heart for obedience.

As this readiness deepens, the disciple begins to see the world differently. Beauty becomes gift rather than possession. Relationships become sacred trusts rather than instruments of security. Work becomes participation in God's creativity rather than a ladder to self-worth. Even suffering becomes transformed—not sought, not welcomed, but not feared. The detached heart does not imagine that pain means abandonment. It understands that pain is an unavoidable part of love in a fallen world. Suffering becomes a place where detachment and trust meet, where the soul learns again that hope rests not on circumstances but on Christ.

Detachment ultimately clears the way for love. The attached soul loves selectively, conditionally, and fearfully. It cannot give fully because it fears losing what it holds. It cannot receive fully because its hands are full. It cannot rejoice fully because it is haunted by the possibility of loss. The detached soul, however, is capable of a love that is wholehearted and enduring. Its freedom allows it to love people rather than use them, to serve rather than manipulate, to bless rather than grasp. The one who has been freed from the tyranny of comfort becomes capable of the uncomfortable compassion demanded by the Gospel—the compassion that visits the sick, feeds the hungry, welcomes the stranger, forgives the enemy, and carries the burdens of the weak.

This is why the Beatitudes begin with poverty of spirit. "Blessed are the poor in spirit, for theirs is the Kingdom of heaven" (Mt 5:3).

The Kingdom belongs to the detached because only the detached can receive it. Those who cling to comfort cling to a counterfeit kingdom, one that crumbles at the slightest tremor. Poverty of spirit is not a virtue reserved for monks or mystics. It is the entryway into Christian existence. It is the recognition that everything belongs to God, that everything comes from God, and that everything returns to God. The poor in spirit are those who live with open hands, receiving and surrendering with equal trust.

St. Augustine captures the radical beauty of this freedom when he says, "Love God, and do what you will." The phrase is often misunderstood. Augustine does not mean that detachment eliminates moral boundaries. He means that detachment purifies desire so completely that the will aligned with God's love becomes incapable of choosing against Him. The whole person—mind, heart, and will—is ordered toward the One who created him. This is the fruit of detachment: the healing of desire. The heart that once loved many things chaotically now loves one thing rightly, and in that love, all other loves are redeemed.

The modern world struggles to imagine such freedom. It equates detachment with deprivation, self-denial with repression, poverty of spirit with weakness. Yet the saints show us that detachment strengthens the soul. It equips us to face loss without collapse, to face temptation without compromise, to face death without despair. Detachment was the strength of martyrs, the stability of monks, the courage of missionaries, the endurance of parents, the fidelity of spouses, the wisdom of elders. It is not a virtue for the elite; it is the necessary posture for anyone who desires to follow Christ without reserve.

Memento mori makes this truth shine with unmistakable clarity. When the Christian remembers that death will take all that is temporary, he becomes free to invest in what is eternal. He becomes free to love without fear, to serve without calculation, to pray without distraction. Detachment becomes not an ascetical burden but the natural fruit of wisdom. It is the recognition that life's true treasure is not found in what can be possessed but in the One who cannot be lost. Every day becomes a rehearsal for the final day. Every surrender becomes preparation for the final surrender. Every act of love becomes a step toward the One who is Love itself.

The tyranny of comfort begins to crumble when death is remembered rightly. The heart that once clung fiercely to the things of earth begins to release them gently. Gratitude replaces entitlement. Simplicity replaces excess. Peace replaces anxiety. The soul becomes attuned to the movements of grace, alert to the presence of God, ready for the Bridegroom. The Christian no longer asks, "How much can I keep?" but "How freely can I give?" No longer "How can I avoid suffering?" but "How can I love in the midst of it?" No longer "How can I preserve myself?" but "How can I offer myself?" Detachment becomes not the shrinking of life but the blossoming of it.

And when death finally comes—as it will for each of us—it will not arrive as a thief but as a threshold. For the detached soul, death is no longer the violent tearing away of identity; it is the final unburdening, the final letting go, the final offering of the self to God. It becomes, in the words of St. Francis, "our sister death," the gentle hand that leads us to the One we have sought all our lives. The Christian who has practiced detachment is ready for this moment because he has already died the first death. He has surrendered his idols, loosened his grasp, purified his loves. He has lived as a pilgrim longing for home.

This is the freedom Christ offers. This is the promise of the Gospel. To detach from what cannot last is to enter into what cannot end. To loosen one's grip on earth is to strengthen one's hold on heaven. To forsake the tyranny of comfort is to embrace the joy of communion. The remembrance of death does not darken this path; it illuminates it. It reveals the brittleness of earthly joys so that the soul may seek unbreakable ones. It exposes the fragility of worldly securities so that the heart may anchor itself in God. It prepares the Christian not simply to die well but to live well—to live awake, free, and ready.

The world cannot understand such freedom. But heaven rejoices in every soul that discovers it. For the detached heart, the one that holds nothing back, becomes the heart that God Himself can fill. And once filled, it becomes the heart that can love without measure, without fear, without end.

19

Urgency Without Panic, Love Without Delay

There comes a point in every believer's life when the quiet insistence of grace becomes unmistakable. It does not shout. It does not threaten. It simply presses upon the heart with a clarity that is impossible to ignore: *Now is the time.* Scripture speaks this way with a kind of divine sobriety. Paul writes to the Corinthians, "Behold, now is the acceptable time; behold, now is the day of salvation" (2 Cor 6:2). He does not say tomorrow. He does not say when circumstances settle or when emotions stabilise or when life becomes more convenient. He anchors salvation to this very breath, this moment held in the hand of God. Heaven's grammar has no future tense for conversion. Grace always speaks in the present.

The remembrance of death prepares the soul for this holy immediacy. It strips away illusions, postponements, and self-protective rationalisations until the real question stands exposed: What am I doing with the time I have been given? Not theoretically. Not eventually. But now. The Christian who has learned to number his days gains a heart of wisdom precisely because he sees that love delayed is love diminished. Forgiveness postponed is forgiveness threatened. Repentance deferred is repentance weakened. Memento mori does not crush the soul beneath fear. It liberates the soul to finally take God seriously.

The early Church lived with this electric sense of immediacy. Acts tells us they "devoted themselves" daily (Acts 2:42). Not occasionally. Not when schedules allowed. They sold possessions, reconciled relationships, shared meals, prayed fervently. Why? Because the resurrection had shattered the illusion that life could be lived in leisurely neutrality. Christ had conquered death. The world was passing away. Eternity was already pressing into time. They acted as though every choice mattered because it did. Their joy was urgent joy, the joy of people who understood that the Kingdom was not an event to wait for but a life to enter now.

This is the spirit that permeates the entire New Testament. "Today, if you hear His voice, do not harden your hearts" (Heb 3:15). The author doesn't say "avoid heresy" or "avoid error." He says "avoid delay." Delay is the beginning of hardness. Delay is the quiet stiffening of the soul against the touch of God. Delay creates distance. Sin grows in delay. Acedia hides in delay. The devil does not need to convince us that holiness is unnecessary—only that holiness can wait. Patristic tradition often attributed to the enemy a single favourite word: *tomorrow*. Tomorrow you will repent. Tomorrow you will forgive. Tomorrow you will pray. Tomorrow you will repair what is broken. Tomorrow you will follow Christ fully. Tomorrow you will give your heart without reserve. Augustine knew this temptation intimately. His famous lament, "Late have I loved You," is not a poetic flourish but a confession of years surrendered to hesitation. He did not despise God; he simply postponed God. And postponement nearly cost him his soul.

Christ's own ministry speaks with that same rescuing urgency. He calls fishermen in the middle of a workday, and "immediately they left their nets" (Mk 1:18). He sees Zacchaeus in a tree and says, "I must stay at your house today" (Lk 19:5). Not tomorrow. Not when Zacchaeus had more time. That very hour salvation entered the man's home. The paralysed man lowered through the roof is forgiven not after a lengthy inquiry but at the sight of faith (Mk 2:5). The thief on the cross receives paradise "today" (Lk 23:43). Everywhere the Gospels reveal this startling tenderness: grace hurries. God does not delay to forgive. God does not delay to heal. God does not delay to love. The only delay in the spiritual life comes from us.

This is why Christ warns so sharply about postponement. It is not that He delights in severity. It is that He sees what delay does to the human heart. He speaks of the servant who says, "My master is delayed," and begins to live as though his life belongs to himself (Mt 24:48). He speaks of the wedding guests who decline the feast because each has something else to attend to first (Lk 14:18–20). He tells the parable of the fig tree wasting season after season in fruitlessness (Lk 13:6–9). He mourns over Jerusalem not because of its sins alone but because "you did not know the time of your visitation" (Lk 19:44). The tragedy was not mere disobedience; it was the failure to recognise grace when it stood before them.

In the parable of the Good Samaritan, Christ reveals urgency in the language of mercy. The priest and Levite delay. They see the wounded man. They understand his need. They grasp the immediacy. But they postpone love. And the postponement becomes a refusal. The Samaritan, by contrast, "had compassion" and "went to him" (Lk 10:33–34). Compassion moved his feet. Charity accelerated his steps. Love is always in a hurry because grace is always in motion. The priest and Levite were not cruel. They were not malicious. They simply hesitated. And a neighbour nearly died. Indifference rarely looks like hatred. It usually looks like delay.

This is why remembering death becomes the great school of love.

Nothing reveals the fragility of time like the awareness that our hours are numbered. Nothing awakens the soul like the recognition that opportunities to love are not infinite. "The time is short," Paul says (1 Cor 7:29). Not because he desires to frighten the Church, but because he desires to free her from illusions. Married, unmarried, mourning, rejoicing, possessing, lacking—whatever the circumstances, the Christian must live with a readiness that refuses to chain the heart to anything temporary. Time is short. Love is eternal. Therefore act with holy urgency.

Urgency is not anxiety. Anxiety is rooted in fear: fear of not achieving enough, becoming enough, acquiring enough, proving enough. Anxiety rushes because it believes everything depends on the self. Urgency, by contrast, is rooted in love. It does not rush; it moves with clarity. It does not panic; it responds. It does not scramble; it chooses. Anxiety drains the soul because it clings. Urgency strengthens the soul because it releases. Urgency trusts the God who holds every moment and who will not waste a single tear offered to Him.

Christ desires this urgency because He desires our freedom. He does not want disciples who postpone joy, postpone holiness, postpone reconciliation, postpone mission. He wants disciples who live awake. "Do not let the sun go down on your anger" (Eph 4:26). Forgive now. Not because the other person deserves it. Not because the wound is small. But because the heart was not created to carry bitterness into another day. Death reveals this with irresistible clarity. The hours of our life will end. The people we struggle to forgive will also face judgment. Love delayed is love lost.

A soul that lives with holy urgency begins to see every hour as gift. It prays not because prayer fits into the day but because prayer shapes the day. It forgives quickly because resentment feels too heavy for a mortal creature to carry. It repents willingly because holiness feels like breath. It acts generously because possessions are recognised as borrowed. It speaks truthfully because lies taste bitter in the mouth of someone who knows he will meet Christ face to face.

This urgency is the joy of the saints. It is what propelled Francis to rebuild a ruined church. It is what sent Patrick back to the land of his captivity. It is what moved Thérèse to offer every small sacrifice as an act of love. It is what inspired the early martyrs to face death with serenity. The remembrance of death did not distort their joy. It purified it.

The saints understood something that modern Christians often forget: urgency is the natural fruit of love. A soul in love does not delay, because delay wounds intimacy. When Augustine urges, "Do not be slow to convert to the Lord, and do not put it off from day to day" (*Sirach* 5:8, a verse he quotes repeatedly), he is not speaking from fear of punishment alone, though that fear is not unholy. He is speaking as a man who finally discovered how much joy he had forfeited through procrastination. He learned the cost of postponing conversion. It was not merely the risk of dying in sin; it was the years in which his heart remained restless and unfulfilled. Delay robs God of glory and the soul of joy. This is why Augustine speaks of his late conversion not with shame but with grief: not "I was almost condemned," but "I could have loved You sooner."

The remembrance of death becomes, for this very reason, the antidote to spiritual sluggishness. When the Fathers counsel, "Keep death daily before your eyes," they do not intend to create gloomy Christians. They intend to create focused ones. Clarity comes when eternity is allowed to speak. The noise of lesser desires—comfort, distraction, the compulsive craving for control—begins to loosen its grip. The soul becomes lighter. The heart becomes decisive. John Climacus, in *The Ladder of Divine Ascent*, teaches that remembrance of death "is a daily death," not in despair but in freedom. To die to the illusions of tomorrow is to begin living with the simplicity of discipleship today.

Christ Himself teaches this principle with a tenderness that is easy to overlook. When He calls His disciples to follow Him, the Gospels record a pattern: *immediately*. "They left their nets immediately" (Mk 1:18). "He called them, and they left the boat and their father and followed Him" (Mt 4:22). Christ's invitations are not coercive; they are compelling. His presence makes postponement unthinkable. The fishermen follow at once not because they are reckless, but because they perceive that the grace of God is passing by. When grace moves, the only dangerous response is hesitation.

This is why the Christian tradition has long regarded "later" as the most perilous word a soul can speak. "Later" is how love cools. "Later" is how duty fades. "Later" is how the heart becomes divided. "Later" is how the devil finds space to whisper alternatives. Evagrius names this spiritual strategy with surgical clarity when he describes the demon of acedia persuading the monk that "the day is long and the evening far off." The man believes there is time to delay prayer, delay charity, delay repentance—yet no one knows if he will live to see the evening. Here acedia and postponement become indistinguishable. A soul that expects endless tomorrows becomes incapable of giving itself today.

Jesus reveals the gravity of this danger most starkly in His parables. The ten virgins fall into tragedy not because they hated the bridegroom but because they delayed preparation. They assumed they had more time. The slothful servant buries his talent not out of rebellion but out of fear disguised as caution. The unfaithful servant squanders his stewardship because he believes the master is delayed. The fig tree wastes year after year with the quiet presumption that fruit can come later. Each parable ends not simply in judgment but in a terrible realisation: time has run out.

These are not stories meant to terrify; they are stories meant to awaken. Christ does not tell parables about delay because He delights in exposing failure. He tells them because He knows how strong the temptation to delay truly is. Love delayed becomes love endangered. Faith delayed becomes faith diluted. Repentance delayed becomes repentance uncertain. Christ is urgent because His mercy is urgent. He desires our salvation more than we do.

The modern world, with all its comforts, has become skilled at making postponement seem reasonable. Everything can wait. Everything can be rescheduled. Everything can be revisited. But the soul is not designed for that rhythm. The soul flourishes in immediacy. Jesus says, "Follow Me," and discipleship begins that moment. Forgiveness begins that moment. Conversion begins that moment. Charity begins that moment. Holiness begins that moment. Eternity meets time not in tomorrow but in the now that God offers as pure gift.

Yet holy urgency is not frantic. Christ does not say, "Hurry," as though the Kingdom were a race of speed. He says, "Watch." "Stay awake." "Be ready." The readiness He commands is not frantic motion but interior clarity. It is the disposition of one who keeps a lamp lit not because night is terrifying but because the Bridegroom may appear at any hour, and meeting Him is joy. The early Christians prayed "Maranatha"—"Come, Lord Jesus"—because their hearts were attuned to this readiness. They wanted Him to come. They longed for Him. Nothing in their lives was worth delaying His arrival.

A soul that remembers death begins to rediscover that same longing. Death becomes not merely an end but a meeting. Not merely a judgment but a revelation. Not merely a moment of reckoning but a moment of arrival. When death is remembered rightly, the heart becomes capable of urgency that is not fearful but loving. It forgives quickly because time is fragile. It reconciles boldly because divisions waste precious hours. It prays deeply because prayer is the only preparation for eternity. It offers itself generously because the world passes away and only love remains.

Paul captures this beautifully when he writes, "It is already the hour for you to wake from sleep" (Rom 13:11). *Already.* Not someday. Not eventually. The night is far gone. The day is at hand. Wakefulness is the posture of a soul that knows death is coming but Christ is coming sooner. Wakefulness is the fruit of wisdom, and wisdom is the daughter of remembrance.

This final chapter draws near to its task with this conviction: that urgency is not a burden but a gift. It is the grace that cuts through lethargy, excuses, hesitations, and half-measures. It is the divine summons that transforms ordinary life into holy life. The remembrance of death does not take away peace; it gives peace— because it frees us from the fantasy of endless tomorrows and teaches us to live the only day God has given: today.

The Gospels describe this spiritual immediacy with a kind of quiet boldness. When Jesus calls Levi from the tax booth, the narrative moves with stunning simplicity: "And he rose and followed Him" (Lk 5:28). There is no negotiation, no calculation, no delay. Grace entered his life, and he responded with the obedience of the moment. The Fathers loved this scene because it captures the essential character of discipleship. Christ's call always meets us in the present tense. He does not ask whether we will follow Him next year, or after our circumstances improve, or once we have rearranged our lives to a more convenient configuration. He speaks now. He invites now. He loves now. And He asks for our hearts now.

This immediacy is not harsh; it is tender. Christ knows the fragile nature of the human heart. He knows how easily affection cools, how quickly distractions multiply, how naturally the soul slips into half-heartedness when it is not anchored by a decision made today. Augustine reflects on this dynamic when he confesses his own reluctance to surrender fully. He describes a voice whispering, "Soon…soon…just a little longer," even as grace stirred within him. That whisper, he realised, was not benign. It was the quiet rot of delay. It was the slow corrosion of desire. It was the voice that kept him from joy. Grace was not strengthened by postponement; it was threatened by it.

Christ understands this danger better than we do, which is why His appeals are so often urgent. When He says, "Today salvation has come to this house" (Lk 19:9), He is not merely making a statement about Zacchaeus. He is articulating a principle: salvation comes *today*—whenever a heart responds without delay. That is why Scripture consistently binds salvation to the present: "Now is the acceptable time; now is the day of salvation" (2 Cor 6:2). The Spirit works in the now because the now is the only moment in which love can be chosen.

Remembrance of death makes this truth transparent. When the Christian remembers that life is fragile, that time is short, that eternity is near, the soul discovers a simplicity it did not know it lacked. Small resentments lose their force. Grudges begin to crumble. Indifference becomes intolerable. The heart begins to ask different questions: Does this matter in eternity? Does this decision align with the love I hope to offer Christ when I meet Him face to face? Does this delay honour God, or does it reveal a quiet resistance to grace?

A person who remembers death begins to recognise that delaying forgiveness is a kind of spiritual contradiction. To hope for God's mercy in our final hour while withholding mercy today is to misread the entire Gospel. Jesus teaches us to forgive "seventy times seven" not because forgiveness is easy but because forgiveness is the clearest sign that a heart has awakened to reality. If death could come tonight, how could we allow anger to persist? If Christ could call us home before morning, how could we permit divisions to remain un mended?

The remembrance of death makes forgiveness urgent—not as an obligation but as liberation.

The same is true of repentance. Those who postpone conversion rarely do so from malice. They simply imagine a future in which they will feel more willing, more ready, more resolved. But willingness grows when repentance begins. Readiness is the fruit of obedience, not its prerequisite. When the prodigal son "arose and went" (Lk 15:20), he was no more prepared than we often feel. His heart was still bruised, his motives still mixed, his shame still raw. Yet he acted. He moved. He turned toward the father. The father did the rest. Remembrance of death teaches us to make that turn today, not because God is impatient but because His mercy is too beautiful to postpone.

Action, too, takes on a new clarity in the light of mortality. Acts of charity, hidden sacrifices, small obedience's—all the gestures of love that seem insignificant in the world's eyes—become luminous when we remember that every hour carries eternal weight. Basil the Great once said, "The time you have is the time of your salvation." If this is true, then every moment holds an opportunity for love that will never return in the same form again. The cup of water given, the kindness offered, the prayer whispered, the interruption endured—these become treasures stored in heaven, imperishable, carried into eternity. To act now is to refuse waste. To love now is to invest in the Kingdom that does not pass away.

Yet urgency without panic requires a deeper transformation still. It requires the reorientation of desire. Panic is the fruit of fear; urgency is the fruit of love. Panic arises when we think God is harsh. Urgency arises when we know God is beautiful. Panic is anxious motion. Urgency is steady attentiveness. Panic tries to earn salvation. Urgency responds to grace. The Christian who remembers death does not rush; he prepares. He watches. He prays. His heart leans gently toward the Lord, the way a bride awaits the return of her beloved. This is why urgency is ultimately peaceful. It is the readiness of a heart that has arranged its affections around the one desire that cannot disappoint.

The Christian life lived in this readiness becomes a quiet testimony to the world. It is a life marked by presence, by attentiveness, by generosity, by spiritual fragrance. People notice. They see a person who forgives quickly, serves joyfully, prays steadily, and loves without hesitation. They may not articulate it in theological terms, but they sense something alive, something awake. They encounter a person who has not postponed conversion to a distant future but has allowed the present moment to be touched by eternity. This is the witness the world needs. Not frantic Christians, not panicked Christians—but Christians who live as though Christ truly is coming, and as though meeting Him is the joy for which they were made.

The remembrance of death sharpens this witness because it frees the soul from the tyranny of trivialities. Much of the world's anxiety comes from clinging to what cannot last. People hurry because they fear loss. They panic because they feel behind. They grasp because they believe everything depends on this moment's success or failure. But the Christian who lives in the light of eternity sees differently. He knows that the only losses that matter are those of love withheld, grace resisted, mercy delayed. Everything else is dust and passing breath. When the heart is freed from lesser fears, it finally has room to cultivate the one fear that Scripture calls holy—the fear of losing communion with God. This fear does not paralyse; it purifies. It makes the heart attentive, reverent, awake.

The saints lived with this clarity. Their urgency was never frantic because it was rooted in a deep awareness of God's nearness. Think of Francis of Assisi, who urged his brothers to obey "quickly and joyfully," not because God demanded haste but because love cannot bear delay. Think of Thérèse of Lisieux, who saw every small moment as the arena of love. Think of Isaac the Syrian, who wrote that the heart becomes wise when it realises "each hour is the hour of judgment," not in terror, but in wonder—because each hour is also the hour in which mercy can be chosen. Their lives were not rushed; they were radiant. They lived with the time of eternity, not the time of anxiety.

This interior freedom creates a paradox in the Christian life: the more deeply a person lives with the awareness of death, the more fully he lives now. To remember death is not to disengage from the world; it is to engage it with truer sight. It is to see people as precious, not obstacles. It is to see time as a gift, not a burden. It is to see suffering as a place of communion, not abandonment. It is to see forgiveness as liberation, not loss. A heart formed by memento mori becomes spacious. It becomes simple. It becomes unhurried in its love because it has stopped postponing love.

When Jesus warns of the dangers of delay, He is not issuing a threat but revealing a truth about the structure of the human heart. Delay reshapes desire. Every postponement makes the next one easier. The will weakens by hesitation. The affections cool by neglect. The conscience grows dull through inaction. Augustine's lament in the *Confessions* captures this decay: "I was held back by trifles... They plucked at my garments of flesh and whispered, 'Do you cast us off?'" The whisper of delay always comes from trifles—small attachments that promise comfort but steal freedom. Christ confronts this whisper not with impatience but with mercy. He exposes its power so that we may be freed from it.

The temptation to delay does not evaporate through fear of judgment alone. Judgment awakens us, but love moves us. This is why urgency must be grounded in desire. Fear may shock the soul into awareness, but only love sustains obedience. The Psalmist captures this beautifully: "I hasten and do not delay to keep Your commandments" (Ps 119:60). It is not dread that drives haste; it is delight. The law becomes a joy, and joy refuses to wait. When the

Christian sees obedience as participation in the life of God rather than obligation before a judge, urgency becomes natural. It is the movement of a heart drawn toward its source.

Yet Christ does not romanticize the struggle. He knows the human heart becomes sluggish. He knows spiritual drowsiness returns. He knows distractions multiply. This is why the Gospels repeatedly call the disciple to watchfulness—not as a heroic effort but as a posture of love. "Blessed is that servant whom the master finds awake when he comes" (Lk 12:37). Watchfulness is not simply staying morally alert. It is staying relationally attuned. It is listening for the footsteps of one you long to see. It is living with the awareness that every moment of fidelity is a step toward the homecoming for which we were made.

This relational urgency transforms everyday life. The Christian who lives in readiness forgives quickly not because he is naturally virtuous but because he cannot bear to bring a divided heart into the presence of the One who reconciled him at such cost. He repents quickly because sin feels foreign to a heart shaped by grace. He acts quickly because love tastes too good to postpone. The delays that once seemed harmless now feel incongruent with reality. Eternity draws near, and the soul adjusts its pace accordingly.

This is not a burden. It is liberation. The world measures time by productivity. The Kingdom measures time by love. The world fears running out of days. The Christian fears running out of opportunities to love God in this life. That is why urgency is ultimately joyful. It is not the rush of one who fears punishment; it is the readiness of one who longs for union. It is the tempo of a heart aligned with eternity.

The remembrance of death gives this joy its proper shape. When the Christian understands that life is a pilgrimage with an appointed end, every hour becomes sacramental. Time is no longer a neutral backdrop for activity; it becomes the arena of salvation. Each decision, each encounter, each act of love becomes a thread in the tapestry of eternity. The early Christians understood this with remarkable clarity. They did not romanticize death, nor did they flee from it. They saw it as the horizon that gave their choices weight. This is why the Acts of the Apostles describes the early Church as living "with glad and generous hearts" (Acts 2:46). Their joy came from urgency, not from comfort. Their readiness came from the nearness of Christ, not from escape from suffering. They lived as though Jesus truly meant what He said: "Be ready, for the Son of Man is coming at an hour you do not expect" (Lk 12:40).

This readiness expresses itself most profoundly in charity. Love that acts quickly carries a distinct fragrance. It is uncalculated, generous, almost reckless by worldly standards. It does not delay kindness until it is convenient. It does not postpone generosity until it feels sufficient. It does not wait for the perfect moment to console, to encourage, to serve. Love that knows death is near becomes swift. It moves the way God moves—quietly, steadily, immediately. Christ did not wait for the crowds to become worthy before healing them. He did not postpone compassion until they understood His mission. He acted because love could not wait. A disciple formed by memento mori learns to imitate this tempo.

Urgency also reorders priorities. A person who remembers death feels the quiet pressure of eternity pressing against the trivial pursuits that consume so much of modern life. Noise becomes less appealing. Distraction becomes distasteful. Endless scrolling feels like spiritual suffocation. The heart begins to hunger for what endures—Scripture, prayer, repentance, silence, sacrament, meaningful work, authentic relationships. These are not simply "holy practices." They are the things that will matter at the hour of death. They are the things that prepare the soul to meet the Lord. A heart trained by memento mori begins to see through the false urgency of the world and into the true urgency of the Kingdom.

This clarity transforms how the Christian views his own weaknesses. Instead of being discouraged by imperfection, he becomes motivated by grace. Every fall becomes an invitation to rise quickly, not gradually. Every temptation becomes an opportunity to turn to Christ now, not after repeated failure. Every sorrow becomes a call to trust, not an excuse to withdraw. Urgency makes the Christian resilient. It teaches him that holiness is not achieved by grand gestures but by immediate fidelity in the moment grace is offered. The devil's favourite word, as the Fathers often remarked, is "tomorrow." God's favourite word, as Scripture repeatedly proclaims, is "today."

The remembrance of death also purifies hope. Hope is not optimism; it is endurance toward a promised future. But when hope is postponed—when a person imagines he will trust God later, or surrender later, or believe more deeply later—hope becomes diluted. It loses its force. The saints guarded their hope by acting on it, not dreaming about it. They believed the promises of God enough to stake their lives on them now. They did not wait for perfect circumstances. They did not wait to feel ready. They responded to grace with the immediacy of faith. This is why their lives seemed ablaze. They were not extraordinary by nature; they simply refused to delay trust.

This refusal extends even to the smallest matters. A heart living with holy urgency learns to speak words of encouragement before the opportunity fades. It learns to apologise before pride settles in. It learns to thank God for blessings before they are forgotten. It learns to practice patience before irritation takes root. It learns to begin prayer before distraction sets in. These small obedience's accumulate into a way of life. They become the daily rhythm of a soul that knows it does not have infinite tomorrows. They become the training ground for the final act of surrender at death.

Most importantly, urgency awakens desire. The Christian who lives in readiness begins to long for Christ with increasing intensity. This longing is not morbid or escapist. It is the natural fruit of love. Just as lovers who are separated count the days until reunion, the soul counts the moments until the Bridegroom's arrival. This desire does not diminish the responsibilities of life; it ennobles them. It turns work into offering, sacrifice into communion, service into anticipation. The remembrance of death becomes the remembrance of the One who conquered death. The heart, trained by urgency, becomes spacious enough to hold both longing and fidelity at once.

Christians who live this way do not panic about the end; they prepare for it with joy. They do not fear the moment death comes; they see it as the culmination of every yes they have spoken throughout their lives. They do not arrive at their final hour as strangers to God, but as those who have been moving toward Him with every act of love. Their hearts have learned the tempo of eternity.

This longing reveals why urgency without panic is the true mark of a soul prepared for God. Panic imagines a distant Judge who surprises us with severity. Urgency knows a present Bridegroom who draws near with love. Panic fears punishment. Urgency desires communion. Panic rushes because time is against it. Urgency moves steadily because eternity is for it. The difference is not psychological; it is theological. It is grounded in who God is. Christ is not the master who delights in catching His servants asleep. He is the Bridegroom whose joy is to find His beloved awake, expectant, leaning forward in hope.

The early Christians internalised this truth so deeply that the remembrance of death became their way of remembering Christ. For them, death was not merely the boundary of earthly life; it was the threshold of union. This is why the New Testament closes with a cry that the Church never stopped praying: "Come, Lord Jesus" (Rev 22:20). That prayer is the distilled essence of urgency: it is the refusal to delay love. It is the soul saying, "Do not wait, Lord. I am ready to receive You." The one who prays in this way knows that the purpose of every day is to deepen this readiness—not through fear of the end, but through love of the One who will meet us there.

A heart shaped by this longing begins to measure its life by grace rather than time. Instead of asking, "How many years do I have left?" it asks, "How much love can I give today?" Instead of asking, "When will I finally change?" it asks, "What grace is God offering me this moment?" Instead of asking, "How can I secure my future?" it asks, "How can I entrust my future to God now?" This shift does not diminish responsibility; it sanctifies it. It frees the Christian from the false urgency of the world—the urgency of accumulation, achievement, self-preservation—and reorders life around the urgency of the Kingdom.

It is in this spirit that forgiveness becomes one of the clearest expressions of holy urgency. To forgive quickly is to refuse the slow poison of resentment, which hardens the heart and dulls its capacity for grace. Forgiveness is not merely an act of obedience; it is a preparation for death. No one wants to stand before Christ carrying the weight of bitterness. No one wants to meet the Lord with a heart divided by grudges. The remembrance of death makes this painfully clear. It reveals that forgiveness is not primarily for the one who wronged us; it is for the one who hopes to die in peace.

Repentance takes on the same luminous quality. The person who postpones repentance imagines that sin becomes easier to abandon later, but the opposite is true. Delay strengthens attachment. Hesitation deepens habit. Waiting for a better moment only ensures that repentance becomes more difficult. This is why the Fathers saw immediacy as essential to spiritual freedom. "Do not say, 'Tomorrow I will repent,'" warns the *Sayings of the Desert Fathers*, "for you are not promised tomorrow." The point is not fear, but liberation. The sooner the soul returns to God, the sooner it rests. The sooner it confesses, the sooner it heals. The sooner it obeys, the sooner it delights.

Urgency without panic also transforms everyday work. When a Christian knows death could come at any hour, small tasks are no longer meaningless. A mother calming a child at night, a labourer doing honest work, a student struggling to learn, a priest preparing a homily, a neighbour offering help—these are not interruptions to spiritual life. They *are* spiritual life. They are opportunities to love in ways that will echo into eternity. When the Christian remembers this, even the most ordinary task becomes infused with hope. The remembrance of death sanctifies the mundane because it reveals the eternal significance of the present moment.

This is where joy enters. A heart that lives urgently becomes surprisingly joyful because it is no longer enslaved to the illusion of limitless time. It savours blessings more deeply. It cherishes relationships more tenderly. It prays more sincerely. It notices beauty. It becomes grateful in ways it never was before. This joy is not shallow; it is Eucharistic. It receives life as gift. It sees every sunrise, every breath, every act of grace as something that will not be repeated. Gratitude is urgency's natural companion. The one who knows he is dying learns how to live.

Yet the deepest joy comes from love. Love chosen today. Love offered now. Love not postponed. Love that prepares the soul for the final encounter with its Lord. This is why urgency is the crown of memento mori. It is the virtue that transforms death from a threat into a horizon. It turns the fear of endings into anticipation of fulfillment. It allows the Christian to live each day as though it were both penultimate and ultimate—penultimate, because life continues; ultimate, because this day may be the last one offered for love.

This is why the remembrance of death, when rightly understood, reaches its crescendo not in fear but in readiness. The Christian who lives with urgency becomes the kind of person who could meet

Christ at any moment and not feel ashamed to look upon His face. Not because he lived flawlessly, but because he lived faithfully—quick to repent, quick to forgive, quick to love. His life becomes a long practice of saying yes to God in small and great ways alike. Death, when it comes, simply gathers all those yeses into one final surrender.

The tradition has always spoken of this readiness as the soul's true freedom. Freedom is not doing whatever one wishes; it is the capacity to give oneself without hesitation. Death exposes whether this freedom is present. A heart entangled in worldly anxieties, grudges, attachments, and delays meets death reluctantly because it has not learned how to yield. But a heart that has lived with urgency learns the art of surrender long before its final hour. It has practiced dying in the only way that matters—dying to sin, dying to pride, dying to procrastination, dying to the illusion that it will live forever. Such a heart discovers the paradox the saints cherished: when one dies daily, death loses its sting.

The Gospels reflect this in the simplest of gestures. The widow placing two coins into the treasury (Mk 12:41–44) acts with urgency because she knows God deserves her whole heart today, not when she becomes richer. The woman who anoints Jesus' feet (Lk 7:36–50) acts with urgency because she refuses to postpone love. The centurion who says, "Lord, I am not worthy" (Mt 8:8) acts with urgency because he recognises the moment of grace standing before him. Each of these figures teaches us the same truth: holiness belongs to those who respond the moment grace appears.

This is the beauty of memento mori. It purges hesitation. It awakens courage. It strengthens desire. It quiets fear. It draws the soul into the present moment, where grace is alive and God is near. It transforms the spiritual life from a series of postponed intentions into a living dialogue between God and the soul. The disciple who remembers death stops waiting for ideal conditions. He forgives now, because mercy cannot wait. He repents now, because conversion cannot wait. He loves now, because Christ is present now. His life becomes a single thread woven between two moments: the moment he awoke to grace, and the moment he will awaken to glory.

What emerges from this way of life is not a frantic Christian, but a luminous one. Urgency without panic produces serenity. It produces clarity. It produces a soul that can look at death without flinching, because it has already practiced meeting Christ in every moment of every day. Death no longer appears as an abrupt intrusion, but as the final invitation of the One who has been calling all along.

The last words belong to Jesus Himself: "Blessed are those servants whom the master finds awake when he comes" (Lk 12:37). Blessed—not terrified, not frantic, not exhausted, but blessed. Awake, ready, longing, living in the fullness of the present. This is the blessing memento mori offers. This is the grace of urgency. This is the life Christ desires for His disciples—not a life lived in fear of the end, but a life lived in love toward it.

When the Christian finally stands before Christ, urgency ends and union begins. The Bridegroom lifts the veil of time, and the soul discovers that every moment of fidelity was preparing it for this encounter. What death takes away, love restores. What time limits, eternity fulfils. The disciple who lived without delay at last hears the voice for which he has been waiting: "Well done… enter into the joy of your Lord" (Mt 25:23).

And the one who remembers death throughout life knows exactly what this means.

Epilogue

There is a prayer whispered in the shadows of ancient monasteries, a prayer carved into the memory of Christian ascetics from the deserts of Egypt to the forests of Russia. It is not long. It contains no ornament, no poetic flourish, no elaborate petitions. It is a single line, severe in its truth, luminous in its hope:

"Lord, let me die before I die."
No one knows exactly who said it first. Some trace it to the earliest desert wanderers who withdrew into silence to confront the inner terrain of the soul. Others hear in it the echo of Paul—"I die daily" (1 Cor 15:31)—the apostle who understood that the Christian life is a slow and deliberate surrender of everything that cannot enter the Kingdom. Still others identify its spirit in the Syriac tradition, especially Ephrem and Isaac, who speak of the "death of the heart" as the beginning of wisdom. Wherever it comes from, the prayer remains the distilled essence of memento mori. It is the whole Christian vision compressed into a single paradox. It is the invitation Christ Himself extends in the Gospels: lose your life, and you will find it.

The monks prayed it for a simple reason. They knew that natural death is unavoidable, but spiritual death is chosen. They knew that the man who refuses to die before dying arrives at the gates of eternity unprepared, his heart still clinging to illusions he should have surrendered long ago. They knew that the Christian who practices dying—dying to sin, dying to pride, dying to delay, dying to the self that imagines endless tomorrows—discovers death transformed. What once appeared as an abyss gradually becomes a threshold. What once summoned fear begins to stir longing. What once felt like loss begins to feel like home.

To say "Lord, let me die before I die" is to pray for freedom. It is to ask God to loosen the knots that bind the heart to passing things. It is to ask for the grace of detachment—not as a rejection of the world, but as a reordering of affection toward what endures. It is to recognise that the self we defend so fiercely must be surrendered if we are ever to receive the self God intends to give. It is to admit that the greatest obstacle to holiness is not ignorance but resistance: the slow, stubborn refusal to let go of the false self that sin has shaped.

This death of the false self is not morbid. It is the beginning of life. Paul declares, "You have died, and your life is hidden with Christ in God" (Col 3:3). The Christian life begins with death—the death of the old Adam—and continues with a lifelong pattern of surrender. "If any man would come after Me," Jesus says, "let him deny himself, take up his cross daily, and follow Me" (Lk 9:23). Daily. Not occasionally. Not when convenient. Every day requires a small death, a letting go, a relinquishing of the illusion that life belongs to us. This is the death the monks sought, the death Augustine described when he wrote that his conversion required the crucifixion of "the old man"—the self enslaved to disorderly loves.

The paradox is simple: the more a person dies to sin, the more alive he becomes. Sin narrows the heart; grace widens it. Sin suffocates desire; grace breathes it into flame. Sin isolates; grace binds. Sin blinds; grace illuminates. The world imagines holiness as suffocation, but the saints knew holiness as space—the spaciousness of a soul no longer trapped by its own compulsions. They died before dying so that death would not catch them unprepared, still clinging to shadows. They wanted death to find them already half-resurrected.

EPILOGUE

The remembrance of death intensifies this desire. When a Christian remembers that his days are numbered, that his breath is fragile, that his life is brief, he sees with clarity what he should have seen all along: pride is absurd, resentment is wasteful, delay is foolish, sin is small, love is everything. Memento mori becomes not a threat but a lens. It reveals the truth that was always present: the soul must be prepared for God. Not someday. Not eventually. Now. While breath remains.

This is why the epilogue to the Christian life is not fear but longing. The desert elders were not grim men; they were men aflame with expectation. They looked at death not with shrinking dread but with the vigilance of those waiting for a friend. They practiced dying not because they despised life but because they desired eternal life too deeply to be distracted by lesser things. When they prayed, "Lord, let me die before I die," they were asking to be purified of everything that would keep them from meeting Christ with unclouded joy.

Death, for them, was not the end of life but the unveiling of love.

Gregory of Nyssa speaks of this when he writes that the soul, freed from earthly attachments, "runs swiftly to the Bridegroom." Augustine captures it when he says that the heart is restless until it rests in God—and the heart can only rest when it is stripped of all that is not God. Even Aquinas, with his serene clarity, reminds us that the beatific vision requires a purification that cannot be bypassed. No soul enters heaven carrying disordered loves. Something must die before glory can be seen.

The saints understood that death merely completes what we began in life. If we have practiced surrender, death will feel like surrender fulfilled. If we have practiced repentance, death will feel like coming home. If we have practiced vigilance, death will feel like recognition rather than surprise. If we have practiced love, death will feel like the final ascent into the arms of the One we loved imperfectly but sincerely.

But if we have practiced delay—if we lived in acedia, in half-heartedness, drifting through grace with a divided heart—death becomes an interruption of a life that was never truly begun. Jesus warns of this with sobering directness: "Be ready, for the Son of Man comes at an hour you do not expect" (Lk 12:40). Readiness comes from dying daily. Readiness comes from vigilance. Readiness comes from the refusal to postpone conversion. Readiness comes from the quiet courage to say, every morning, "Lord, kill in me whatever keeps me from You."

This is the death before death.

And when that death has taken place—when pride has been humbled, when grudges have been relinquished, when sloth has been pierced, when illusions have been shattered—then the Christian meets physical death with a serenity the world cannot comprehend. Natural death becomes the doorway through which the true self steps into the fullness of the life for which it was made.

When the Fathers spoke of death as homecoming, they were not indulging in poetic comfort. They were naming a reality that becomes visible only to the soul stripped of illusion. A person who dies before he dies—who has surrendered the ego's endless self-assertion—begins to see that natural death is simply the moment when the veil thins and the truth of things emerges. Augustine describes this as the soul "going forth to the joy of its Lord," a joy proportioned to its freedom. The more a person has laid down his false attachments, the more eagerly he runs. The less he has surrendered, the more he must be untangled. Death reveals what the heart has chosen.

The Christian who has practiced dying discovers that death is not rupture but return. Scripture uses the language of home again and again. Jesus speaks of His Father's house. Paul speaks of being "with Christ, which is far better." The author of Hebrews describes the saints as "strangers and exiles," longing for a better country. Death, then, is not the collapse of meaning but its consummation. It gathers the scattered pieces of a life lived in fragments and brings them into unity. It is the moment when the promise God has been speaking since baptism—"You are Mine"—is finally unveiled without shadow.

But that unveiling presumes a heart trained to recognise the One who speaks. This is why the Church has always seen memento mori not as a grim discipline but as a schooling in vision. When we remember our death, we remember our meeting. When we remember that our days are numbered, we remember that our life has direction. When we remember that time is limited, we remember that time is filled with grace. Death does not diminish life; it clarifies it. It tells the truth about what is passing and what endures. It sharpens love. It cleanses desire. It sifts the trivial from the eternal.

This is why vigilance matters. Vigilance is not anxiety dressed in piety; it is love awake. Jesus does not say, "Panic, for you do not know the hour." He says, "Watch." Watchfulness is the posture of a heart waiting for someone, not something. The vigilant Christian is like the wise virgins who kept their lamps lit—not because they feared darkness, but because they longed for the Bridegroom's arrival. The monastic tradition called this *nepsis*, the guarding of the heart. It is the discipline of noticing: noticing grace, noticing temptation, noticing the small movements of love that beckon us to respond now, not later.

The vigilant heart is sober, but its sobriety is joyful. Sobriety, in the Christian sense, is clarity. It is the refusal to be intoxicated by the illusions of the world—wealth, status, distraction, comfort, control. It is the refusal to drift through life as though eternity were a distant rumour rather than the horizon of every breath. Sobriety sees clearly that death is not the enemy of joy but its tutor. It teaches us what matters. It teaches us whom we must become. It teaches us that love must not be postponed.

A life lived in this clarity becomes beautifully simple. The Christian stops scattering himself across a thousand minor concerns and begins to live from the centre. He forgives more quickly because he knows resentment is dead weight. He repents more honestly because he knows God already sees the truth. He prays more frequently because he feels the nearness of the One who loves him. He serves more readily because he sees in every person an opportunity to love before time runs out. He begins to live with the gaze fixed where it belongs: on the One who will meet him at the end.

This simplicity produces peace. Not the peace of comfort or control, but the peace of alignment. The soul that has practiced dying discovers that it no longer fears the stripping away of lesser things. It has already surrendered them. Its treasure is not threatened by loss because its treasure is Christ. This is why the saints could face death with serenity—even joy. They had died before dying, and so death could not surprise them. It could only complete what grace had begun.

This interior freedom does not negate grief or the natural sorrow that comes with parting. The Church never denies the human weight of death. Jesus Himself wept at Lazarus' tomb. But beneath the grief lies something deeper: hope. Hope is the virtue of those who know that death is not an end but a passage. Hope is the virtue of those who have tasted resurrection in this life—the resurrection of a heart awakened, a will strengthened, a soul purified. Hope is the virtue of those who have learned that the God who calls them through death is the same God who carried them through life.

In the final hour, everything unnecessary falls away. Only the essential remains. Only love remains. The soul that has practiced dying recognises this immediately. It recognises the voice calling it. It recognises the Presence drawing near. It recognises the One it has sought in prayer, in repentance, in sacrament, in silence, in longing. Death becomes an unveiling—not of terror, but of truth. Christ stands before the soul, and the soul understands that all the small deaths it embraced in life were preparing it for this moment of fullness.

This is the meaning of the monastic prayer.

It is not a cry of despair.

It is the cry of desire.

It is the cry of someone who does not want to arrive at the threshold of eternity still clinging to what must be left behind.

"Lord, let me die before I die"—

let me lay down everything that would keep me from You.

Let me surrender now, so that surrender later is simply love fulfilled.

Let me be purified now, so that glory is not delayed.

Let me wake now, so that death does not find me sleeping.

Let me love now, so that meeting You is joy without remainder.

To pray for this death-before-death is to ask for the grace of a final simplicity. It is to ask that the heart be narrowed to its single purpose: to belong to Christ without division. When all is said and done, the Christian life is not a contest of achievements, nor a ledger of perfection, nor a catalogue of avoided sins. It is a deepening surrender. It is the slow brightening of desire. It is the soul learning, sometimes painfully, sometimes gently, that nothing matters except to love God and to die in that love. Everything else—every success, every failure, every sorrow, every joy—serves this one end.

This is why Scripture places so much emphasis on readiness. Not readiness in the sense of calculation or foresight, but readiness in affection. Jesus asks whether He will "find faith on earth" not because He doubts His disciples' intelligence but because He knows how easily the human heart drifts into forgetfulness. Readiness means the heart has learned to look for Him. It means the inner eye has been trained to expect His coming. It means the soul has been shaped by desire more than by fear. When death approaches, such a soul does not scramble to assemble a final repentance; it steps forward with the familiarity of one who knows the path. It has walked it a thousand times.

The life that prays "Let me die before I die" becomes a life that sees death as the completion of every daily surrender. Think of each moment of forgiveness, each act of hidden charity, each whispered repentance, each tear of longing, each relinquished grudge, each humbled pride—these are small funerals, small deaths, small relinquishments of the false self that resists God. And these small deaths accumulate into a single posture. They gather the soul into readiness. They prepare the heart so thoroughly that when natural death comes, it does not feel like an intruder but like the final chord in a melody long practiced.

For the Christian, death is not an interruption of life but the unveiling of its meaning. It reveals what we have loved. It discloses what we have become. It gathers the scattered desires of the heart and shows which ones were true and which ones were illusions. This revelation is not meant to terrorise but to complete. Christ does not come at the hour of death to condemn the soul that has practiced repentance; He comes to finish what love began. Thomas Aquinas reminds us that the beatific vision is not a reward but a fulfillment—the flowering of a desire planted by God and cultivated by grace. The soul that dies before dying is simply the soul that has allowed this desire to grow unobstructed.

This is why the saints could speak of death with such tenderness. Francis of Assisi called it "Sister Death," not because he romanticised suffering but because he recognised in death the final gate through which the soul enters its true homeland. Catherine of Siena said the soul who has died to self "goes to God as to a wedding feast." Even the martyrs, facing violent ends, wrote of a strange sweetness, a clarity, a certitude that what lay beyond was not darkness but Day. Their serenity was not stoicism; it was recognition. They met death already half-transfigured.

The Christian who lives with memento mori learns to see the world in this same light. Time becomes precious, not because it is scarce but because it is meaningful. People become luminous, not because they are perfect but because they are eternal. Suffering becomes instructive, not because pain is good but because Christ meets the soul most powerfully when all illusions fall away. Gratitude becomes instinctive. Prayer becomes natural. Love becomes urgent. Life becomes sacramental. Death becomes familiar.

When such a soul approaches its final breath, nothing essential is unfamiliar. The gestures of surrender that death requires have already been practiced. The letting go of control, of pride, of plans, of possessions, of reputation, of fear—these things have been happening for years. Death simply completes them. It becomes the final assent, the last yes, the full release of the heart into the One it has been longing for. It is the moment when faith becomes sight and desire becomes union.

Imagine that hour. Not with fear, but with Christian realism. The room grows quiet. The noise of the world recedes. The soul stands where every saint has stood, where every Christian will stand. And what rises from the depths is not panic but recognition. The One who comes is not a stranger. His voice has been heard in Scripture, in conscience, in sacrament, in silence, in sorrow, in joy. His face has been half-glimpsed in prayer and in the poor. His wounds have been contemplated. His love has been tasted. His mercy has been trusted. The soul does not shrink back; it steps forward.

All the small deaths have prepared it.

All the small surrenders have shaped it.

All the delays overcome, all the temptations resisted, all the sins confessed, all the loves purified—these make the soul fluent in the language of surrender. And in that final moment, the prayer of the monks becomes the soul's own: "Lord, let me die before I die," and now, "Lord, let me live in You forever."

The grace of memento mori is not melancholy. It is readiness. It is the joy of a soul that has arranged its life around the One who will meet it at the end. It is the peace of knowing that death cannot take anything from the Christian except what must be left behind. It is the serenity of discovering that death does not have the final word; Love does.

In the end, everything in the Christian life comes down to readiness for love. Not readiness for judgment in the sense of courtroom fear, but readiness for communion. Readiness to be seen completely. Readiness to let go of the masks we have worn, the illusions we have carried, the sins we have nursed, the grievances we have justified. Readiness to allow Christ to love us with a love so consuming that it burns away every falsehood. This is why the monks prayed to die before dying. They wanted to stand before Christ with nothing left to surrender. They wanted every part of them to be already yielded, already simplified, already oriented toward the Kingdom. They wanted death to be not a wrenching loss but a final unveiling.

The remembrance of death teaches us that time is mercy. God gives us days so that we may learn how to give Him our hearts. God gives us seasons so that we may practice the detachment that death will one day complete. God gives us moments of clarity—moments when mortality becomes unmistakable—so that we may wake from spiritual sleep and choose what matters. Every day is a grace offered to the soul. Every morning is the invitation to begin again. Every breath is a reminder that we still have time to love, to forgive, to repent, to let go, to return.

"Lord, let me die before I die" is the prayer of someone who understands this mercy. It is the confession of weakness and the cry of longing. It is the recognition that holiness is beyond our strength but not beyond God's. It is the admission that the heart is too entangled to free itself. It is the surrender of one who places his hope not in his own discipline but in divine compassion. God hears this prayer not as desperation but as desire. And He answers it through thousands of small graces: moments of humility, opportunities for repentance, gentle revelations of our attachments, quiet invitations to deeper trust.

Each of these graces is a rehearsal for death. Each one prepares the heart to meet Christ. When the final hour comes, the soul that has cooperated with these graces finds itself strangely at peace. The fear of death may flicker, but beneath it lies something steadier: recognition. The soul recognises the One who calls because it has heard His voice so many times. It recognises the path it must walk because it has walked it daily in prayer and penance. It recognises the surrender it must make because it has surrendered a thousand times in small ways. Death becomes the moment when practice becomes fulfillment.

This is the culmination of memento mori.

Not fear.

Not morbidity.

But freedom.

Freedom from the tyranny of lesser loves.

Freedom from self-deception.

Freedom from delay.

Freedom from the illusion of endless tomorrows.

Freedom to stand before Christ with a heart already half resurrected.

And so the book ends where the Christian life begins: with a prayer.

Not a complicated one. Not a long one.

A prayer as ancient as the desert and as urgent as the present moment.

A prayer that carries within it all the longing of the human heart.

MEMENTO MORI

A Final Prayer
Lord Jesus Christ,
You who conquered death by dying,
teach my heart the holy art of surrender.
Strip from me now whatever death will strip from me later—
every pride, every fear, every delay, every false security.
Let me die to sin before I die in the flesh.
Let me die to the world before I leave the world.
Let me die to myself so that I may finally live in You.
Grant me vigilance: a heart awake to Your presence.
Grant me sobriety: a mind clear in the light of eternity.
Grant me love: a desire so strong that no attachment can rival it.
Grant me the grace to live each day as the threshold of our meeting.
And when my final hour comes,
let it be the hour for which my life has been preparing—
the hour when all my yeses gather into one,
the hour when faith becomes sight,
the hour when the Bridegroom lifts the veil,
and love becomes all in all.
Lord, let me die before I die.
And then, O Christ,
let me live forever in You.
Amen.

About the Author

Matthew Sardon is a Catholic writer based in Melbourne, Australia, formed by the depth and breadth of the Church's spiritual heritage. His path has taken him through years of study, prayer, and immersion in both the Roman and Byzantine traditions, giving him a single, integrated Catholic vision rooted in Scripture, nourished by the Fathers, and shaped by the Church's unbroken life of worship.

His work centres on biblical theology and exegesis — exploring how the ancient Word speaks with living power — but it also engages the pressing questions of the modern world. In an age marked by confusion and restless searching, he writes to help readers find clarity, refuge, and strength in the Church's tradition: the wisdom that has shaped saints, sustained families, and offered meaning to every generation.

Alongside his theological works, Matthew creates children's stories that open young hearts to faith and wonder through simple narrative and timeless imagery. Whether speaking to adults or children, he writes with the same purpose: to reveal how grace transforms the human heart and how the truths of the faith illuminate every corner of ordinary life.

When not writing, he serves in his local Catholic community, continues his theological studies and formation for ministry, and spends time with his family — seeking to live the beauty he teaches, one act of love at a time.

You can connect with me on:
🌐 https://matthewsardon.com